INDIE AUTHOR CONFIDENTIAL 1-3
SECRETS NO ONE WILL TELL YOU ABOUT WRITING

M.L. RONN

Published by Author Level Up LLC.

Version 5.0

Cover Design by Pixelstudio.

Cover Art for Volumes 1-3 © pevunova / Depositphotos.

Editing by BZ Hercules.

Time Period Covered in This Omnibus: 2020

Special thank you to the following people on Patreon who supported this book: Jon Howard, Megan Mong, and Lynda Washington.

Some links in this book contain affiliate links. If you purchase books and services through these links, I receive a small commission at no cost to you. You are under no obligation to use these links, but thank you if you do!

For more helpful writing tips and advice, subscribe to the Author Level Up YouTube channel: www.youtube.com/authorlevelup.

ABOUT THIS SERIES

This isn't your typical writing self-help book. This series is a compilation of lessons learned from an indie author trying to walk the path to success. Follow author M.L. Ronn (Michael La Ronn) as he navigates what it means to master the craft of writing, marketing, and running a profitable publishing business. Learn from his successes and failures, and learn about things that most successful authors only talk about behind the scenes.

CONTENTS

VOLUME 1

VOLUME 1

INDIE AUTHOR CONFIDENTIAL

Secrets No One Will Tell You About Being a Writer

VOL. 1

M.L. RONN

INTRODUCTION

This book is a gamble.

I'm not writing to market.

I'm not writing about the usual things you'd expect to see in a book for writers.

Instead, this book is a captain's log of sorts with lessons I've recently learned on my writing journey.

This book idea came to me in March 2020, during the dark, early days of the COVID-19 pandemic, when I was trying to focus my energy on productive activities rather than reading the news.

I recommitted to learning and improving in all areas of my writing life while the world was shut down. Every week, I wrote down lessons I learned about writing, marketing, and more. I decided to turn those learnings into an ongoing book series.

I'm a big believer in the concept of "evolving publicly." I don't hold myself out as a guru. I've built my nonfiction writing business model on sharing information with the community as I learn it. In many ways, I'm "documenting" my writer's journey, as Gary Vaynerchuk often suggests.

Today, writers don't document their progress until they're

successful. One of the bestselling books for writers of all time, *On Writing* by Stephen King, wasn't written until he was already a household name. This is true of virtually every book for writers written by a mega-successful author.

It would be ludicrous for an unknown writer who isn't making a living from their work to write a book about becoming a successful writer, right? Right?

Yet that's exactly what I'm doing.

Success is the result of many decisions and advantages that pile onto each other. New writers who want to walk the path of successful writers can't see all those decisions. All they can see are the big, most recent ones. They don't see the failures, bad decisions, bad luck, or important revelations that led to success.

Maybe by writing this series, I can uncover more clues about what it takes to be successful and share those with the community.

Instead of waiting to write the *one* book about success, I'm writing my first one now, and I'm publishing often.

Like I said, this book is a gamble. It's contrary to how we typically do things in our community.

I also recognize that it may seem presumptuous for a (largely) unknown writer to claim they're going to be successful. I may be an unknown, but I've accomplished a lot so far: I've written over 50 books of science fiction and fantasy and self-help for writers, I host a YouTube channel for writers with over 25,000 subscribers and counting, and I managed to build a writing career while raising a family, working a job at a Fortune 100 insurance company, and attending law school classes in the evenings. So I'm not a complete newbie with unrealistic expectations; I'm working hard toward a successful writing career, and I hope this book will reflect that.

My hope is that you'll find ideas and lessons in this book that you'll never find anywhere else. You won't hear other influ-

encers in the community talking about this stuff publicly. It's
not marketable, and it's probably not what their communities
want.

I tend to live on the fringe, and I'm comfortable there. If you
are looking for more basic writing advice, you won't find it in
this series. Check out my other books for writers instead. But if
you want something different, unusual, entertaining, and
perhaps a little controversial, keep reading.

How This Book is Organized

As a writer, my mission is to create content that entertains
and/or educates my audience, preferably both. I do this by
focusing on five strategic priorities:

1. Become a world-class content creator
2. Become a world-class marketer
3. Become a technology-driven writer
4. Become a data-driven writer
5. Become the writer of the future

I believe these five priorities are most important for me to
have a long-term sustainable career.

I need to master the craft of writing and content creation,
which will take the entirety of my lifetime. I'm not in a hurry,
but I have a quiet urgency to learn as much as I can quickly.

I need to keep finding ways to sharpen my marketing. Every
author must learn to do this.

I need to harness technology to make my writing business
more efficient. In a world where technology is rapidly evolving,
writers also have to keep evolving. The biggest advantage we
have in the market is that we can be nimble. How can we
embrace streamlining, automation, and outsourcing so that we

can remain nimble no matter how the sands of the industry shift?

I need to harness data to make better decisions that will keep my business profitable. Data is all around us, but how can we capture it and make it more useful? Authors and data don't always mix, but in our rapidly evolving future, data will become ever more important. In fact, I suggest that we'll need to start thinking of our books as data, just like we learned to think of them as products.

And finally, I need to become the writer of the future. The indie writer in 2040 is going to look drastically different than he or she looks today. How will they be different, why will they be different, what trends do we need to pay attention to, and what do we need to do to position ourselves today so that we can thrive tomorrow?

This Book Came from a Wake-Up Call

For me, the pandemic was a wake-up call to start thinking about the future.

Traditional publishers found themselves in dire straits because of their business model. Indie authors experienced record sales numbers because the pandemic favored *their* business model. The comparison between traditional and self-publishing could not have been more contradictory, but that contrast got me thinking...every industry sector experiences a fall at some point. Indies aren't invincible.

My revelation was that I can't continue to do the same things I'm doing today and expect to still be growing in 2030 or even 2040. As great as the increased sales feel, I don't want to wake up one day in the future and be in the same situation traditional publishers are right now—facing the extinction of my business because I failed to adapt and take advantage of trends and emerging technology.

I'm leaning into the discomfort of change even though I don't have to.

I'm giving you a fair warning that sometimes I venture down paths that don't immediately make sense. At times, you may think "Huh?" That's okay.

On the Meyers-Briggs Test, I am the rarest of personality types: INTJ, which stands for Intellection, Intuition, Thinking, and Judgmental. My spirit animal is an octopus, which describes me perfectly if you've ever read any of my books or met me in person.

On the Clifton Strengths Assessment, my five strengths are Strategic (Thinker), Intellection, Futuristic, Achiever, and (wait for it) Learner.

Because of my personality type, I tend to think long-term, and I connect dots that don't seem connectable. For a long time, I thought there was something wrong with me because most people don't think this way. I've learned that it makes me unique. The more you double down on your strengths, the more successful you will be, so that's exactly what I'm doing with this book.

What's in This Volume

From deep dives into mega bestseller fiction techniques to sneaky copywriting tricks to the power of databases, this volume is wide-ranging.

The contents reflect my soul-searching to find the best path forward for my author business during the panic of the pandemic.

This book is organized by my strategic priorities, with about

12 lessons in each section. The chapters are concise and to the point so you can absorb the lessons quickly.

The *Ideas You Can Steal* section contains ideas that I think could be game-changers if the right people took them on. I invite you to dream with me in this section.

And lastly, I have included links to the content I created during the time I wrote this book. I'd love it if you checked it out.

As a final note, this book assumes that you have basic knowledge of certain concepts such as ebook aggregators, metadata, artificial intelligence, and cryptocurrencies, to name a few. I do my best to explain most of them at a high level, but if you need a primer on all the basic industry terms that indie writers need to know, consider reading my book, The Indie Writer's Encyclopedia. It'll help you grasp any concepts I don't cover in-depth in this book.

Thanks for reading this very experimental book. My sincerest hope is that it helps you in some way.

M.L. Ronn
Des Moines, Iowa
July 15, 2020

BECOME A WORLD-CLASS
CONTENT CREATOR

BECOME A VIRTUAL APPRENTICE

In a pandemic world, it's hard to keep a mentorship going. You can't exactly meet your mentor for coffee.

Most people are too busy and too stressed out in a pandemic, so why not develop a virtual apprenticeship instead?

Pick a mentor you admire that has a strong Internet presence. Study every single thing that person has written or done and take copious notes.

Learn one or two things per week. You'll be amazed at what you've learned by the end of the year.

I've done this for years with fiction writing. I have studied mega bestsellers for the last few years, and I have learned a lot from practicing their techniques.

This year, I started doing the same thing with marketing and copyright, after hearing some advice from Dean Wesley Smith. I want to improve my marketing and my knowledge of copyright.

For marketing, I started with Seth Godin. I already read his blog every day, but there's much more I can learn. I consumed as many of his blog posts and videos as I could, and I read a few of his books.

For copyright, I took a copyright law class in my final year of law school. The other students weren't interested in the topic and just wanted the credit; I was the most engaged student in the class because copyright law was the main reason I went to law school. Each week was really just a conversation between me and the professor because no one else participated. I came with a lot of questions and was always the first to volunteer to dissect cases. I got a first-class copyright education from a practicing copyright attorney without having to pay legal fees.

With my marketing and copyright "masters," I pretended that I knew nothing and absorbed everything they taught me. I tried new ways of thinking and new ways of approaching my business as a writer.

For example, Seth Godin published a blog post about "bridges and tunnels." Bridges are monuments that stand the test of time and are revered by the public. Tunnels are invisible because they are underground, and not as glorious. However, tunnels are more important because they signify progress. How much better are all of our lives because of sewers, subway systems, and other infrastructure that lay beneath the surface of our busy society? The lesson in Seth's 100-word blog post was that you need both bridges and tunnels as an entrepreneur. Your bridges will attract attention, but it's your tunnels that will truly advance you in life. That got me thinking about what my bridges and tunnels were as an authorpreneur. I decided at that moment that I needed to stop building bridges during the pandemic and focus on tunnels—the world was too anxious to admire any bridges. If I focused on my business and improved my invisible infrastructure, I could emerge from the pandemic and build even bigger and more beautiful bridges. That got me thinking about ways to be more efficient, which led me to my book sales database project, which was my banner accomplishment for the year. All of that happened because of a 100-word blog post that I read in the mindset of a virtual apprentice.

When you study someone for as long as I did, you start to intuitively know how they will respond to questions you have. When you have a question, you can use the virtual mentor in your head. When I read copyright cases now (something I do once a week), I imagine what my professor would think about the cases, and the Socratic questions he would ask.

Virtual apprenticeships are a great tool, and in my opinion, a secret weapon.

IRAC—A UNIQUE WAY OF LEARNING CRAFT

I fell behind with my law school classwork and found myself studying all day. From sunrise to sunset one Saturday, I dissected twenty cases.

When I finished studying, I should have gone to bed, but I did some chores and listened to an audiobook—I think it was one of *The Dresden Files* audiobooks. I heard a chapter that captivated me, and I wondered how the author did it.

Then my mind immediately tackled the problem the same way I would tackle a law school case, which led me to a new way of thinking about the writing craft.

In law school, when studying cases, lawyers are trained to use the IRAC method, which stands for Issue, Relevant Law, Analysis, and Conclusion.

The first element in any case you must understand is the issue at hand. Court justices usually state the issue at the beginning of the case, but not always. Lawyers are trained to spot issues quickly. An example of an issue would be "To what extent should an employer respond when an employee faces death threats and harassment at the workplace?" or "Is an advertisement copyrighted?"

The second element you must understand is the relevant law and why it is at issue. In other words, what is the law that both sides are arguing over?

The third element you must understand is the analysis. How did the court analyze the issue and relevant law, and what is their reasoning?

The fourth element is the conclusion, also known as the holding, which is the decision the court made.

Law school students learn the IRAC method because you have to answer law school questions in the format. They internalize it and carry it with them throughout their lives.

What if you could apply IRAC to fiction writing as a way to dissect how an author wrote a passage of fiction? What if it could help you improve your craft?

I brainstormed the idea and came up with an IRAC of my own: Issue, Relevant Books, Analysis, and Conclusion.

Let's say that you read a scene where a beloved character dies at the hands of the villain. It's a sad scene, but it enthralled you and you want to know how the author did it so you can do something similar in your novel.

First, what is the issue? Who is the character, what level of importance do they have, how do they die, and when do they die? In this case, the issue might be "How do I kill a supporting character at the hands of a villain at the end of a novel?"

Note the specificity. It's a supporting character, not a main character. The character dies by the villain, not by disease or bad luck. And the character dies at the end of the novel, not in the prologue or in the middle. But for this problem, we're focused on a narrow issue: how to kill a supporting character at the hands of a villain at the end of the novel.

Next, in what books can you observe this issue at work? Start with the current book you're reading, but there may be other books you've read in the past or will read in the future that use the same technique.

Next, analyze the passage and break it into a series of steps. Think of it like a recipe. Then do the same thing for other relevant books and compare the recipes. The commonalities are the essential ingredients for replicating the scene in your fiction. But do note the differences between the books because those can give you clues on how to stylize your implementation of the technique. Maybe Book 1's dying character is a best friend, but Book 2's character is a love interest. If your character is a family member, their death is going to elicit a different response that would be somewhere between the death of a friend and a lover.

Finally, take the commonalities that you find and write them down as your conclusions. Then, as you keep reading more books in the future and see additional character deaths, you can update your conclusions.

Follow this method and you'll become a pro at spotting issues in fiction right away. It worked wonders for me.

I developed this method for studying mega bestsellers' work. If I could learn from the top authors in the world, I could improve my craft exponentially.

Anyway, this was a major breakthrough for me and I produced a series of fiction craft videos on YouTube that delve into issues like how to write minor characters, fight scenes, and more. You can view it at www.authorlevelup.com/irac.

HOW TO WRITE MINOR CHARACTERS LIKE THE MAJOR BESTSELLERS

I received a question from a YouTube subscriber requesting for me to do an IRAC deep-dive into a specific craft issue. She had a lot of minor characters in her novel and felt like she was "collecting people."

The issues were: how many minor characters is too many, and to what extent do I need to develop each minor character in a story?

In discussing the issue with the subscriber, we discovered that she was talking about walk-on characters, not minor characters. A walk-on character is a character who serves a singular purpose but doesn't do very much in the story other than help it move forward in some way.

In reviewing a few relevant books by mega bestsellers, I learned some important lessons.

To answer the issues, there is no limit to the number of walk-on characters you can put in your novel. Every writer is different and each story has its own demands.

With developing walk-on characters, I learned the following lessons:

- 5 out of 6 of the walk-on characters had names.
- Each walk-on character had an obvious, singular purpose in the story.
- Almost every walk-on character had NO physical description. Instead, the author used a smart character tag (such as an attorney carrying a briefcase). The authors left the rest to the readers' imagination and were careful not to contradict any images the reader formed in their heads.
- The more you visualize a character, the more the reader thinks they are important.
- Visualization equals importance, but dialogue and action do not. So while readers ascribe importance to a character depending on the level you describe them, you can have a walk-on character talk and perform as much action on the page, and readers won't ascribe those as importance. This means that the best way to convey walk-on characters is through dialogue and action.
- In the books I reviewed, each walk-on character appeared three to four times on average.
- All the walk-on characters I studied received zero character development.

These observations were based on studying the walk-on characters in three books, but they were helpful to understand.

You can watch this video as part of my IRAC playlist on YouTube at www.authorlevelup.com/irac.

EXTERNAL LINK VALIDATION IN CALIBRE

I've often said that Calibre is one of the most underrated ebook tools on the Internet. The app started as a way for readers to easily side load books onto their e-readers, but it's also a stellar ebook formatting tool for people who need a free solution.

Calibre has an external link validation tool that will check all of the links in your book to make sure they are valid. I first discovered it several years ago; I didn't have a need for it at the time, but I took a mental note.

When I was finalizing my book *150 Self-Publishing Questions Answered*, I had a large resources section with many external links. I had double-checked the links, but I wanted extra peace of mind since I was writing the book for The Alliance of Independent Authors (ALLi). Since ALLi is a nonprofit, I wanted to make sure the book left a good impression on readers.

I used Calibre's external link checker, and sure enough, it found two broken links that I had missed.

I published the book with confidence that all the links were valid, which will result in a more positive reader experience.

LESS FLEXIBILITY REQUIRES MORE CREATIVITY

After I used the external link validation tool in Calibre, I realized that even though all the links in my book were valid today, they might not be valid a year from now.

Since the book was being published by ALLi, I knew I would have less flexibility in making updates.

Instead of putting my resources section at the back of the book like I originally planned, I removed it from the book and put it on an unlisted webpage on ALLi's website. This way, we could easily make changes to the resources without having to republish the book. This would also help the book remain evergreen. Ultimately, it's an extra step for the reader, but a better long-term experience for them.

SPRINKLE IN THE QUIRKY

I was reading a book about a technical topic that honestly could have been bland and boring: Microsoft Excel's Power Query. But the author had such a great writing style and he used practical examples that were so helpful that I couldn't stop reading. I consumed all of his books in an afternoon.

One of the ways he reeled me in was with his first chapter. He talked about where he was born, where he's lived and worked—you know, all the usual stuff. And then he talked about how he made a ghost pepper peanut butter cookie that won a bunch of awards, and how he likes to tell stories at storytelling events on the weekends. Those two little details were so interesting and quirky that I wanted to keep reading. I wanted to get to know the guy, even though he was talking about a dreadful topic. I ended up reaching out to him and we struck up a great friendship.

Sprinkling in interesting details about yourself when you get a chance is a great idea. It's also a great idea to do this with characters. Wouldn't your readers be intrigued if your protagonist said they created an award-winning ghost pepper peanut butter cookie?

WRITING WITH THE AUDIOBOOK IN MIND

I have produced around 15 audiobooks, so I know a lot about what it takes to create one.

But it wasn't until I narrated my own audiobook that I truly understood what I was doing wrong.

Writing for ebook and print is easy—we do it without even thinking. But there are unique things you have to keep in mind when writing for audio.

I like to use bulleted lists in my nonfiction books. I like how clean they look on the page. However, they are shockingly difficult to narrate. I feel bad for the poor narrators that had to navigate them in my early nonfiction books.

I discovered a few key tips to write books that translate better into audio: shorter sentences, fewer commas per sentence, no bulleted lists, and no parenthetical asides unless they are at the end of a sentence. Each of these elements serve as speed bumps that make it hard to narrate effectively, which translates to a poorer experience for audiobook listeners. Learning to adjust my writing style will be a big adjustment for me, but it will make a big difference in listeners' enjoyment of my audiobooks.

HOW A SIMPLE AUDIOBOOK NARRATION TRICK DOUBLED MY PROFIT

In recording my first audiobook, I accidentally narrated the first few chapters too fast.

I spoke too quickly and had no idea I was doing it. I tested my audio while mowing the lawn and I couldn't keep up with my voice.

I imagined what a fast-talking audiobook might sound like to a listener—probably not good. People listen to books while they're commuting, doing chores, taking their dog on a walk, or exercising. They need time to hear and process the message.

When I re-recorded those chapters at a slower pace, I was surprised at how much longer they were; a 30-minute chapter lengthened into 42 minutes.

Multiply those results by the entire book, and you get 12 minutes by 15 chapters, which is 180 minutes, or 3 hours! All because I narrated the book *correctly*.

A comfortable pace is easier to listen to, and therefore more accessible. Longer audiobooks command higher prices, which means more profit.

MY #1 FAIL FOR THE YEAR

I took a gamble in recording the audiobook version for *150 Self-Publishing Questions Answered*. The book had just been copyedited, so I felt confident that the proofread wouldn't result in too many errors that needed to be re-recorded in the audiobook version.

Since this was my first audiobook, I needed to know if my equipment worked and if I could pull it off. I was eager to start recording, and the proofreader was taking longer than expected.

I took a risk and recorded the audiobook version before the proofreader was finished.

Huge mistake.

I had to rerecord nearly 75 sentences, which was an administrative nightmare. It was, without a doubt, my most expensive mistake of the year. It took approximately eight hours to fix everything. I didn't get much sleep that week, and I was extra cranky.

To put the eight hours in perspective, I can write 2,000 words per hour toward a novel. I lost 16,000 words, or 22% of a potential novel.

Very expensive mistake.

PROFESSIONAL INDEXERS: A NOBLE PROFESSION

Did you know that there is such a thing as a professional indexer?

Their sole job is to create indexes and glossaries for ebooks and print. There's even an American Society for Indexing, with other similar organizations around the world.

According to their website, their membership is open to "all interested persons: professional indexers, editors, publishers, librarians, and anyone else curious about indexing."

You can find indexers on websites like Upwork, or even with a simple Google search.

Indexing is a noble profession that will one day be lost to artificial intelligence, and future generations of writers will never know it existed. Yet it's so intriguing.

I discovered the professional indexer profession as I was producing my book *150 Self-Publishing Questions Answered* with The Alliance of Independent Authors (ALLi). ALLi is a non-profit organization for self-published writers with a mission of ethics and excellence in self-publishing, and they hired me as their Outreach Manager. The book, a joint effort between me and ALLi, is written in a question-and-answer style and addresses the most common self-publishing questions. ALLi has a blog with over 2,000 helpful articles, a podcast network of over 200 episodes, and a YouTube channel with hundreds of self-publishing advice videos. The organization sits on a figurative goldmine of advice, so I pitched a book that tapped into and organized the wealth in that mine. The goal was for the book to serve as a value to their members as well as drive new membership and revenue to the organization. (If you're not a member, join ALLi today at www.authorlevelup.com/alli. We'd love to have you.)

Because of the book's unique nature, I suggested to ALLi that an index could be useful for readers who want to use the book as a resource in the future. Fortunately, ALLi was already in the process of putting indexes in their existing books for writers.

I thought we could find someone to do an unremarkable index in Microsoft Word. Little did I know that my suggestion would open the door to a new galaxy for me. The indexer created a "glindex," which is a hybrid between a glossary and an index. Who knew?

The indexer not only did a great job, she incorporated the index into my Vellum file, which amazed me because I don't have to go through her if I want to make future edits to the book. The "glindex" took the book from good to great because it improved its intrinsic value.

I will be including "glindexes" in all of my writing books moving forward where it makes sense. Though there is a cost, it's a simple way for me to improve the value and utility of my books so that they serve as a helpful resource even after readers finish reading. Plus, almost no one in the indie space is doing it.

AUTHENTICITY MATTERS

During the George Floyd protests and racial unrest here in the United States, I decided to break one of my main rules.

I NEVER talk about race, politics, religion, or current events. I am not in the business of polarizing people. I accept everyone in my community regardless of who they are or where they come from...except if they spew hate, of course.

I decided to make a video and share my story of how racism has affected me. I kept it short and to the point, but I got pretty vulnerable. You can view it at www.authorlevelup.com/racism.

I was afraid the video would be taken poorly. I was also afraid that I would have been misunderstood or maligned for talking about my blackness.

Instead, the video was one of the best performing videos on my channel. Many of my black subscribers commented that they had the same experiences and felt validated. Non-black subscribers appreciated hearing the story. I received a flood of fan mail.

Yes, there were trolls. A few dozen people disliked the video and probably unsubscribed.

Two people told me to go back to Africa, and three people

acted as if a race problem didn't exist in the United States; I banned those people immediately from my channel. Eliminating them makes my community a better, safer, and more inclusive place.

I learned that sometimes it's okay to break your own rules and let your guard down.

UPDATING OLD CONTENT

In 2014, I did a video showcasing the writing gear and equipment I use. It wasn't a popular video, but it did drive decent affiliate income. For example, I sold a lot of Blue Yeti USB microphones from that video, which netted me nice sales commissions.

In 2018, I did an updated video to showcase my new gear since I had made some updates over the years. It drove more affiliate income.

As my YouTube channel grows, I plan to start doing these types of videos annually because they're easy to do, and equipment questions are some of the most common fan mail questions I receive.

BECOME A WORLD-CLASS MARKETER

HOLDING OUT VS. GETTING IT OUT

This isn't a marketing lesson per se, but it is.

When you're working on anything, you have two choices.

You can work on it until it is good enough, and then release it.

Or, you can work on it until it is better than good enough, and then release it.

With "good enough," you're trusting in your creative process.

With "better than good enough," it's usually perfectionism.

But there are times when "better than good enough" is your only option.

This year, I began recording my own audiobooks. Fortunately, I have a prior career in music with a lot of exposure to audio engineering, so it was easy for me to get started.

However, I quickly ran into trouble with getting my voice to sound like what you hear in professional audiobooks. That said, the audio quality was still serviceable, and I could have easily put it on the market.

But the sound quality didn't meet my personal standards. I decided it was best to spend money and get some help. After working with an audio engineer, we got my audio to sound clean and smooth, almost like what I imagined in my head. Now I know exactly how to replicate this sound in the future without having to hire an engineer. While the audio wasn't celebrity audiobook narrator quality, it was good enough that I felt comfortable releasing it.

I didn't allow myself to fall into the trap of perfectionism—the process of getting help took two days. If I didn't hold out for those two days, I would have let myself and readers down. My audiobook wouldn't have been nearly as good.

So, while I never recommend perfectionism, there is a time and a place for holding out. You just have to have the courage to know when to draw the line and push your product into the world.

EASY REPURPOSING

When I was promoting my book *150 Self-Publishing Questions Answered*, I had the opportunity to do a guest blog post on ALLi's' blog. But it didn't make sense to write a 1000-word blog post about how I wrote the book. I didn't think people would be interested. I felt it was better to lead with value.

I asked if it would be okay to make the blog post an excerpt from the book. I copied and pasted 1000 words from the book, with a short introduction and call-to-action at the end of the post that promoted the book with buy links.

Additionally, I included the audiobook sample that aligned with the excerpt so readers could listen if they chose. Since the audiobook is not exclusive to Audible, I can do whatever I want. It was a simple but effective way to promote the audiobook.

Overall, creating the content took about 15 minutes, which was a win.

SURVEYING MY AUDIENCE

I came up with an amazing idea. I found a way to auto-calculate your book sales without any data entry, and I found a way to create a book sales database that houses all of your sales reports at the click of the button so that you analyze them to your heart's desire.

I thought authors would love it, so I did a 12-week-long blog series chronicling my adventures in building the database and I even did a three-part YouTube series on the idea.

I asked my audience to take a survey about how they track their book income, and out of my entire 20,000 to 30,000 member audience, only six people took the survey.

Six people.

No one was interested enough in the topic to even click on the survey link.

Even though I built the database for myself (and it was a game-changer for me), I decided that it was something the majority of my audience wasn't interested in. I also blame the pandemic; people were distracted and focused on other things.

I proceeded with the project anyway because I believed it

was important, but surveying my audience gave me realistic expectations about how a book sales database product might perform with my community.

ADVANCE REVIEW COPY TRICK

When promoting my book *150 Self-Publishing Questions Answered,* I started promoting the ARCs about a month before I sent them out. I talked about it on my podcasts and YouTube channel.

I used Book Funnel's Certified Mail feature, which was very, very cool because it automated the entire process. The open rates on the emails Book Funnel sent were above-average too.

I also sent readers a link to the audiobook MP3s, even though the audiobook wasn't published yet. It's a nice value-add I haven't seen anyone else do.

COPYWRITING TRICK

When email marketing, short sentences keep readers moving down the page.

One to two sentences per paragraph is all you need.

If you start with a compelling subject line and hook, readers won't be able to resist scrolling.

Putting a simple call-to-action at the bottom of the email makes it even better, preferably inside a button.

Arial size 16 or 18 is the perfect font that has worked wonders for me.

Almost no photos is better because it keeps the focus on your copy.

Anyway, if you've gotten to the bottom of this, be sure to join my email Fan Club and you can see the copywriting lessons I've learned in action.

THREE-STEP SALES METHOD

I read a book called *New Sales Simplified* by Mike Weinberg. I bought it because I accepted the role of Outreach Manager at ALLi. My job was to reach out to companies with services for authors to entice them to join ALLi as Partner Members. It's a sales-driven role, and I've never been in a true sales job. In fact, I've never thought of myself as a salesman. I wanted to read a book that could mentor me before starting the role.

The core message in *New Sales Simplified* is that sales is three steps:

1. Pick a target
2. Employ weapons
3. Develop a plan of attack

Battle symbology aside, the book offers some interesting perspectives of what it means to be a salesperson. It offered many fun thought experiments and gave me ways to stretch myself into a skill set that always made me uncomfortable.

I needed to pick a list of organizations to target. In my case, I focused on organizations for writers. There are a lot of writer's organizations, but most of them cater to traditionally-published writers. Many of them recognize the rise of indie authors but don't know how to help members that have indie aspirations. If ALLi could build inroads with those groups, it could be a win-win.

By focusing primarily on writing groups, I could learn their "language" and get better at selling ALLi's services to them, even if I failed in my first few prospects.

I'm still too new to rate myself in the Outreach Manager role, but the three-step sales tip was helpful in shifting my mindset.

BE A BAT

A flock of bats lives near my house. They circle my roof occasionally, and they freak my dog out.

Bats are nearly blind and can't see well. They use echolocation to get information about their surroundings. They send out sound waves, and those waves reflect off surfaces and back to the bat, giving it a perception of its surroundings—a tree branch, predator, or its next meal.

Creating and marketing products is like echolocation. You send things into the world, like sound waves, not knowing whether they will ever return.

Think about how many sound waves a bat sends out that never come back. The same is true with marketing our books. Some marketing tactics work; others fail and we almost never know why.

When we do receive a signal—sometimes it's an unexpected win. It could be an audience we never considered, or a new marketing platform, or something as simple as a reader comparing your book to a well-known book you've never heard of before.

It's almost always worth paying attention to every signal because following them allows us to fly more confidently, even when we can't see.

USING MY ASSETS

I have more communication channels than your average writer: a YouTube channel, three podcasts, a (not frequently updated) blog, multiple mailing lists, and three websites. I need to do a better job of utilizing them to promote my work.

I was watching YouTube and observed two different mega influencers use subtle video editing tricks to promote their books. They displayed a banner ad at the bottom of the screen with the book and a URL. While it only showed for a few seconds, it was a smart and unobtrusive way to advertise the book. This got me thinking about additional ways I can use my communication channels as vehicles to promote my work—without being spammy about it, of course.

THOUGHT ANCHORING

Let me know what you think about this conversation.

Me: "I have this great tool that will help you aggregate all of your sales reports and add them up so that you don't have to do data entry ever again."

Random Author: "Whoa! Sign me up!"

Me: "Cool. I just need you to run this Excel macro, wait 10 minutes, and you'll be amazed."

Random Author: "Excel macro....? Nope. See you later."

Me: "Don't run away. Trust me on this. I've simplified it so that all you have to do is click a couple buttons. No code required."

Random Author: "Really?"

Me: "Think about it like this. Isn't the process of uploading a book to Amazon, Kobo, Google, etc. complicated?"

Random Author: "Sometimes."

Me: "If you can upload a book to six different retailers, then you can click a few buttons on my Excel spreadsheet."

What's wrong with the conversation above?

Have you ever been pitched a course by an online marketer, and they say something like "Normally, I'd sell this course for

$600, but because I'm not doing this for the money, I'm charging only $200. People told me I'm nuts for doing this."

That's price anchoring. Give people a higher price and then they will keep referring to that when you give them the lower one. They automatically think the lower price is a better deal, when it's just a marketing tactic.

You can do that with thoughts too.

In marketing my book sales database product, I started way too technical and scared people off.

What I should have started with was "You're an author. You get 10-15 sales reports every month, and what are you supposed to do with them? I surveyed a bunch of writers who told me that they spend an average of 4-5 hours doing their sales reports each month. What if I told you I built a tool that will take all your sales reports, roll them together, add everything up, and give you one report that will tell you how much money you made and how many books you sold?"

Yeah, not my finest marketing moment. I'm not hard on myself, though, even though I squandered an opportunity to sell the product to a gigantic influencer in the self-publishing space. My explanation scared them off.

You live and you learn. Every product is different and you have to find the right way to message it.

GAUGING PAIN LEVELS

Jim Kukral, former host of the *Sell More Books Show*, always said, "If you've got a toothache, what's your pain level?" How bad will you let something get before you go to the dentist?

The general wisdom is that if people's pain level is high, they're more willing to do something about a problem they're facing. If you have a product that solves their pain, they're more likely to buy it.

However, there is such a thing as a friction level.

If a person's pain is a 10 out of 10, and they encounter a solution that will solve 100% of their problem, but it's too difficult to implement, they won't do it. They'll live with the pain because there's too much friction.

Imagine you're on the verge of bankruptcy, and I offer to give you a million dollars. It will solve all your money problems forever. However, in order to get the money, you have to receive ten root canals at the same time. Most people would choose bankruptcy.

I learned this first-hand when building my book sales database. I shared the idea with about 10 different major influencers in the industry in addition to my audience. No matter how I pitched the product, I couldn't get people excited about the problem, even though they admitted that tracking their sales reports was a major problem for them.

I had to learn how to reduce the friction, or rather, give the *perception* that friction didn't exist.

Marketing is Like Going to the Eye Doctor

I've learned that sometimes your marketing doesn't connect and you have to keep shifting the message.

When I built my royalty database, that's what I called it—a royalty database.

I showed it to a fellow influencer, and he didn't get it. Even though he admitted it would have been immensely helpful, it looked scary to him.

I showed it to another influencer, but this time, I made the demo less technical. It still looked scary, but she saw the potential and gave me good advice.

Feeling more confident, I showed it to three more influencers, and instead pitched it as a way to "automate your monthly royalties."

Influencer 3 loved it and offered me money on the spot.

Influencer 4 loved it and put me in contact with her assistant to discuss logistics.

Influencer 5 gave me the advice that made me realize my mistake: "It's interesting. I do think people would want this—at least those who understand what you are talking about."

I discovered that no matter how well I simplified it—and trust me, I oversimplified this damn database—it either scared or confused people.

I stopped talking about Excel. I stopped talking about databases. Instead, I called it the "Author Income Dojo." It's the place where you go to kick your sales reports' asses.

Let me ask you this: what's your most popular book?

What did you earn on that book last month?

What have you earned on that book year-to-date? Is it profitable?

If you can't immediately answer these questions, you're not alone. I mean, let's face it: you probably publish your books on many retailers and you get a ton of sales spreadsheets every month. You don't have time to read them because your time is best spent writing.

What if I told you that I built a tool that takes all your sales spreadsheets, combines them, and gives you amazing insights to your book sales?

Throughout this chapter, I kept shifting the message, much like when you go to the eye doctor and they ask you, "Which looks clearer? One or two?"

I learned to be persistent with my messaging.

JUST KEEP TALKING

Sometimes, people don't act on your message because you didn't refine your message, or because you didn't have the right messaging, or because you caught them at the wrong time, or because they were having a bad week, or because they were too busy, or because they just lost a family member, or because you were ahead of your time, or because you were behind your time and therefore ahead of your time for when people find renewed interest in your subject matter, or because...

You'll never truly know why, though some wonderful readers will tell you what they think occasionally.

But if you keep talking about the book you believe in, eventually, people will pay attention.

I learned this lesson first-hand in my professional life at work this year, where I am an insurance consultant who specializes in insuring the restaurant industry.

It's amazing how quickly circumstances can change.

Restaurant owners resisted things like self-service kiosks, contactless ordering, and artificial intelligence to serve their patrons. They didn't understand why the technology was needed.

Most restaurant owners would have told you, "Wait a minute. You're telling *me* that I should de-incentivize people from coming into my restaurant by telling them to order at a kiosk? You think I should develop a mobile phone app that senses when my customer is approaching so I can give them a special, or ping them on their way home with a coupon so they'll swing by? Are you kidding me? Where am I going to get the money for that, and how can you prove it will work?"

And they would have been right...before COVID-19. Prior to the virus, restaurants were all about in-person experiences— good waiters, good decor, a nice atmosphere, and so on. Those things are irrelevant in a time of social distancing.

If I was a startup trying to get people to buy my contactless ordering software before the pandemic and getting nowhere, I'd be doing a lot more talking during the pandemic era.

Circumstances change, often in ways you can't imagine. That's why you have to keep talking and marketing, even if it's hard.

THOUGHTFUL QUESTIONS

So much in life is all about asking the right questions.

Seth Godin is great at ending his blog posts with a thought-provoking question.

Once, he was talking about the coronavirus and how difficult it is to concentrate during the pandemic. He ended the post with "When it's all over, what will you have done and contributed?"

Throughout the day, I reflected on that question and answered it for myself. Then I wrote a blog post with some words of encouragement for my audience and asked them the same question. A few people commented and said it was exactly the post they needed to read.

Thoughtful questions are a great way to plant seeds in your readers' heads, but also a great tool for engagement.

What's the question you need to ask your readers today?

BECOME A TECHNOLOGY-DRIVEN WRITER

PERSONAL THANK-YOU VIDEOS

I celebrate when people buy my courses. Of all the content I create, I consider it the best compliment when someone likes me and my content enough to buy one of my courses.

I discovered a neat little mobile app called Bonjoro that allows you to send a personal video to someone. They receive an email notification and can watch it in their browser.

I started sending personal thank-you videos to everyone who signed up for my courses. In the video, I say their name, tell them thank you, and that if they have any questions to email me. I give the link to my contact form.

Fifty percent of my customers were floored. The other fifty percent probably never saw the videos because of spam filters.

Sure, this kind of thing isn't scalable, but it's a free and easy way to show your audience that you appreciate them.

LOCALIZED LINKS MAKE YOU MORE MONEY

This lesson is something I've known about for a while, but finally got around to implementing it.

I localized my Amazon links so that the links direct you to the Amazon storefront of the country where you live. It doesn't make sense to send UK readers to Amazon.com if they can't buy from there. They need to be routed to Amazon.co.uk.

Localization also works with the Amazon Associates affiliate program, which is the main reason I implemented the solution.

I know this is simple and likely something everyone knows. But I didn't think spending money on a link localization service made financial sense for me until recently, especially for my fiction book sales alone. My novels receive decent affiliate clicks, but not at a scale to justify $100 per year. However, my YouTube channel is growing, and my increasing affiliate commissions there made me finally take another look at localized link services.

Upon implementing localized links, I saw an instant return on my investment, mainly driven on YouTube by people who bought books I recommended or wanted to know what gear I used. It wasn't anything huge, but I did see a few commissions here and there in other countries that I never would have seen otherwise. Quick math indicated that I would break even on the investment in the first year. If I continue doubling down on YouTube and affiliate links, the service would pay for itself in the second year.

THE POWER OF MIND MAPS

Mind maps are an underappreciated and underutilized tool. I use them all the time for brainstorming.

I happened upon a free course on copyright law from Harvard Law School on YouTube. The professor created an enormous, interactive mind map outlining the essential concepts of copyright law. He shared it for free. I often refer to it when I am reading copyright cases for leisure. You can find it at www.authorlevelup.com/harvardcopyright.

I was intrigued by the idea. A mind map is powerful because it is a *map of your mind*. It's the equivalent of showing your work in algebra class—you are showing someone your thought process around an idea.

How often do people share their thought processes in a transparent way? For example, if you want to know how someone is successful, you have to study their lives and recreate the path. You'll often find gaps. But what if that person shared mind maps that served as snapshots on their journey? Something as trivial as an everyday decision could shed great insight into how that person thinks when they are more successful and you want to study their path.

I experimented with mind maps in this vein, but I haven't come up with anything that was worthy of sharing yet. However, as I explore futurism more, I think it's a perfect way to convey long-term thinking and visualize the future of writing.

COMMAFUL: WATTPAD FOR THE NEXT GENERATION

I had the pleasure of collaborating with Commaful, the world's largest multimedia storytelling app. Young people love it, and teenagers between the age of 13-17 comprise the biggest demographic of the app's user base. The app is similar to Wattpad in that users can write stories, but they can add interactive backgrounds, images, and GIFs. The stories read like little text movies, and the platform makes Wattpad look like your grandpa's writing site. I couldn't help but wonder if this is the distant future of writing. It's a novel app but part of what I believe is a bigger trend of easy-to-create, more interactive multimedia content.

Commaful wants to foster and encourage writing so they invited me to produce a couple writing advice videos for their blog.

Prior to making the videos, I spent a weekend with the app, trying to see what advice writers on the platform needed. I made a story of my own and shared it on social media. Then I realized that the app could be an incredible way to make a text-driven book trailer because you can create one in minutes and embed it on social media. Viewers don't have to have the Commaful app to see your story.

It's always a good idea to see what young people are into, because their likes will manifest themselves in the future, whether you like it or not.

AUDIOGRAM

I have been listening to podcasts since 2008. I was a podcast listener before it was cool, before Apple launched its podcast app, before all the Internet marketers jumped on the bandwagon, before *Serial*, and before Google announced that it would start indexing podcasts in search results.

A challenge with podcasts has always been how to share them. Audio used to be so expensive to host and stream that you had to hope people had enough patience (and bandwidth) to listen to your show.

In recent years, I've seen podcasters use YouTube and Soundcloud to share snippets of their shows on social media. Now I'm seeing more people use audiograms, which are audio snippets that promote the show, usually with a visualized waveform so that viewers have something to see while they're listening. Podcasting services such as Anchor offer an easy audiogram creation tool, and there is a company called Audiogram that specializes in this technology.

It's hard not to see Google offering something like this in their search results. Audiograms may be how Google serves audio content in the future, cutting up snippets of podcasts it thinks are relevant to a given search—much like what happens with video searches where Google returns 1-2 minutes of a relevant YouTube video that might answer your question. This could potentially disintermediate the podcasting format as we know it, making podcasting truly mainstream while reducing people's attention spans, driving a trend toward shorter content. It would be cataclysmic for long-term podcast listeners like me, but it's probably the future. I'm ready for it.

MERGING EMAIL AND TO-DO LIST

At the time of this writing, I receive 1,200 emails per month, which is around 40 per day. Most days, I can manage the volume, but when I fall behind, it can take me weeks to catch up.

I tend to change my email client like you change the arrangement of furniture in your living room—once every few years.

This year, I experimented with an email client that mixed email with a to-do list. I'm not a huge to-do list fan, but I found an app called Sortd that provides the best of both worlds. It's not perfect, but it did help me stay productive for a while.

DATABASE INTEGRATION: ONE TRUTH

I got tired of filling out marketing forms and having to put the same information about my books into them every time. When you're marketing your book, it's staggering how many times you need links, ASINs, book descriptions, and so on. You have to input this information into contact forms, your website, and more. I often forget little things like price or trim size, and I find myself looking them up often, which takes too long.

I decided to build a book database in Microsoft Access that houses all of the information for my books so that I can keep everything in a central location. Any time I have questions about my book details, I fire up the database. I can even export data in any form I want to.

I still have to copy and paste, which is tedious, but the database is just the first step in a long-term strategy.

The database can also become the engine for my website. Imagine loading a book into the database, and then pushing it to your website. Your website would then auto-create a page for your book, with all of the correct information, populated from the database, with the ability to update it as needed. This is absolutely possible—I used to work for a web development company and we did SQL server integrations for clients all the time. My next website iteration will have this functionality.

Next, imagine a browser extension that pulls from your database and auto-populates forms with your book information. All you have to do is choose which book it populated and verify that the information on the form is correct. This would save you time when you're marketing the book or sharing it on social media.

Next, imagine entering your book into a database and then being able to publish your book to book retailers from the database instead of signing in to a dashboard. That technology exists; traditional publishers use it every day. It's the future for indie authors. More successful and prolific writers will demand it. Distributors like PublishDrive recognize this need and already quietly offer bulk uploads and database integration so that you can publish by uploading a specially-formatted ONIX file.

As I scale my business, it's increasingly important to maintain fewer records with more accurate data. One day, when I have over 100 books, I need one version of the truth that preferably serves as a Swiss Army knife for whatever I need it to do.

Building my database was the first step in that future I want to create for myself.

EXCEL MACROS

I've always been afraid of Microsoft Excel. Its interface isn't suited to my thinking style. I don't consider myself as someone who has strong data analysis skills, but I'm trying to improve.

When I built my book sales report database, I threw my fears aside and dove into learning it.

I took interactive Excel courses, watched hours of Excel videos on YouTube, and read Excel books. I even learned how to write Visual Basic for Applications (VBA)—something that makes most people run away screaming. As part of my sales database project, I wrote over 10,000 lines of VBA code that worked very well. I also hired a few programmers to help me with the most difficult parts, and they taught me a lot.

I learned that macros, while scary, are amazingly useful. They save time by helping you automate mundane and repetitive tasks.

Sales reports are the definition of mundane and repetitive. I don't know anyone who enjoys digging through them. I created macros that manipulated sales reports from multiple retailers into something more palatable that you can use to make data-driven decisions about your sales. I created the tool for myself but found that others can use it too.

I harnessed the power of macros and automation, and my business is much better for it. I now have access to more data, so I can improve my data analysis skills.

Not bad for a guy who barely knew what a macro was before he started the project.

SOMETIMES, YOU JUST CAN'T HELP PEOPLE

This chapter isn't what you think it is—a rant about human nature and some writers' indomitable stubbornness and inability to accept that they have flaws...

Instead, I'm talking about book and product development.

Every once in a while, you get this amazing idea to solve a problem.

Maybe you write a book that, on paper, is the sweet spot in an underserved fiction genre.

Or maybe you come up with a unique nonfiction book or course that helps your audience do something.

There will be a time when you simply can't help the people you want to because of factors out of your control.

Maybe the idea is too expensive or too technical for the average person. Or maybe you can't reach the people you want to reach because it's too difficult to find them.

In any case, you have a choice: keep moving forward and hope you'll succeed, which isn't likely, or you stop and abandon the project.

I ran into this problem with my sales report tool, Author Income Dojo.

I was tired of dealing with complicated sales reports every month and I wanted a simpler solution. I scoured the planet for a solution, and I wouldn't stop until I found one.

I did, and I wanted to share it with the community.

While it was a complete solution for me, it was a partial solution for others.

Essentially, it worked perfectly for Windows users, but for Mac users, it involved installing Windows on your Mac.

Yikes.

I tried to develop an alternative solution for Mac users, but I couldn't make it work even after consulting with two Microsoft Certified MVPs.

Macs just aren't built for the type of tool I created, and there was nothing I could do about it.

As a result, I couldn't help the average Mac user in my community.

Asking people to install Windows on their computers is a big ask.

This was an example of not being able to help people. It happens a lot, unfortunately.

THE DANGERS OF WEB SCRAPING

This year, I partnered with a Silicon Valley-based developer to build a tool that could help me with my writing business. It involved data mining and web scraping, and it would have been a game-changer for me, and possibly the writing community. We didn't pursue the project for legal reasons.

Web scraping is when a "bot" takes information off a website and provides it to the owner for any number of reasons, mainly for competitive intelligence.

Companies like Amazon and Google didn't like web scraping back in the old days because it caused problems for their servers. This is why Amazon, Google, and major websites offer Application Programming Interfaces (APIs). An API is like a plug-socket arrangement where your program is the plug and the website is the socket. When you connect to an API, you agree that your bots will follow certain protocols and rules. Companies provide data in exchange for your bots playing nice with their servers.

The problem with our project was that we could use APIs, but our particular use case was not technically a sanctioned use of the APIs. That left us with the choice to use the APIs for our purposes and hope we wouldn't get caught, or to scrape data from them, which was also against most sites' terms of service. Both choices were unpalatable.

Compulife Software, Inc. v. Newman, **F.3d** , 2020 WL 2549505, (11th Cir. May 20, 2020) was the kind of case we were worried about. In that case, the plaintiff compiled insurance company rates that were publicly available and then wrapped them into a database that it then provided to customers to get life insurance quotes, I presume as a comparative rater so customers could get multiple quotes from different companies at the same time.

The defendants, Compulife's competitors, created bots that scraped the database to discern the workings of Compulife's proprietary product, which was protected as a trade secret.

Normally, if a hacker did this, they would glean some important data, but a key fact in this case is that the bots were able to scrape 42 million computations of the potential data in the database, giving the defendant an immense competitive advantage and the ability to reverse engineer what Compulife had created.

In my case, the web scraping was innocent and for my own commercial use.

In the Compulife case, the scraping was nefarious.

You can see how the same technology can be used for both good and evil.

The programmers and I left the project at "this is a really messy legal issue right now, but the courts and legislature will have to address it at some point because APIs are the future. If average people can't use APIs to get data that they own, that's not the world we want to live in." We didn't like the legal and ethical crossroads we found ourselves at.

Not only was our decision the correct one, it was right on time given the Compulife case, which came out soon after we halted the project.

Is something a trade secret if it's based on publicly available information?

You may be wondering why I care about this.

Well, the information on a book retailer's website is public, isn't it? For example, your book's metadata can be scraped easily off Amazon, and also obtained through Amazon's Product Advertising API. How would you feel if someone could access the information about all your books that is available publicly and use the data to gain a business advantage over you? (News flash: they already can.)

And couldn't one argue that retailers don't own that data, that it's merely facts created by authors? *Shouldn't* authors have a right to gather their own facts and use them for whatever purpose they desire?

In the insurance industry, insurance agents have "agency management systems" that allow them to manage their customer accounts with different insurance companies. The software is a customer database that downloads insurance rates and policies and allows the agent to make changes to the customer's policies.

Why don't authors have "book management systems" that do the same thing with their books? Why log in to a retailer's dashboard when you can log in to a database on your computer that communicates with the book retailer instead?

In short, authors are going to need more access to data about their books in the future to make business decisions. Retailers have that data, but they limit our access to it. When I think about who might disrupt Big Tech like Amazon and Google, I think of companies whose business model is democratizing data (ironically, which is how the Big Tech companies started, but they hoard data now). That, or evolving technology and market forces, will push Big Tech to grant access to more data via APIs.

This project was another example where I was ahead of my time.

TEXT SPINNER AI

A text spinner is software that takes a source text, modifies it slightly, and produces new material that someone can then pass off as their own. Text spinners are used all the time for plagiarism.

Using a text spinner is also clearly copyright infringement. However, if the software used AI, it prompts the question of who owns the copyright to the spun material.

This issue came up when Pamela DuMond, a bestselling romance author, sued author Emma Chase over copyright infringement. DuMond alleged that her romantic comedy novel, *Part-Time Princess*, was copied by author Emma Chase, whose romantic comedy novel is *Royally Screwed*, published by Simon & Schuster.

In addition to copyright infringement, DuMond and her attorneys alleged that Chase and Simon & Schuster used text spinning software to write *Royally Screwed*.

The complaint contains very convincing side-by-side comparisons of both novels, showing plot points, passages, and even character names that are a little too similar to be a coincidence.

If the allegations are true, this is potentially a bombshell case. Did Chase use the text spinning software before submitting the novel to Simon & Schuster? If so, why didn't the publisher's team catch it? Didn't they practice due diligence? Wasn't there a warranty clause in the publishing contract that says the author warrants that the work doesn't infringe on anyone's copyrights, and a hold harmless and indemnification clause that stipulates that the author will hold the publisher harmless for any claims arising from copyright infringement? These are boilerplate clauses in any publishing contract that typically can't be negotiated away. If those clauses are present in the publishing contract, then why is Simon & Schuster defending the case instead of cutting ties with the author and asking to be dismissed from the lawsuit? Wouldn't allegations of plagiarism (especially by software) run contrary to the publisher's brand, and therefore be toxic to them? Why are they doubling down on their legal defense team?

Or...did Simon & Schuster's staff use the software? Who used it, who condoned it, what did all of those people know and when did they know it? Did the CEO know? Are other big publishers doing this? If so, who else have they plagiarized?

And more pragmatically—who owns the copyright to the infringing material? The publisher or the AI?

These are all allegations, of course, and I'm not making any accusations. I'm simply asking the questions. But something smells funny. Good attorneys are like bloodhounds—they'll uncover the truth.

This case, while still young at the time of this writing, has earthquake potential on the level of the big publisher price-fixing collusion lawsuit in 2009.

The Passive Guy did a great analysis of the case on his blog and he opined that it could also shape the future of how copyright infringement cases are tried. It would also have broader implications on text spinner software and copyright ownership.

I don't know the answers, but it's an interesting problem.

PUBLISHED BOOKS ARE REAL ESTATE

Your published books are like real estate. They need to be managed just like a landlord manages their properties.

A good landlord always knows what's going on at their properties. They know if pipes are leaking, what dates someone is moving in or out, or when a roof needs to be updated.

Do you know what's going on with your book on Kobo right now? What categories is it in? How about Google Play? What's the discounted price Google is selling your book at right now?

Exactly. You probably don't know. I didn't either, until this year.

Many authors think about the management of their published books as an administrative problem—one that is solved manually or by an assistant. I suggest that this is not an administrative problem; it's a data problem.

The best way to manage your books is to condense them into data points. Look for issues with the data points and manage them accordingly.

To use a simple example, if your book's price should be $2.99, but it's $3.99 at one retailer, that's a problem you can easily solve if you aggregate all your prices into one place to review them. The wrong price will stick out. We can solve this problem and others like it with data tools like Excel and Access, or long-term, dedicated software.

It took a long time for the indie community to think about books as products. I also believe it will be important to think about our books as data too.

BECOME A DATA-DRIVEN WRITER

CLEAN AND MESSY DATA

Our goal is clean data. But when data comes to us, it's often messy.

Think about the sales reports you receive every month. They're not exactly easy to read.

I struck a friendship with a Microsoft Excel MVP, who is one of the top Excel experts in the world. Businesses pay him to consult on data problems, and he makes a good living at it. I learned a lot from chatting with him.

In order to get data clean, we have to do what data analyst professionals call "data wrangling," "data cleansing," or "data munging." This means cleaning up headers, deleting unnecessary data, converting currencies, and so much more so we can get our sales reports to a readable state.

So if we wanted to clean up our sales reports, we'd find a way to standardize them so that they're easier to read, say the same thing, and can be connected. We can do this in many ways, but Microsoft Excel is the tool that can help us do it most effectively.

Without clean data, you can't make decisions, just like you can't see through a dusty window.

EASY DATA ANALYSIS QUESTIONS

I was fortunate enough to have a mentor at work this year who helped me improve my data analysis skills. The mentor taught me to ask a couple of basic questions when looking at any dataset.

What is the data saying at first glance?

Where are the outliers?

If you look "under the covers," what do the outliers tell you?

Does this data make sense given what we know?

What data isn't here?

How do we validate what *is* here?

These are all basic questions, but they helped me make sure I was approaching a work project with a difficult data set correctly.

YOUTUBE ANALYTICS LESSONS

I've learned a lot about my YouTube audience, which has evolved rapidly over the last year as I've brought on new subscribers.

Sixty percent of my audience is age 25-44.

About 40% of my audience is female, but they tend to be more engaged in the content and therefore post more often.

About 20-30% of my views are from outside the United States, with many watching me from the United Kingdom, Canada, Germany, and surprisingly, India.

A sizable percentage of my audience is people of color, but I can't quantify that.

Many in my audience are aspiring writers or have published a handful of books. Most are indie.

My YouTube subscribers like me best when I am exploring writing app technology, sharing transparent stories about my journey, or doing deep dives into fiction craft. When I stray away from those, my YouTube stats suffer.

I've learned to find the sweet spot between content I want to produce versus content my audience wants. This year, I learned to shift non-marketable topics on my podcast, *The Writer's Journey*, where my listeners are more open to listening to unusual ideas. With YouTube, I will stay in my sweet spots, which, fortunately, align with my passions right now.

POWER QUERY

Owning a Mac has many advantages. Doing data analysis isn't one of them.

I didn't know Excel Power Query existed until this year because the Mac version of Excel doesn't have it.

Wow, is it powerful!

Hook up Excel Power Query and Microsoft Access with Microsoft Power BI, and you'll have a data analysis engine that is unrivaled in the indie community. To do this, you have to run Windows 10 on a virtual machine if you own a Mac, however.

If you have no idea what I just said, look it up. You'll thank me for showing you that you've been doing "data" wrong your whole life.

DATABASE NORMALIZATION RULES

This lesson may sound like Greek, or it may not. Let's give it a try, shall we?

In learning database management, the first thing I learned was the fundamental concept of database normalization, which is a universally-accepted approach to building and maintaining databases. The following three rules will ensure that you lay a good foundation for your database.

It's best to think of a database as a series of interconnected tables. Each table should be tall and narrow, meaning they only store the minimum amount of data that is needed.

Rule 1NF states that each cell should only contain a single value. For example, instead of a full name, there should be two fields, one for the first and last name.

Rule 2NF states that data not dependent on the primary key should be moved to a separate table. The primary key is a unique identifier on a particular table that links it to other tables in the database. An employee ID is a classic example of a primary key. An employee ID identifies a name, title, address, and possibly more—and each of those items are stored in separate tables. If you have a table that represents which of your employees helped which of your customers, there should be one table for employees and one for customers; this way, you can link the tables together rather than storing everything on one table. The primary key for each table might be an employee ID and customer ID, respectively.

Rule 3NF states that data that can be derived from other fields should not be stored. For example, on the employee table, you shouldn't store a field for employee initials. You can calculate that with an equation using the employees' first and last name fields.

Anyway, these were the ground rules I followed when building my book database.

Maybe it can help you at some point in your journey.

DATABASES ARE COPYRIGHTABLE

People copyright databases all the time. It's not terribly helpful for most people to know this, but it was helpful for me when I was building my book database because I now understand the true sales and licensing potential.

ONIX, METADATA, AND DATABASES

I have a subscription to LinkedIn Learning and happened to encounter a course on metadata and book publishing.

The course was like the Matrix. It validated all of my database work. It turns out that traditional publishers also manage their books in databases. They use an industry-standard markup language called ONIX, which stands for Online Information Exchange. An ONIX file contains all of a book's or books' metadata and stores it in a special format so that publishers can, with a click of a button, send their books to distributors, retailers, bookstores, and other trading partners.

I always thought there was some poor soul at a publishing house who had to upload and manage the publishers' books on various dashboards. That's not how it works, at least for large publishers.

ONIX is generally exclusive to traditional publishing circles, but the truth is that indie authors can use it too.

In fact, the book database I developed was a crude version of ONIX without realizing it.

Then I discovered through the course that there is professional metadata management software that was designed to help publishers manage this problem. It costs less than $100 (at the time of this writing).

That's when I realized: why develop my own format when I can use the industry standard?

By adopting the industry standard, I can integrate a future database more easily with my website and also bulk upload my titles to a future retailer without any additional effort.

Learning about ONIX was a critical step in my database journey.

DATA DOESN'T GET WRITERS EXCITED

I've doubled down on learning data analysis this year, but I learned that most writers don't want anything to do with data. It scares them. I get it.

How can one motivate people to get excited about data? I believe it's possible if you show them the benefits and give them a tool that helps them bypass the worst part of data analysis, which are data entry and data cleaning. I think many authors would actually be pretty good at data analysis if you visualized it for them. It's not hard; the challenge is getting to the visualization, which requires a few steps. Every step is friction.

POWER BI AND DASHBOARDS

While working on my sales database tool, I discovered Microsoft's Power BI product. BI stands for business intelligence. Outside of data analyst and data science circles, few people know what Power BI is or that it even exists.

You can feed data into Power BI and visualize it in sophisticated yet easy-to-create dashboards. You can create any chart or graph you can dream of, for less time and effort than it would take you in Excel. For example, I can visualize all of my book sales on a geographic map. Some book retailers collect the states, provinces, or ZIP codes of their readers. In the United States, I can see what cities and states my readers are from; for Canada, I can see what territories my readers live in. That's very, very useful.

After building my sales report database, I fed it into Power BI and created a visual dashboard that showed my sales data in an instantly understandable format. It's an indispensable tool, one that I can use for all areas of my business, not just book sales.

Imagine hiring a developer to help you integrate your book sales, website analytics, email newsletter statistics, and any other metric you need to track onto an organized dashboard on Power BI, using APIs and (legal) web scraping. Imagine waking up with a monthly digest of your vital business data. Wouldn't that be a game-changer? That's what I'll be working on in the future.

I have been saying that learning database technology is possibly the biggest breakthrough I have made in my business since publishing my first book. A sound database is the Swiss Army knife for the writer of the future.

RANSOM ATTACKS: A GROWING THREAT

Ransom attacks are on the rise. I talk about this exposure at length in my course *Writing in Hard Times*. I believe it is an emerging threat for writers, but I don't talk about it publicly for fear of bad guys hearing it.

A ransomware attack is when a cybercriminal gets access to your computer and then shuts it down and makes you pay money to get access back.

Many people think ransomware attacks only happen at large organizations. I've read industry statistics that somewhere around 60-70% of ransomware attacks are actually on small businesses.

Writers are small businesses. In fact, we're what the industry calls "micro small businesses."

It's just a matter of time before ransomware creators realize that self-published writers are worthy targets, so start preparing now.

The average ransom for a large business is somewhere between $100,000 and $400,000. For self-published writers, I imagine that the ransom would be a couple hundred dollars. Why? Because the bad guys want to make sure you can pay the ransom. Their entire business model (if you want to call it that) is predicated on their marks paying them.

If a ransom attack happens to you, you have three choices.

First, you can try to disinfect the computer yourself using Internet research or by hiring a computer technician.

Second, you can pay the ransom.

Third, you can abandon the computer.

None of those choices are ideal, so make sure your work is backed up to alternative sources so you have more flexibility.

I'll link to two informative videos I found while researching this topic for my *Writing in Hard Times* course that will help educate you on this topic. You can find them at www.author levelup.com/ransom

AI IS COOL, BUT IT'S ALSO SCARILY DECEPTIVE

Few emerging technologies hold promise like artificial intelligence and machine learning.

Many people are placing blind faith in artificial intelligence, hoping that it will eventually solve many business problems.

The writing community is no different. Perhaps the biggest impact that AI and machine learning can make is in editing. Imagine not having to hire a copyeditor in the future, but instead running your book through a sophisticated algorithm that catches most major errors. That will be a reality one day.

But not today.

You can see AI at work in Microsoft Office. PowerPoint will recommend ideas for slide designs based on your content; Excel will show you data based on questions you ask it; Outlook will show you emails that need attention.

Grammarly, the ubiquitous grammar app, is driven by artificial intelligence and machine learning. So are your smart speakers. All the aforementioned technology is promising, but it's still too new to drive true efficiency.

Most AI applications I have seen for writers have been basic at best, but the marketing makes them look better than they are.

A friend of mine is a Microsoft Excel MVP and he warned me about how AI and ML in Excel in particular is new and prone to mistakes and false positives.

That said, I believe it's very, very important *not* to dismiss emerging technology based on its quality. Think about how many people laughed at the first iPhone because it was slow compared to "dumb" phones at the time. Who's laughing at the iPhone now?

Quality is a red herring that distracts people from the real reason the technology exists.

I consulted on a project to build a custom app for writers this year. In my conversations with the developers (who were extremely talented), I learned that artificial intelligence needs massive amounts of data to be successful. A data engineer can't just build an AI algorithm. They need to feed the AI engine, and that engine is like a coal furnace. Someone's got to constantly feed the beast.

All that data has to come from somewhere. Therefore, companies make their apps available for free to the public with a façade of helping people solve simple tasks, but with the real goal of aggregating data to make the AI engine more effective.

The conversations I had with folks around AI behind closed doors were eye-opening, and a little frightening.

The next time you see a glitzy new app that promises to use the power of AI to help you succeed in life, first ask yourself what data it is taking from you. Second, ask yourself how they're going to use it. Third, consider the very real possibility of whether this company will be around in five years or if they will be sold or acquired—along with your data. Fourth, consider for what reason they might be acquired. If you can step through that mental exercise and come to an answer, you now understand the company's true motive. Then, make your decision accordingly on whether the app is truly worth your time.

Understand that the quality may not be where you expect it to be, but that quality is a red herring. History shows that the quality will *always* improve. The more people use a software with artificial intelligence and machine learning, the smarter it gets over time.

Also, consider this. In the business world, entrepreneurs pitch products to investors. Investors get irritated when an entrepreneur walks through the door with no experience in the industry they're entering. The entrepreneur wants the investors' help and contacts to learn the market.

As a general rule, investors don't like to pay to educate entrepreneurs. It's expensive and usually doesn't end well.

Are YOU okay giving away your data —which has immense value, by the way—to help train an AI with no real benefit in return?

With AI services, you are an investor, and you must choose where and with whom to spend your data.

Remember that when AI becomes more prevalent in the publishing community.

I'm a strong proponent for AI, but I do worry that writers won't truly understand the technology and its risks when bad actors are involved.

BECOME THE WRITER OF
THE FUTURE

ALIGN YOUR BUDGET WITH YOUR
STRATEGIC PRIORITIES

This year, I spoke frequently on all my communication channels about my 2020 and beyond strategy.

My five strategic priorities are to become a world-class content creator, to become a world-class marketer, to become a technology-driven writer, to become a data-driven writer, and to become the writer of the future.

Every project I take on fits into one of those categories.

To cement my strategy further, I revised my budget for 2021 to align with my strategic priorities. This way, I'm putting my money where my mouth is.

How much do I allot for each priority? That was an interesting mental exercise, but necessary. I decided that for the next two to three years, I need to invest more money in data, technology, and futuristic items because we are currently in hard economic times. Looking ahead, I want to emerge from this period with significant advantages. In two to three years, more of my budget will shift toward production and marketing.

FOUR AREAS AI CAN HELP WRITERS OF THE FUTURE

One of the things I have enjoyed most this year is learning about artificial intelligence. I've had conversations with some smart people who have given me great advice.

As I look at the indie publishing community, I think there are four major areas where AI can help us.

The first area is a replacement for developmental editing. Before you come to my house with an angry mob, hear me out...

There are already companies that offer AI developmental editing software. They work by comparing your manuscript to bestselling books. While the quality is questionable *today*, remember my prior comments about quality for emerging technology. It's a red herring. At some point, the quality will improve and there will be a company that wins in the space. This kind of technology will render developmental editors irrelevant, though it won't eliminate the profession.

If you can pay software less than $100 to glean insights about your story's weaknesses, why would you pay several thousand to an editor to do the same thing?

Quality is irrelevant. The main reason that authors pay for developmental editors today is because there's no other good alternative. If they have a choice between an expensive editor and affordable software that is *good enough*, they'll choose the software. Also consider that many authors who hire developmental editors are new and aspiring writers, who, ironically, have the least money to spend because they don't have book sales yet.

The same is true with copyediting and proofreading, but I think the horizon for AI replacing a copyeditor is much further away. It is extraordinarily difficult to program the rules of English into software. Many have tried; most have failed. So far.

The second area is writing assistance. AI has the potential to help us become better versions of ourselves. I don't need AI software that gives me generic spelling and grammar recommendations. I *do* need software that can look at all of the mistakes I've made in my past writing and help me avoid making them again. That would save me editing costs and help me create cleaner books. AI models need a lot of data, so this isn't likely possible until someone finds a way to generate better models that require less data.

Further out, imagine integration with biohacking technology. What if my writing app could track my vitals during writing sessions and tell me when it's time to stop writing because I'm too tired? Or maybe it could sense when I'm distracted and gently redirect me to another function in my writing business instead where my attention would be more productive, like marketing? If I ignored it and wrote anyway, the app could mark those sections with a recommendation for my editor to pay more attention to them and why. It would know my error rate and compare that to my vitals over time. In a sense, your writing app could assume a function similar to a nurse. Your editor would become more like a (true) book doctor, treating areas of the manuscript that are most problematic. In the future, if the book has been run through developmental editing software and more sophisticated grammar and spellchecker software based on prior mistakes, an editor's approach will have to be different and more holistic.

The third area is marketing assistance. Marketing today is manual. I believe AI can help.

Amazon Advertising (and pay-per-click advertising in general) for example, is an area where AI can make a big difference in authors' lives. Every decision with ads is data-driven. If you give a human and an AI a data-driven decision, the AI will win (almost) every time. I love the idea of running my ad reports through an AI that can recommend things like daily budgets, keywords, categories, and so on.

Your first instinct to this might be, "If everyone uses AI for their ads, then they'll become less effective." I don't think that's true. Every book has its own unique audience. We already know that authors aren't truly competitors. If you and I write similar books, readers will eventually want to read them both because they want content that is more similar than different.

Pay-per-click advertising is a discovery tool, so if advanced software can help you get your books discovered, it could help with the discoverability problem and make the "long tail" of book discovery fatter, which means that authors who sell almost no copies of their work can find a bigger audience. Multiply this across the entire industry and you have a bonanza if a developer can get this right.

I also think about software that can monitor any activity around you and your books on the Internet, and provide that to you as a daily report, like Google Alerts but way more powerful. It can send bots to every corner of the Internet, across search engines, podcasts, video sites, and retailers to see what people are saying about you and your books. Maybe it employs sentiment analysis so it knows what's positive and what's negative.

Amazon already uses this technology in its product reviews section.

The fourth area is writing to market. It takes a lot of time to figure out where your book fits in a given market. I do extensive market research, but it seems like no matter how hard I work, I always miss a few books that are similar to mine. It would be nice if AI could do market research. It doesn't have to be right one hundred percent of the time, but if it can make connections that I wouldn't have made otherwise, it's worth it.

There are other ways AI can help indie authors, to be sure, but these are the major areas I am interested in.

BRANDON SANDERSON KICKSTARTER

Many people are celebrating Brandon Sanderson's Kickstarter to create a leather bound edition of one of his books, which funded in minutes and made him several million dollars. It's an amazing success, and I wish him all the best with it.

Dean Wesley Smith argues that it will make Kickstarter pay more attention to publishing projects, which have historically had a high failure rate. Dean has been fairly successful at Kickstarter, integrating it into his regular product creation schedule.

I wonder if that will be a model for the future: write a book, run a Kickstarter to fund limited editions, rinse, and repeat. Kickstarter could become part of your launch strategy, occupying a similar place as Patreon—a fringe revenue source (for most people), but one you can use to drive value for your biggest fans.

DIRECT SALES INTEGRATIONS

I'm finally getting around to integrating direct sales on my website. I've used a few different direct payment services over the years, but I've never been happy with them. They cause too much friction, and the good ones can be expensive.

I used to have a direct store called Michael La Ronn Direct, but I disabled it because it was too much trouble to maintain and readers didn't like it. I decided that I wouldn't do direct sales again until I could do it right.

I rediscovered Payhip, which is affordable and intuitive. They've improved the platform considerably over the years.

My goal is to implement it onto my website by end of the year.

I'm leaving money on the table by not doing direct sales, and I recognize that. There were too many other projects with a better ROI that I kept pushing this down on my priority list. But since this year is an infrastructure year for me, now is the time to implement direct sales again so that I can improve my earnings.

I will also need the ability to accept cryptocurrencies and blockchain transactions in the future, but I'm not ready for that yet.

BACKGROUND ELIMINATOR

An affiliate network I participate in sent me an email about a new affiliate that promised to use AI to eliminate unwanted background noise during conference calls. Crying babies, barking dogs, loud spouses, and so on. The affiliate network promised that the product was a slam dunk for people working from home due to the pandemic, and I bet the claim was true.

The email came at an interesting time because I happened to notice similar technology in other places that week.

Eliminate background noise with the help of artificial intelligence.

Adobe Premiere offers this technology with its sound healing feature. I once watched someone eliminate a telephone ring from a piece of audio. It was as if the ring was never there. This is why Adobe is a pioneer in AI.

Now, this new affiliate offered that same technology, but in real-time. They've probably been in business for a while but are just now starting to get traction. Companies like that don't just come out of nowhere.

Around the time I wrote this chapter, I also happened to be on a Microsoft Teams call; while I was setting up my microphone, I noticed a green screen feature that allowed me to change my background to something more pleasant, like a beach, a fake conference room, or even outer space. While it wasn't a true green screen replacement, it didn't look bad.

Background and background noise replacement in real-time. I believe this is the start of a bigger trend that is going to catch fire in the next few years.

What if a podcast recording app allowed you to eliminate background noise, therefore allowing you to record anywhere, like a busy park or a crowded food court? What if it could make your voice sound better too?

What if a video editing app could replace your background and lighting without the use of a green screen?

In case the trend isn't clear, let me explain.

If you look at the history of audio and video recording, it is all about democratizing the medium so that more people can create in it. Only film broadcasting studios could shoot high quality video until digital cameras came along. Podcasting as we know it today was possible twenty years ago, but only if you had the money to afford sound equipment and the know-how to operate it.

Today, anyone can make high-quality videos on their smart-phones; they can use those same smartphones to record podcasts with apps like Anchor.

Now we have a new wave of technology that will make it easier for people to record anywhere without fear of distracting background noise or unprofessional backgrounds. Imagine what this could do in developing countries, or for those people who are too self-conscious to put themselves into the world for fear of loud children or lack of space to create green screen videos.

As the price of smartphones and audio and video decrease and the quality of their signal capture increase, we have more content creators who will feel empowered to make content that they otherwise would have never considered. And that's a good thing.

If the technology quality advances significantly, we might even see a world where people can narrate studio audiobooks thanks to background noise elimination. Is it a stretch? Maybe, but's it interesting.

SUBLICENSES

When you license your copyrights, sometimes the people or companies you license your work to may want to license your work again. The classic example might be a publisher signing a deal on your behalf to get your book into audio.

Whenever possible, you want to control sublicense situations, and you don't want a licensee signing rights on your behalf. This can be negotiated into a licensing contract.

If you're looking at a contract, it may be a useful thought exercise to think about potential situations where a sublicensing situation can come up.

It's also worth thinking about how sublicensing works on the sites you use every day. For example, if you post a photo to Instagram, you're giving Instagram (and anyone who uses it) a license to embed your photo anywhere. What if someone embeds your photo on their website instead of paying you for it, but your photography business is based on licensing your photos for a fee? There was a lawsuit about this very topic this year.

Part of being the writer of the future is understanding how the contracts you sign today will impact your career ten, twenty, or thirty years into the future.

LICENSING YOUR PERSONA

I spoke with a company this year about licensing my voice to read audiobooks. They make AI versions of your voice so that readers can choose who reads their audiobooks to them. The technology is advancing so fast that soon you won't be able to tell it's an AI. It reminds me a lot of when GPSes introduced custom voices like Homer Simpson and Samuel L. Jackson to narrate turn-by-turn directions.

That seems to be where audio is headed—one market for standard, traditionally-narrated audiobooks, and another for cheaper versions narrated by AI.

While the talks with the company didn't work out, I learned a great deal about which direction I need to pivot. I need to create hours and hours of high quality audio narration so that I can put myself in a position to license my voice for this technology. This way, readers can choose to hear my voice narrate ALL of my books, whether I narrated them traditionally or not. There are many interesting opportunities that can spring from this technology.

COPYRIGHT EXPIRATION

I was working with an author to help him publish a book. He wanted my feedback, so I reviewed his cover, book description, and more.

I then noticed that his book was a reimagining of another book that was published in 1926.

The question both of us were curious about was: could he do this?

There were two issues: the first was whether the original book was in the public domain or not. Per the United States Copyright Act, works published prior to 1925 are in the public domain. Works published prior to January 1, 1978 could have been extended 95 years of protection from the publication date if the registration was renewed in the 28th year of publication, but they cannot get more than 95 years of protection from the date of publication.

What I learned in doing a copyright search was that a revised version of the book was registered in the 29th year, so the heir to the author's estate missed the window. From what I could tell, even though the copyright office granted the registration, the book entered the public domain. Only the new and revised parts of the book would have been protected. Even if the book didn't for some reason enter the public domain, it will in 2021.

But the author I was working with didn't copy any of the text from the book, so ultimately, he would have been fine. There was no copyright infringement. We were simply curious.

The second issue, which was the real issue, was whether the book title was trademarked, not as a book title, but as a brand. This was a self-help book. Sometimes self-help gurus will trademark books not as books, but as brands that include books. While you can't trademark a book title, you CAN trademark a brand, which means you can authorize someone to take down a book that has a trademark in the title.

After performing a trademark search, this did not appear to be the case, so the author will probably be fine.

But it begs another thought: it's just a matter of time before the trademark wars reach publishing.

I've been concerned for quite some time about trademark trolls wreaking havoc on merchandise sellers on Etsy and Amazon.

The dangerous part about trademarks is that they work retroactively; if you publish a series today and someone secures a trademark on a series title five years from now, they can make you take your book down or change your series title.

So far, the community has taken a strong stance against authors trying to secure trademarks for series titles. Those efforts have been successful, but someone will break the pattern at some point, creating a watershed moment.

We may eventually reach the point where some authors may have to proactively trademark elements of their work to avoid this problem, which will drive up the cost of publishing. It could create haves and have-nots, where trolls actively trade-mark series titles of successful books by have-nots who can't afford trademarks. The trolls will extort those authors to make money or to silence voices they don't want to be heard.

I hope this future doesn't become a reality.

SHERLOCK AND ENOLA HOLMES

In 2008, author Nancy Springer published a series called *The Enola Holmes Mysteries*. It followed a character she invented named Enola Holmes, who is the fictional sister of Sherlock Holmes. The story follows her as she solves mysteries. Sherlock Holmes, Dr. Watson, and Mycroft Holmes make regular appearances in the stories. The books were so popular that they were adapted into a major motion picture film.

The estate of Sir Arthur Conan Doyle sued for copyright infringement. They sued Springer, Penguin, Netflix, the movie production studios, and the screenwriter and director, alleging copyright *and* trademark infringement.

The character Sherlock Holmes is in the public domain. However, the last ten short stories that Conan Doyle wrote are not. The estate argued that Conan Doyle wrote these stories after World War I, when he decided to change the essence of Sherlock Holmes. Holmes had a reputation for being aloof and somewhat cold; Conan Doyle changed that and made him warmer.

Because the books and film portray Holmes as kind, the estate alleged that the author committed copyright infringement because the Holmes that appears in the Enola Holmes Mysteries exhibits character traits from the latter Holmes, which are still under copyright. They also alleged violation of trademarks around the Sherlock Holmes brand because the name Enola Holmes could create customer confusion and therefore lead consumers to believe that the *Enola Holmes Mysteries* are affiliated with the Conan Doyle estate, which they are not.

There are a lot of moving parts to this case, but the most interesting takeaway for me was the trademark infringement allegations. I've said for the last two to three years that we are going to see more trademark claims against authors—primarily because more authors will start to secure trademarks as a defensive gesture. And once you own a trademark, you have to defend it or you'll lose it. This will create a legal environment where the "haves" can afford to secure trademarks and enforce them while the "have-nots" will have no choice but to acquiesce to any demand because they cannot afford the legal costs.

That is a terrifying future. At least with copyright infringement, you won't be sued unless the other person can make a compelling case against you. There are certain barriers to frivolous lawsuits. Those barriers do not exist with trademarks.

I worry about the precedent a case like this could set if the Conan Doyle estate wins, but at the time of this writing, it's too soon to tell.

Another unspoken element of the case that gave me pause was the contractual arrangement between the author and the publisher, Penguin Random House.

Like the case I explored earlier, I have questions. Did the publisher's legal team not do any kind of due diligence? Or were they confident that if a lawsuit arose, they could afford the risk?

Most importantly, did the author have a hold harmless agreement with the publisher? I'd wager not, especially if

Penguin was aware of the potential conflicts—which they probably were. I can only hope she had a solid contract.

Years ago, my very first novel (which I never finished) borrowed significantly from the public domain. It featured many public domain characters, and I thought the concept was pretty cool. However, I scrapped the project for the very concern that Conan Doyle's estate is suing for now—I worried at the time that copyright might extend to character traits, as not all the characters in the story had bodies of work that were *completely* in the public domain. Jeeves, the famous butler, also appeared in the story.

Throw in movies, spin-off books, and other media created through the ages around public domain characters and I worried that I could have been sued for something very little that I could never anticipate.

After reading this lawsuit (whether the estate succeeds or not), I am very glad I scrapped that novel, as a very kind and generous Mr. Holmes did make an appearance.

GROUP REGISTRATION

In June 2020, the United States Copyright Office promulgated a rule that allows writers to register up to 50 short works (100-17,500 words) published online in a single registration.

This is a pretty big deal for freelancers, bloggers, and journalists, who until now, had no easy way to register their content. It also has implications for self-published writers.

For example, if you publish short stories on your website (like a Ray Bradbury Challenge) or if you give short stories away every week on your blog like Kristine Kathryn Rusch does, you can now register those works, assuming they are text-only and published within a 90-day period. This does not apply to books; for most self-published writers, it applies to blogs.

I mostly had questions as I read the final rule from the Copyright Office.

My understanding is that a group registration will explicitly list each of the individual works directly. Is there a benefit to publishing your work online first (such as on your website) and then registering the work as a group? Would this give you potentially better and stronger copyright ownership than registering all of the stories under a single collection whose public registration record does not specify the individual works except in the sample you provide to the Copyright Office? Not sure if I know the answer.

Also, what about podcasts and video works? My YouTube channel has almost 300 videos. There's no way I'm registering each video separately. My podcast *The Writer's Journey* has 52 episodes per year, and my podcast *Writing Tip of the Day* has around 275 episodes per year. As is, I can't register them easily.

I can't help but wonder if we'll see group registrations introduced for podcasts and web content at some point.

WHAT MIGHT THE FALL OF INDIES LOOK LIKE?

I mentioned in the introduction of this book that one day the self-publishing sector will fall on hard times, much like traditional publishers are experiencing with the pandemic.

What will that look like?

What events would precipitate a decline in indie author income?

I don't know. Global economic recession or depression is my first thought.

A close second is a trend away from books toward more interactive experiences—gaming, movies, or even virtual reality in the long-term. Authors who don't pivot will be left behind.

Also, another event that might initiate this is Amazon taking some sort of action that hurts all authors, such as reducing its sales commissions, or restricting the 70% commission to KDP Select authors only, or introducing some sort of new sales commission scheme that drives authors to make less money overall. This happens all the time.

Another might be a traditional publisher "come back." Maybe the pandemic forces traditional publishers to figure out that they need to start innovating and spend a lot of money on technology and marketing value-adds for its authors, enticing more people to seek traditional publishing (and sign the same old terrible contracts). Perhaps innovation technology gives them a clear market advantage over indies, maybe through artificial intelligence. They'll undergo a brand refresh as well.

It's also not hard to imagine a political event that precipitates a societal distaste for self-publishing, such as a self-published writer who commits a mass murder and leaves behind a trail of books that espouse hatred and very obvious motives. I pray to God that never happens, as it would turn governments and public sentiment against indie writers.

But honestly, I don't know what an extinction event for indies would look like, or how bad it would be. It's worth asking the question, as when it happens, it will seem like it came out of nowhere, but will have been glaringly obvious in retrospect.

I think the sole reliance on the book as we know it is a liability. I also think not diversifying your books across all retailers is another warning sign. KDP Select is a game of musical chairs. You don't want to be playing the game when the music stops.

Other than that, I don't know, but it will be very, very interesting to see how resilient the indie community is through the decades.

HOW LONG WILL SMARTPHONES LAST?

Will the smartphone be with us forever?

While they have helped to improve our lives, there is growing evidence that they may be harmful to our health.

It's not implausible to imagine younger generations, perhaps those that haven't been born yet, seeking to abandon smartphones in favor of more experience-driven technology that is less obtrusive and allows them to interact with their environment. That technology could take many forms, many of which haven't been conceived yet, so it's not worth exploring them.

Might the smartphone be a "old folk thing" to our descendants? Will we reminisce what it was like to have iOS and Android devices much like we reminisce about rotary and flip phones today?

If the "handheld device" as we know it were removed from our lives, how would that change how we write, publish, and market? In other words, how does the device-less writer write and reach the device-less reader?

Audio and voice are the first technologies that come to mind along with augmented and virtual reality.

In the future, could people turn anything into a speaker or a screen? Will vibrations become a part of our nonverbal communication? Or will we avoid that altogether and control technology with our minds?

IDEAS YOU CAN STEAL

PLANNER FOR WRITERS

I've always thought that a dedicated physical planner for writers would be a great idea. I bought a Passion Planner last year and loved it. There's something pleasant about writing your goals down on pen and paper.

My hunch is that a planner that helped writers track their word counts, their book's progress, and maybe their emotional state in addition to the usual planner items would be well-received in our community. Especially if it was beautiful.

Planners are consistently a top product on Kickstarter. If the right author did it, they could get it funded, no problem.

CROWDFUNDING IN REVERSE

Kickstarter needs no introduction.

But what if there was a Kickstarter in reverse?

What if there was a site where customers could post problems they wish there was a solution to? What if entrepreneurs could review the problems, find ways to solve them, and then submit proposals with an explanation of what they can do, a completion date, and a dollar amount? The platform would facilitate an automated interview process where customers could ask questions and the entrepreneurs could revise their proposals if needed. Then the customers would pledge a dollar amount to fund the proposal they want to see turned into reality. If the project funds, the entrepreneur receives half the money upfront and the final half upon delivery of the project and an 80% or higher customer satisfaction rate.

It could be a discovery platform for entrepreneurs looking for problems to solve, and a win for customers who can articulate needs that entrepreneurs may not have thought of.

A platform like this would have tremendous benefits for writers. It could be a clever way for us to drive competition between writing apps, for example. If writing apps don't evolve to do what we want them to do, let's pay someone who will do the job. There would be unlimited potential.

GIVING YOUR BOOK AWAY ON TORRENT SITES

A torrent site is a special type of peer-to-peer file-sharing protocol that takes a single file and breaks it into many pieces that your computer has to download. Your computer downloads those pieces from other downloaders' computers all over the world, and once it has all the pieces, it reassembles them together so that you can open the download. It is a highly sophisticated form of file sharing, and while it is legitimate, it is often used for illegal purposes, such as film or pornography downloads. Torrent sites such as "The Pirate Bay" are considered seedy underbellies of piracy.

What if you gave your books away on a torrent site? What would happen?

I have no idea because I've always chickened out at the idea. But I would think a genre like LitRPG could find a new audience on a torrent site. If you accept pirates as they are—a different but valid audience for your work—then interesting things could happen.

Torrent sites are not for the faint of heart, but maybe there's something there.

A BOOK COVER DESIGN YOUTUBE CHANNEL

Have you ever noticed how so many self-published authors choose to design their own book covers, yet there are almost no proven resources for them to learn the art of cover design?

Sure, you can learn design fundamentals, but that doesn't teach you how to design a book cover. Not specifically.

If I were a (good) book cover designer, here's what I would do.

I would start a YouTube channel teaching the ins and outs of book cover design. I'd show how I design my covers, letting people watch live as I designed a cover. I'd also teach the nuances of Photoshop, GIMP, or other design apps, and I'd teach authors design theory and how to make their book covers better. I'd teach how to design tasteful ads and other marketing materials for their books too. I'd write *the* definitive book on cover design and make *the* definitive premium course. That doesn't exist yet.

My content would make a real difference in authors' design skills, and therefore their sales.

I'd also expand the channel into book formatting since it's complementary. Heck, I might even find a formatter co-host who does separate videos on the channel but in the same style so we could build our volume and ad revenue quickly. We could team up a few times a year and do a *This Old House*-style segment where we take an author who has a horrendous cover and interior formatting, and revamp it free of charge as a way to market the channel and give back to the community.

The channel would be a resource for the industry, but most importantly, it would be the primary way I get clients. I'd have so many clients that I'd be booked months in advance.

As I said before, I'd have to be a good designer. Good designers are rare.

Design is a completely foreign world to authors. A book cover design channel on YouTube would be the only one of its kind, and therefore easy to stand out.

IP PATROLLER

I mentioned in the data section how it's a good idea to think about your books as real estate.

Landlords that have a lot of properties hire property managers. Property managers take care of the maintenance, screening for tenants, and any other issues that come up at a property.

Why not have *intellectual* property managers? Instead of a person, I believe this can best be accomplished with software.

Let's say that there's an app called Rover. Rover knows every intimate detail of your books because it connects to your book database. Rover patrols all of the retailers where you publish your books, looking for any problems. If Rover sees the wrong price, he alerts you via email. If the HTML in your book description breaks, he lets you know. He'll even check to verify that the right version of your book is for sale. If you *don't* hear from him, you'll know that everything with your books is fine.

Rover might even keep watch on the other books in your genre, and he could alert you when trends change and your book needs to adapt; he could let you know when it might be time to change your cover, for example. Rover could be a short and long-term tool.

Rover is what I call a yet-to-exist class of software called intellectual property management applications. These apps would treat your books as data and alert you on discrepancies. In a perfect world, they could fix the problems for you, but that's unlikely to happen.

Once, I did a book promo but forgot to change the price from $0.99 back to the original price. I didn't find out about the problem for six months. I lost a lot of money—four figures worth of income. Rover could have spotted that problem immediately and thus saved me money.

In talking about this concept on my channels, my experience is that most indie authors don't understand the need for this software yet, mainly because they don't have enough books for it to be a problem yet. But if our mantra as a community is that we want to make a career out of writing, that means a decent amount of authors will be prolific enough to have this problem long-term.

BOOK MARKETING BROWSER PLUGIN

We need our book metadata often. We may need to give readers a specific link to Barnes & Noble, or fill out a promo form with all our Book 1's basic details, or send our book information to a podcast host.

I envision a browser plugin that gives you easy access to all of your book metadata so that if you need it, you can select the book in the plugin, and the plugin will auto-populate most of the book's info for you. The plugin might also automatically take you to any folders on your computer for that specific book so you don't have to click around to find the right folders.

Think of it like a password wallet like LastPass, LogMeIn, or the Safari keychain, but for your books. Pick the book you want, and the plugin auto-populates as much data as it can. If desired, you could export data from the plugin too. You could also integrate the plugin into a database so that the database feeds the plugin.

Database idea aside, I don't believe this would be too difficult to program.

AUTHOR MARKETING CO-OP

I received a question from an author who asked if there were "self-publishing marketing co-ops." The author had experience with buying advertising through a local small business co-op and wondered if the indie community had the same thing.

A co-op is when multiple businesses pool their money to create a marketing outreach that is bigger than any of the businesses could achieve by themselves. For example, when I moved into my new house, I receive a generous book full of coupons from small businesses in the area—restaurants, insurance agents, contractors, garden centers, and more. Each business paid their fair share to produce the book. If you shop with one of the businesses, you're more likely to shop with another because they have referral programs.

While I don't think that there is a formal way to do this at the moment, I do think indies can pool their collective dollars for marketing. Authors do it for box sets and compilations all the time. It would be interesting to see authors find new ways to cross-promote each other using some kind of co-op. I think this could be particularly effective if all of the authors used direct sales. It would also be interesting if a book retailer tried this with authors in the same genre, using their platform to boost the sales of the authors, perhaps at an affordable rate for the authors to purchase the service.

MICROSOFT EXCEL FOR WRITERS

Microsoft Excel and (most) writers don't mix. However, there are many authors in the community who are masters at Excel. It would be great if one (or a few) of them wrote how-to books or created easy-to-consume courses to help the community get better at data analysis and get the most out of Excel.

There are books and courses out there, but I find that they are more complicated than most authors need. It's also hard to apply the concepts in general audience Excel videos to our situation as writers. It would be great to learn from someone who understands the community.

The simpler, the better. The goal should be to help authors feel more confident in Excel. If they can walk away with a basic framework of how to manipulate data, and maybe a few tips and tricks that they can use every day, I think an Excel book or course for writers could do well. At a minimum, it could recoup the cost of production.

PERSONALIZED EDITING RULES ENGINE

Before I share this idea, I acknowledge that it's not easy to reduce the English language into code. Our language has chewed up and spit out legions of programmers and data scientists trying to solve this problem.

That said, I do think there is more we can do.

In my line of work as an insurance consultant, one of my responsibilities is to review the company's business rules engine. The engine is an IBM product called ODM, which stands for Operational Decision Management, which is an engine that maintains a series of if-then rules that serve as the "brain" of the business's operations.

To use an oversimplified example, let's pretend I have an ice cream shop.

If a new customer purchases ice cream, then the system will print a 20% off coupon for their next purchase.

If an existing customer purchases ice cream in an amount greater than $10, they also get a 20% off coupon.

If an out-of-state customer makes a purchase, they receive a print-out with the ice cream shop's website and a call-to-action to share on social media. After all, it makes zero sense to give them a coupon if they're just passing through.

This means that existing customers who spend less than $10 and out-of-state customers don't receive a coupon. These rules would be programmed into the ice cream shop's point of sale system and could be tweaked at any time.

How could we apply this to the English language? As I said before, it would be foolish to try to create a rules engine for the entire English language. That's a fool's errand. But what if you could build an engine whose sole focus was to help you clean up your manuscript by identifying past mistakes your editor had to correct?

I envision the development of this app as a series of steps.

First, you would need some way to classify every word in the English language. You would need the app to distinguish between verbs, nouns, adverbs, prepositions, and so on. There are college linguistics departments that provide open-source libraries that contain this information—Princeton immediately comes to mind. Much of this work has already been done.

The app would also need to know tenses, conditions, as well as context. Take the word *ride*—it can be a noun or a verb depending on the context. This would be the trickiest part. A developer could start with the five hundred most common words in the English language and program those first to create a minimum viable product.

Next, once you have every word properly classified, then you could start programming rules. Let the author do it using an easy way to construct if-then statements, much like Apple iTunes allows you to create Smart Playlists.

The equation would be: **if-then statement + action.**

For example, let's say that my editor makes a change to my manuscript because I wrote the sentence "I want cookie sandwich." I left out the article "a" and the sentence should have said "I want a cookie sandwich."

The rule might read "If noun follows verb, look for [article] between them. If one does not exist, highlight the noun and the verb." The rule would run on every book moving forward to help me catch the same error.

Let's also say that my editor makes a change to my manuscript because I used the word *cadence* incorrectly in a sentence.

The rule might read "If word CADENCE is used, highlight every instance of the word."

Let's say that I have a bad habit of using the same word repetitively.

Take the paragraph "Eating ice cream is important. As a historical national treasure, its importance cannot be under-stated. It is also important to note that only 50 percent of dessert eaters prefer ice cream."

As you can tell, I used *important* way too much.

The rule might read "if ANY WORD other than [common articles, common prepositions] appears more than once within the same 250 word radius, highlight each instance of the word." I can then review each instance to verify if a change is needed. I could also tweak the radius if I wanted. A rule like this could easily be programmed to police your use of the word "I" in first-person stories, as another example.

I could also program rules that catch if I write numerals instead of spelling out numbers. Editors usually have standards on what you should do in a certain situation as dictated by the style manuals they adhere to; these rules could easily be programmed. For instance, if I write the word *forty* when I should use the numeral 40 instead, the rules can easily catch that.

Compared to mapping the entire English language, I think

this alternative could be slightly more doable. It would require you to understand how to form effective if-then statements. Perhaps artificial intelligence could help, but this technology may best be coded by a developer.

This could also be very effective if it could run in real-time while you were writing so that it could alert you to potential problems while you were typing.

If someone could pull this off, a personalized rule engine could be a game-changer for writers wanting to catch more errors in their manuscripts.

AUDIOBOOK TRANSITION TOOL

Writing with the audio version of your book in mind is not a skill that comes naturally to me.

When I recorded my first audiobook, I found several instances in my writing that did not translate well into audio. If I had known that before recording, I would have made changes.

It would be insightful to solicit feedback from a few dozen professional audiobook narrators to find out what irritates them when they're doing their readings.

Take the narrators' feedback, program as much of that feedback as you can into rules, and then create a simple app or Microsoft Word plugin that can scan an author's text and highlight words or sections that won't translate well into audio. You wouldn't be able to catch everything, but you would be able to capture some important items. The author can then make the necessary changes across their ebook, paperback, and audiobook script so that all versions of their book are consistent.

This tool could be integrated into the personalized rules engine I mentioned too.

Since audiobook is a permanent format, it pays to make sure

your book is as perfect as it can be before the narrator starts recording.

BRAND MONITORING SYSTEM

I've yet to find a brand monitoring system that works well.

Google Alerts works sometimes, but it's notoriously inconsistent.

A successful author needs a comprehensive brand monitoring system that alerts them whenever they or their books are mentioned on the Internet. Social media monitoring sites exist, but an author needs more than that. They need to know if an influencer reviews their book on their blog, or if someone mentions them on a podcast or YouTube channel. They also need to know as soon as possible in case they want to take some kind of action, such as sharing it with their audience. It's bad form to thank someone for shouting out your book six months after they mention it...better late than never, but it makes you look silly.

Also, understanding what people are saying about you in real-time helps you make better decisions about your business.

A COMPANY THAT MAINTAINS YOUR BOOKS WHEN YOU DIE

Every author will die, whether they like it or not.

When you die, who will maintain the rights to your books? Who will make sure they remain for sale? Who will update the book covers when they go stale? Who will answer the email when Hollywood wants to make a movie?

If you have a spouse or child who is willing to manage those rights, then that's the answer.

But many authors don't have spouses or children, or they don't have spouses or children who know how or want to manage their books. The result is that, if we do nothing, generations of authors will die, and their books will die with them. That's a shame because books generate income whether we're alive or not, and that's money our families can use.

Imagine a company that says "Sign a contract with us. When you die, we'll take the rights to your books and we'll keep them for sale so that readers can always buy them. We'll take a commission and pass the remaining royalties to your family each month. If you pay us an additional fee, we'll even change your covers and book descriptions as trends change for the next ten years. While you're alive, you keep your rights and we have no interest in your work. When you die, we'll be there for your family."

Basically, it would be a traditional publisher, but for when you die. The product would function like an annuity, but for your beneficiaries.

When you consider that more people will continue to trend toward indie publishing, you have a renewable audience every year.

I'm making this sound simple, but building a company like this would be far from simple. For starters, you'd be in court a lot. The legal fees would be extraordinary. You'd need a solid way of eliminating fraud and the handling of illegitimate children that pop up out of nowhere.

But the right person could start this company and turn it into a unicorn. The company could effortlessly expand into music and the arts. With enough leverage, you could offer a marketplace to Hollywood and other subsidiary rights buyers who can purchase rights cheaply, easily, and without fear of contractual lawsuits, assuming the company could properly vet authors and their estate situations. Beneficiaries would get pleasant emails whenever a right has been purchased, and a nice payday in their bank account along with a copy of the agreement.

The platform could also automate and simplify intellectual property agreements so that no humans ever talk to each other. The company would have all the leverage because it would control the terms at which rights buyers come to the table.

To put the potential vise-grip this company could have on the marketplace into perspective, consider the company Upwork, the freelancer platform. Upwork provides access to talented freelancers, but places a number of controversial restrictions on its users. If users don't like it, then they can leave, but Upwork is the biggest game in town, so they don't want to leave.

Unlike a traditional publisher, who will only promote their top-selling titles, this company could explore artificial intelligence as a way for it to find ways to sell more of *everything* in its catalogue, possibly using AI and machine learning for pay-per-click advertising as I mentioned before. If the AI can purchase ads for even the most obscure books with confidence, with just a minimal return on investment, it would make the company wildly profitable.

All of this could work because authors all over the world have a dream: to get their books published. Many of them want their books to survive them.

CONTENT CREATED WHILE WRITING THIS BOOK

150 Self-Publishing Questions Answered (Book)

This book was written in a partnership between Michael and The Alliance of Independent Authors (ALLi, a nonprofit organization for self-published writers), and it answers the most common self-publishing questions in a conversational question and answer format. The audiobook is narrated by Michael!

Buy your copy at www.authorlevelup.com/150

Writing in Hard Times (Course)

Learn how to future-proof your writing business by learning the basics of risk management for writers. This course draws on Michael's experience in insurance protecting thousands of businesses every day. You'll learn how to protect your business, family, and your data from anything life throws your way. Never get caught off-guard again. As is typical with Michael, this is the only course of its kind in the writing community.

Enroll today at www.authorlevelup.com/hardtimes

. . .

Author Level Up YouTube Channel - Highlights

Watch at youtube.com/authorlevelup.

How Long Should Your Novel Be?

How much does it cost to publish a book?

Beta Readers: The ONLY Video You Will Ever Need

Read Like a Writer

Interviews & Appearances

The Sample Chapter Podcast: Michael discusses his fiction writing process, writer's block, and reads a chapter from his book, *Shadow Deal*.

Inspirational Indie Author Interviews with Howard Lovy: Michael appears in a montage of interviews with thoughts on how to write during lockdown and how to cope with the pandemic.

VOLUME TWO

INDIE AUTHOR CONFIDENTIAL

Secrets No One Will Tell You About Being a Writer

VOL. 2

M.L. RONN

INTRODUCTION

At the time of this writing, the COVID-19 pandemic continues, and I continue my commitment to learning how to level up my game as an author. I also continue my commitment to sharing my lessons learned with you.

Volume 1 of this series covers April through June 2020, which was around the start of the pandemic shutdowns. My learning was unfocused and wandering as I dealt with the early challenges of the shutdowns. My biggest goal was to ensure that my family and writing business would be in a position to weather the figurative storm. That quarter was tough to navigate because everyday life threw a curveball at me.

The easiest thing for me to focus on during the last volume was building my business's infrastructure. It was a great time to work on problems I had put off for a long time, like how to calculate my sales commissions accurately.

This volume (Volume 2) covers the third quarter of the year —July through September 2020. You'll find that my main focus throughout the quarter was still on infrastructure, but late in the quarter, I shifted toward production and writing again.

August through October of this year will be what I affectionately call "Beast Mode." Since I didn't write many books during the first half of the year, I'm aiming for a strong three months with a lot of books at the end of it. I'm going into beast mode so I can have a strong production year despite everything that's going on in the world.

In many ways, the lessons I learned in this volume were preparing me for "Beast Mode," but I didn't realize it until I wrote this introduction. I look forward to sharing the results of my beast mode with you in Volume 3. In the meantime, the infrastructure lessons this quarter were very productive and insightful for me.

My Core Strategic Priorities

As a refresher, my mission is to create content that entertains and/or educates my audience, preferably both. I do this by focusing on five strategic priorities:

1. Become a world-class content creator
2. Become a world-class marketer
3. Become a technology-driven writer
4. Become a data-driven writer
5. Become the writer of the future

I believe these five priorities are most important for me to have a long-term sustainable career.

What's in This Volume

In the last volume, I created a novel way to track my sales. This quarter, I found ways to visualize my sales data.

In the last volume, I also explored the idea of a personalized rules engine for AI-assisted editing of my manuscripts. I had a major breakthrough with that idea. Turns out it's much easier to accomplish than I thought. Shockingly easier.

I cover a lot of new ground too.

I experienced a three-day-long power outage that put my business contingency plan to the test. Because of good planning, I didn't lose momentum on my work-in-progress (though I did lose everything in my fridge). If you don't know what a business contingency plan is, you're in for a fun adventure!

I also made the biggest sales blunder of the year, costing me hundreds of dollars.

I hired a video editor, which was a major level up for my career.

I explored the ins and outs of browser-based writing apps, introducing my community to a new and competitive sector of the writing app space.

I continued my lessons in becoming a data-driven writer by finding new ways to think about my books as data points.

And, I came up with some pretty unique and interesting ideas for you to steal too.

There's plenty to explore, and hopefully, this book will inspire you to think about your writing business differently.

Thanks for reading this very experimental series. My sincerest hope is that it helps you in some way.

M.L. Ronn
Des Moines, Iowa
September 15, 2020

BECOME A WORLD-CLASS
CONTENT CREATOR

MASCULINE VS. FEMININE
PROBLEM-SOLVING

I read a great book called *The Laws of Human Nature* by Robert Greene. It's a guide to understanding human nature so you can build your influence and impact. The book is a modern-day Machiavellian handbook, though I don't think Greene intended for this to be the case.

An early highlight in the book was when Greene explained the difference between feminine and masculine problem-solving. The term isn't meant to be sexist; there are men who use feminine problem-solving and vice versa. Understanding both styles is key to learning how to influence people because you need to change your style to suit others' preferences.

As a general statement, Greene wrote that females tend to have a non-confrontational approach to solving problems. They "feel" their way through problems and succeed by drawing on relationships with others to build consensus. This is the opposite of how males approach a problem, which is usually by throwing themselves into a problem and figuring a way out.

There's no right or wrong way, but it's helpful to know the style of the people you're trying to persuade. I found the advice to be particularly helpful in my job with corporate America this year, but I also think it's true of human nature in general.

What might your characters' problem-solving style look like? Wouldn't it be interesting to capture this little detail accurately on the page?

EDITING TABLE

I worked with a new editor for my book *150 Self-Publishing Questions Answered*, and she did something I've never seen before.

She added questions and comments in the manuscript about areas that didn't make sense, but then she pasted all of her editorial questions in a separate word document formatted as a table, with the comment, page number, and a column for me to respond if I wanted to.

This is an interesting idea because it keeps the manuscript uncluttered from unnecessary back and forth between the editor and me. More importantly, it's an important thing I can do for the editor up-front.

Instead of putting my questions as comments, I may create a separate Word document with my questions referenced there so the editor can answer them there instead of in the manuscript itself. It's an extra step, but it's cleaner.

EASY SOCIAL MEDIA VIDEOS

The website I use for stock images, audio, and video released a new service that allows you to create short videos using their stock content mixed with your own. It's a browser-based video editor, which is a novel idea that I've never seen before. Doubly smart is the ability to integrate it with their powerful content library.

In ten minutes, I had a great-looking social media video with images, audio, and video to promote one of my books.

I could have done this on my own, but the app made it more convenient. The app makes everything look more professional, which suits my goal of becoming a world-class content creator.

This was a pleasant surprise and another tool in my toolbox in the future.

HIRING A VIDEO EDITOR

I decided to hire a video editor for my YouTube channel this year. My schedule was so busy that it was the right time.

I've worked with a dedicated video editor in the past, so I knew what to expect.

My time is best spent strategizing, shooting videos, and connecting with my subscribers. Editing was eating up too much of my time each week, and the quality of my channel was suffering.

The first three videos were really about the editor and me getting to know each other. The videos weren't perfect, but they were much better than anything I could have done myself. Each video took approximately 7-10 hours to plan, shoot, and produce. Now that we're familiar with each other, it takes around 3-5 hours.

It takes me approximately two hours to plan a video, 30 minutes to shoot, 30 minutes to upload and communicate with the editor, and another 30 minutes to watch and provide feedback. That's around 4.5 hours, which, ironically, was about the time it took me to produce a video on my own.

While I didn't save a ton of time, I restructured my time so that it was more profitable. The time spent editing now goes to planning, which means that I can make more videos that will improve my subscriber count, views, and average view duration. I can now spend more time in the comments of my videos, assisting subscribers with their questions. I don't feel "rushed" to make videos like I used to.

By spending time doing the *right* activities, I'm happier and I make more money. It makes for a better experience for my subscribers too.

COURSEWORK

My first course took me almost two months to create. I had never created an online course before, and I wanted to take my time. I paid for it dearly because I stopped producing content for my YouTube channel for a few weeks.

My second course took about two weeks. I learned a lot from my first course, and I worked faster. I didn't get much sleep, but I created a premium course in a fraction of the time.

My third course also took about two weeks, but I improved the quality substantially and got more sleep. I did better planning because I knew what I needed to do and how many sessions it would take me. Even though it took two weeks, it was a leisurely two weeks.

My lesson learned is that you can indeed create a premium course in a short period of time. Courses are perhaps the biggest margin product you can create. Spend 20 hours to sell a course for \$197. If your time is worth \$50/hour, sell four units and you've just made a profit.

I once took a course where a guy sat on a couch in a hotel room for three hours and just talked about how to do something. He did the videos in one take with no editing. The course was very good, even though it wasn't highly produced. Ultimately, I just wanted the information. The production level didn't matter.

While I don't intend to turn my content into a course factory, I learned how to create a valuable course in record time when the time comes.

REDDIT

Lately, I've been following writing communities on Reddit. I use Reddit notifications as a way to generate ideas for new YouTube videos.

If I receive a notification about something, it's because people are talking about it. After I receive the notification and verify that it's on-brand for me, I review the post and look for the pain points.

For example, I saw a post on copyright. You'd think that people would have burning legal questions—but instead, so many wanted to know *how* to do the little copyright symbol on their keyboards. I made a series of copyright videos for authors, and I made sure to include the keyboard shortcuts in the video.

In many ways, Reddit is a streamlined way of doing market research. I'm starting to let Reddit notifications guide my content decisions, at least for the next quarter. Since I'm doubling down on my YouTube content, I need to make sure I'm in sync with what people talking about. I haven't always done a good job of that in the past.

YOUR BOOK AS A SERIES OF DATA POINTS

It took the indie community a long time to accept that a book is more than just a book; it's a product. In order to sell more books, thinking of them as products is useful.

I also believe that books are data. That data has immense power if we are willing to harness it. My sales database project in Vol. 1 of this series was a perfect example of harnessing the data around my books.

But what about my books themselves?

For marketing, this makes a lot of sense. Joanna Penn has said for a very long time that "the book is the metadata." Why should we have to choose silly keywords and categories when book retailers can scan our book and understand it on a deeper level? Amazon and Google are tech behemoths that have mastered the art of search—the keyword system is quite absurd if you really think about it.

At the time of this writing, YouTube engineers have admitted that YouTube's AI software can watch videos and understand them at a fifth-grade level. This means it can absorb the content of your video and make recommendations based on what it can understand. As such, tags are irrelevant there now.

It's just a matter of time before YouTube stops supporting them.

Amazon will follow a similar path eventually. Amazon has some of the best artificial intelligence engineers in the world. It's hard to imagine they don't have software that can read the millions of books on the Kindle platform and make decisions based on what it reads.

The very words we write are data. The purest example of this is a word count or statistics calculator in your writing app. It tells you how many words you wrote yesterday and today. That's data, and you can use that to make decisions. If you wrote 1,800 words Monday but only 500 on Tuesday, then you'll try to do better on Wednesday.

I've always believed that the text we create has unharnessed potential.

For example, in the first book in this series, I posed the idea of a "personalized rules engine," which is an app that can detect errors your editor caught in the past and warn you about them before you send your next book for editing. Once, I used the word "cadence" incorrectly in a sentence. I should have used interval instead. I use the word cadence all the time. Why waste my editor's time with an edit like that when I can fix it myself first?

Sometimes I accidentally leave articles out of sentences. My editor shouldn't have to fix mistakes like that.

This issue kept bothering me, so I decided to do something about it. Like I did with my sales database, I poured my time, money, and energy into solving this problem for myself, not knowing what would happen.

Turns out the solution was simple. I'll explain the technical details in the Technology section, but it involved using natural language processing (NLP), which is a subset of artificial intelligence. Long story short, I partnered with a developer to turn a test sample of editor recommendations *for Indie Author Confidential, Volume 1* into a series of if-then statements. The developer turned those statements into Python programming language commands. We used an open-source natural language processing (NLP) artificial intelligence model that was *free* on the Internet to process the commands into a Microsoft Word doc that had problem spots of the book marked as tracked changes.

Guess how long it took the programmer to do it?

Less than five hours.

In five hours, we harnessed the power of artificial intelligence to translate my words into data, and that data into real-life edits that Microsoft Word, Grammarly, and ProWritingAid couldn't catch.

As I build out my personal rules engine, I can now look at all of my books retroactively and turn many of my edits into code, and that code will alert me to potential mistakes, which will result in cleaner manuscripts and a better relationship with my editor so that she can focus on what really matters—my content and its meaning.

In many respects, if the project succeeds, my personal rules engine will be like a buffer between Grammarly and ProWritingAid and my editor, which is ironic because those apps are supposed to be a "last line of defense" before editing. Now they're the "second-to-last line of defense," I suppose.

A tool like this helps me on my journey to becoming a world-class content creator because it helps me deliver cleaner manuscripts that are more consistent from book to book. It's an invisible and subtle infrastructure change that will make a big difference over the life of my career, which ironically, is also the value proposition that artificial intelligence provides.

HOW TO DIE EMPTY

In a July 2020 guest interview, I received a question about how I remain creative after writing 50 books. The interviewer wanted to know if I've ever run out of ideas or if I struggled with writer's block.

I told her no, and then I gave an answer I've never talked about before.

In 2015, I read a book by Claudia Azula Altucher titled *Become an Idea Machine: Because Ideas are the Currency of the 21st Century*.

I love this book. I've read it several times. The main idea in the book is that coming up with new ideas is like exercising a muscle. The more you do it, the easier it gets. Altucher recommends coming up with ten ideas every day. It's tough at first, but becomes easier over time.

I've practiced that technique off and on over the years. The result is that I have digital idea notebooks with thousands of pages. The last one I checked was around 2,000 notes. That's just one notebook.

I have a notebook for fiction ideas (called my "sketchbook").

In fact, I used to read pages from my sketchbook on my *Writer's Journey* podcast every week for a year.

I have a notebook for business ideas and opportunities I want to pursue in the future.

I have a notebook for other random ideas that don't fit into the other two categories.

And, of course, I have this series, which is a collection of ideas. Every Friday, I receive an automated email reminder to write the weekly chapters of this book—one entry per strategic section with something I learned.

Some weeks, I didn't learn something new in a particular category, so I have to figure out what I'm going to say. I pull ideas out of the air almost every time. I have to think about all the content I consumed for the week and all the random ideas I had. I always ask, "What do authors need? What do I need in my business?" Then the idea comes almost every time. When it doesn't, I just wait a few hours. Usually, ideas come to me in floods, and I struggle to write them *all* down.

Oops, maybe I shouldn't have admitted that...But if you're reading this book, then you probably read the first book in this series, so your very presence here right now proves that my method works.

But, to be honest, I usually have more than one idea per category each week. As I write this, it's the end of July, and I already have around eight entries per category, which is more than double where I should be since each book is supposed to be 12 weeks long.

Anyway, the interview question made me critically examine my idea-generation process, and that's a good thing.

EMPATHY

This lesson is rambling and disjointed, but the topic is not an easy one, so bear with me.

I've struggled over the years with social skills. I've tried to work on improving them.

I wouldn't consider myself as someone who has high emotional intelligence. I care a great deal about people, but I've never been very good in social situations. It's just something I know about myself. It's one of those areas in life where I function, but not terribly well. When you talk to me, I listen more than I talk, mainly because I'm listening to understand. You can see "the wheels turning in my head." I struggle to process information in real-time, and by the time I have processed it, I have missed most of the social cues.

Instead, I tend to "feel" my way through social situations. I can't always read people very well, but I can read their emotions, and I rely on my intuition to help me determine whether I can trust someone or not. I call it social echolocation. Somehow I've managed to do pretty well for myself socially, even though I consider it a disability.

I do much better when I'm creating content. I can take my

time and craft my books to speak to people. I can put myself in other people's shoes much easier when I'm planning YouTube videos and podcasts too. The result is that no one would ever suspect that I'm socially awkward by watching my content.

It's one-way and one-sided, but in a weird way, my content builds so much trust that, when I meet with people, it's a lot easier for me to make connections. If I know which content resonated with them, then I know how to connect and help them on a deeper level. That builds more trust. In a way, I created a shortcut around my weakness and turned it into a strength.

I share this because I think a lot of writers are like me. We don't do terribly well in social situations, but we excel in the written word. It's not that we *lack* social skills; rather, we just have them in another format, and that format is not the common way that society expects them to manifest itself.

I reflected on this because, earlier this quarter, I was on a conference call with a writer who was asking me for some advice.

I've learned over the years not to ask about people's publishing situations. If someone tells me they have a publisher, I *never* ask who the publisher is. If it's a known, scammy publishing company, I have an ethical obligation to point that out to the author, namely because I am so open about self-publishing and I belong to a nonprofit that spends a significant amount of time exposing scammy publishing companies.

BUT...authors typically don't want to hear the fact that they're getting ripped off and their copyrights are getting stolen, even if it's true. The whole conversation just becomes awkward, and I lose the ability to help the author because they get defensive and shut down. I don't really lose much in the exchange other than my time, but I do like to help people if I can.

Like I said, I'm not going to ask about your publishing situation, but if you ask me my opinion, I'll tell you.

Anyway, I was speaking with this author, and we had a great conversation. A few weeks after our call, he emailed me and said his publisher wanted to charge him several hundred dollars for some publicity service that 100% of legitimate publishers do for free. The author asked me what I thought...

A basic Internet search confirmed my hunch that this was in fact a fraudulent situation. My ethical obligation kicked in, and I gave him the most diplomatic answer I could. I basically said, "That's not normal and not something you should pay for. You may wish to consider other ways to market your work without your publisher's assistance." I gave him enough to read between the lines, if he chose to do that. Then I walked away.

As I wrote the email, I tried to imagine myself in the writer's shoes—he probably didn't want to believe that he was living in a lie. He spent a year of his life writing a book, found someone who he thought believed in him and his work, and someone had finally validated him. He probably lived his whole life with the dream of becoming a writer, and he probably spent thousands of dollars already on this scam, possibly thousands he didn't have. In his mind, he was living in paradise, and who am I to tell him that the choices he made are going to come back to bite him later? Who am I to tell him that happiness isn't coming his way after all? If I were him, of course I would feel this way. From his perspective, he can't afford to lose.

You see, that's my problem. I knew all of this, but I said something anyway on the slim chance that maybe it would help him.

I never heard back from that writer, and I knew that would happen. It's not likely you'll ever hear about him either, because he and his book are screwed.

I've seen a lot of people come and go in the last eight years. The writers who leave the fastest are the ones who burn out, who never develop a thick skin, or those who are so embarrassed by unscrupulous people that they can't bear the thought of picking up the pen again.

I thought about this interaction quite a bit over the last few weeks. This guy had an amazing story, and he was very smart. His Achilles heel was that he was so *busy* that he wanted other people to do the work for him.

Writers' ability to place readers into the heads of characters and make readers laugh and cry along with those characters is, in my opinion, the ultimate empathy. In some ways, you could argue that writing is positive manipulation—it's the only kind readers sign up for. But writers also can't see when they are being manipulated. It's an interesting paradox.

There's a saying that scammers prey on the young, the old, and the stupid. Well, they also prey on the "very busy." This is why I constantly tell writers that you're never too busy to take control of your career. Busyness is an invitation for scammers to enter your life. This is why I am particularly careful, and it is also a reason why I have been extremely slow to outsource.

So, to conclude this long-winded chapter, my points are as follows.

If you don't have social skills, it's okay. Your skills and personal value lie in other areas, like writing.

If you have this problem, you will probably struggle to influence people, just like I did with that poor writer.

If you have this problem, you're also probably more vulnerable to scams than most people.

If you're too busy to wear the many different hats that are required in the self-publishing business, you're *especially* vulnerable to scams.

If you don't have social skills and you're too busy to take control of your career, you *will* get scammed. It's just a matter of time.

LESSONS FROM A THREE-DAY-LONG POWER OUTAGE

On August 10, a powerful derecho storm struck the state of Iowa. According to the Google dictionary, derechos are a line of intense, widespread, and fast-moving windstorms and sometimes thunderstorms that move across a great distance and are characterized by damaging winds.

The winds from the storm were approximately between 75 and 115 miles per hour, which is close to that of a category 3 hurricane. Derechos are called "inland hurricanes" for this reason. They are difficult to predict and seem to come out of nowhere.

Imagine my surprise as I was walking my dog and saw a giant gray wall of cumulonimbus clouds rapidly moving across my neighborhood. My dog was afraid—she wanted to go back home as soon as possible, and that never happens!

I gathered my wife and daughter and we hid in my basement until the storm passed. The lights blinked out Monday at 11AM, and we didn't have power again until Wednesday evening.

Do a web search for "Iowa derecho" and you'll see the destruction the storm ravaged on the state. It was unlike anything I've ever seen. There were trees down all over the neighborhood, taking power lines with them. Some trees fell on houses, sheds, and cars. Millions of acres of crops were destroyed, and this was already a bad year for farmers because of the COVID-19 pandemic. Three people died because they were caught in the storm unexpectedly.

The national media largely ignored the storm, but it was devastating to Iowans.

I was lucky. I only had a few tree limbs down in my yard, and I was able to easily pick them up. I also lost about two-hundred-dollars' worth of food in my refrigerator and freezer that spoiled. Other than that, we had to deal with a three-day-long power outage. There were some people in Iowa who didn't have power for weeks.

The outage came at the worst possible time. My phone was at 50%, my power bank was at 25%, and I hadn't yet recorded my content for the week.

However, I have a contingency plan for these types of situations. I keep a power bank to help me keep my phone charged because, during an outage like this, writing on my phone is the only kind of writing I can do.

I was in the middle of a new book, and I didn't want to lose momentum, so I used my phone to write. I could only write in small bursts at a time to save my battery. But I wrote about 300-1000 words each day, which is a win.

I also communicated with my audience that my content was going to be late for the week. I let people know on Twitter and YouTube. I believe it's important to communicate with your audience whenever you can't meet their expectations.

Fortunately, the power came back on and I was able to keep my streaks going without missing any content.

But the outage taught me some valuable lessons.

First, it tested my contingency plans. A contingency plan is a strategy of what you will do when disaster strikes. There are many different disasters that can strike a writer's career—damage to their home, the death of a relative, lawsuits, etc.

Anyway, writing on my phone is an easy way to get words in—since I do that every day, it kept me progressing on my novel. That was the first part of my contingency plan that worked well.

Second, my power bank has continued to prove itself a smart investment. I paid $50 for it on clearance, and it provided power for me when I didn't have access to an electrical outlet. This allowed me to devote 10% of my battery at a time to writing while keeping my phone available for emergency use.

Third, it confirmed my need to purchase a backup generator for my home. I plan to buy one sometime in the next year if I can. I don't need one to power my whole house—I just need it to power my phones, power banks, computers, and keep my fridge running for a few hours a day. I priced a solar-powered generator for about $500, which is useful because we can take it with us on family vacations as well.

Fourth, it allowed me to put my communication plan in action. When I took a YouTube hiatus in 2016, my biggest regret was that I failed to communicate with my audience about why I was leaving. I promised that I would never do that again. That plan largely worked, and my audience appreciated it.

Fifth, it's a great reminder of how life happens and how you often can't do anything about it. Even if I missed my YouTube or podcast content, I would have been fine with it because I communicated with my audience.

Sixth, I had some email successes and failures. I had about 20 emails in my inbox when the storm hit. When I received power back, I had about 100. That's a failure. However, I prioritized fan-mail, responding to fans even when I didn't have power. I even received and accepted two speaking engagements during the outage! My prioritization worked, but I didn't like how many emails I couldn't take action on. So many of the emails I received during the outage required me to be at my computer, which I don't like. I need to find ways to reduce my dependence on my laptop in responding to emails. If I could have remained inbox zero during the outage or close to it, I could have emerged from the ordeal with almost no real loss in productivity other than a lower daily word count. I'll need to think of ways to keep my emails low.

Anyway, I'm glad of where I ended up after the storm. It proves the importance of having contingency plans, particularly for power outages. Consistency is the key to being a successful author; being able to overcome little things like power outages can add up in a big way over the life of your career.

RECONNECTING WITH MY WHY

I wrote a book this quarter that was the most fun I'd had writing a book in years.

I did a YouTube video in early 2020 where I talked about how I created a "learning plan" for myself early in my career. I wrote down everything I didn't know much about, and I went off and learned it. I created deep, nested bullet lists for writing craft, business, marketing, technology, and more. And as I learned a new skill, I crossed it off the list. I made it a point of learning something new every day, and I improved my knowledge base substantially. My audience loved this idea and wanted to see me develop a learning plan for them.

My dilemma was that I didn't want to give people a book full of bullet points. That's boring.

I decided to take a risk. Instead of boring my readers to death, I wanted to convey the pathway to learning in a more instructive and creative way. So I wrote a book that mixes learning with storytelling and entertainment.

The book is called *The Indie Author Atlas: Your Guide to the Five Continents of the Writing World.* Essentially, I took the main bullet points that an author needs to learn and turned them into fictional places, then I wrote about them in the style of a Lonely Planet travel guide. It's a wacky idea, but it was so much fun to write. The book is the only one of its kind.

I mixed fiction storytelling style with my usual nonfiction writing style, which was unusual. Also, the book is written in the second-person POV, which is a first for me. The book contains custom illustrations that I commissioned.

All signs point to this book being either a winner or a complete dud—and that's exactly where I love to be as an artist. People will either "get it" or they'll say "that's the dumbest thing I've ever seen." I love that level of risk, and it's where I perform best, both in writing and business. This scares most authors.

You can trace an early prototype of this book back to my first novel, *Magic Souls: An Interactive Urban Fantasy*. It's a story about a woman who accidentally makes a deal with a demon and has to steal three souls to break the contract, or she'll lose her own soul. The story sounds dark, but it's actually not—it's quite sarcastic and ironic.

The reader controls the heroine, Bebe, as she navigates through various ethical train wrecks, because she has to manipulate and steal in order to save her own soul. One of the characters she has to manipulate is competing on a gameshow—and Bebe has to cheat her way onto the gameshow to get close to her mark. The gameshow is an actual gameshow—and the reader controls Bebe as she competes in various challenges. She can win or lose, and the story changes accordingly.

In the gameshow, the contestants can win different prizes—vacations, household appliances, and so on. Each prize had a short description inspired by television gameshows, accompanied by a public domain stock image.

Here's an example:

"BEBE WON A PARTY BUS PACKAGE!

"You and twenty friends will experience the city like never

before with a Megapimpin' Party Bus! Sure, this party bus looks like a school bus on the outside, but on the inside, it's a chic party room, retrofitted with comfortable seats, changing LED lights, a DJ, free premium alcohol, tinted windows for privacy, and a professional chauffeur who will take you anywhere you want to go. Climb aboard, and whatever you do, don't stop the pimpin'!"

And another:

"BEBE WON A PAIR OF CUSTOM BASKETBALL SHOES!

"Whether you love basketball or not, you'll love these shoes. B-Ball Shoes, Inc. has agreed to design a custom pair of shoes just for you! You'll visit the website and select your colors, soles, laces, bling, and other accessories that will make your shoes unlike anyone else's on the court. If you think your friends will be flabbergasted when they see your new kicks, wait until they see you dunk!"

These write-ups were inspired by hours and hours of watching gameshows as a kid.

Somehow, the memory of the gameshow in *Magic Souls* made its way back to me, and it inspired me to try writing in this style for an entire book.

Whether the book succeeds or not, I had a blast writing it. While writing it, I kept thinking, *This is what pure fun and entertainment feels like.* My hope is that readers will feel my joy when they're reading. If they don't, it's okay. I had an amazing two weeks writing the book, with really high word count days to be proud of.

I NEED A BETTER INTERNET CONNECTION

Being a guest on *The Creative Penn* was one of the highlights of my author career when I appeared on the show in 2016. It accelerated my YouTube channel and increased my income substantially. I'll always be grateful to Joanna for that early momentum.

Imagine my surprise when she invited me to be on the show again in 2020 to promote my book *150 Self-Publishing Questions Answered*.

Joanna is a great interviewer because she reads your books and does a substantial amount of prep work prior to the interview. She also sends you the questions ahead of time, which just makes things easier for everyone. I spent a few days preparing for the show.

I joined the Zoom call and we chatted for a few minutes—everything was going smoothly. Then she started recording and we started the show. Out of nowhere, my Internet decided to stop working!

I had to do some quick thinking—this was only the biggest podcast interview that I did this year...

Luckily, I have an alternative Internet connection. I tried

that, and it didn't work! Thank God my neighbor let me use his Wi-Fi so we could complete the interview. Aside from being out of breath from racing to my neighbor's house, the interview went smoothly. You can definitely hear me out of breath, though. Bless Joanna for her patience and ability to edit the audio smoothly, so you won't even be able to tell that we had an interruption!

It was an incredibly embarrassing moment for me, especially because I pride myself on being professional, and I rarely have Internet issues.

After that moment, I swore that I would never let this happen again on a podcast interview. Ever.

I upgraded my Internet speed and hired an electrician to install ethernet ports in my home. This way, I can hardwire my computer to my ethernet instead of relying on Wi-Fi during a podcast interview. That should solve the problem. And the expense is tax-deductible!

Part of creating world-class content is not having Internet issues. This will improve my professionalism and make it easier for me to do livestreams in the future if I choose to do that.

BECOME A WORLD-CLASS MARKETER

DISTINGUISHING BETWEEN SALES AND SERVICE

I bought a car a few months ago. The salesman was fantastic. He worked with me to find a car that was right for my family, and he didn't try to force me into anything.

A few weeks after we bought the car, we received a threatening letter from our bank because they hadn't received the title yet.

I called the salesman, but he didn't return my calls. I had to call the company's corporate office to resolve the issue, which took longer than I liked.

I don't blame the salesman for what happened. I blame myself.

Salespeople are salespeople for a reason. They get paid to sell. That's when they're at their best. Force a salesperson into servicing the accounts they sell, and you will create one of the most miserable beings on the planet. It's not what they're born to do.

That's why every sales organization needs a servicing department. The proper way to draw the line between sales and service is to do a clean hand-off at the point of sale—let the customer know who they can call if they have a problem. Otherwise, they'll call the salesperson, which sets everyone up for failure.

Why is this important for writers?

Writers are salespeople. We do almost everything in the writing life with the goal of selling more books. Yet there are times when we must also wear a servicing hat. A great example is helping readers side-load books onto their reading devices. This is why Book Funnel became so popular; they created a servicing platform and took side-load servicing away from writers so they could focus on writing and selling more books.

As I scale, I think about the line between sales and service in my business often. I'm at my best when I'm writing, making YouTube videos and podcasts, communicating directly with readers, doing podcast interviews, and strategizing about the future. Yet I receive a fair amount of "how do I" and "where do I" emails from my contact form.

As much as possible, I try to answer common questions on my contact form page to eliminate as many of those questions as possible. I think of it as reader self-service.

In the future, I'll need to find ways to assign certain reader emails to an assistant. I love answering fan-mail, but it's probably not a good use of my time to answer questions like "do you have a video on outlining your novel?" or "which book of yours should I read first?" An assistant (or even an AI) can and should handle that for me so that I can spend my time with the more substantive fan emails. I'm not trying to diminish fan-mail—I love it. But you do have to be more efficient at some point.

KEY PERFORMANCE INDICATORS IN SALES

There's a famous saying about marketing that says that 50% of marketing is effective, but no one knows which 50%.

I know one thing that *is* effective: analyzing your data for trends. Every successful salesperson I've known has this trait, without exception.

I was fortunate enough to have the vice president of sales at a Fortune 100 company mentor me. He always asked about numbers. "It's how I'm built," he used to say. A tactic I learned from him was learning how to quantify (almost) everything you do. If you can't put numbers to what you're doing, you're in the dark. How will you know if a decision is the right one? Your gut is right nine times out of ten, but what about the one out of ten times?

After building my sales report database, I found myself in the pleasant but daunting position of sitting on a mountain of data but not knowing what to do with it. I could do anything I wanted, but I didn't know where to start.

I thought back to the conversations with my executive mentor, and that helped me determine a path.

First, I needed to determine my key performance indicators

(KPIs). A key performance indicator is a signal that shows whether the business is doing well or in trouble.

For my author business, I determined that my KPIs were as follows:

- Total revenue and net units sold
- Revenue and net units sold by book, series, and product lines such as my YouTube channel and online courses
- Percentage of revenue and net units sold from frontlist content and backlist content
- Year-over-year growth
- Profitability of each of my books, which is the amount I have earned to date on the book minus the cost to produce the book
- Revenue and net units sold by retailer
- Revenue and net units sold by country

There are so many other ways I can slice and dice my sales data, but I had to start somewhere.

VISUAL SALES DASHBOARD

I don't do well with raw data. I like spreadsheets, but I prefer to turn them into something useful. In my professional job, I work with a data science team that turns raw data into pretty visual dashboards.

I asked, "Why can't I do the same thing with my writing business?"

I used Microsoft Power BI to create a nice, simple dashboard that gives me access to all my key performance indicators at a moment's notice. It only took me about an hour. I can also export the data as PowerPoint so I have historical snapshots.

It's not enough to analyze the data. Because I'm not a data person by nature, I often forget data points or nuanced details as time goes by. I developed a log that I used to answer a couple of key questions:

- What is the data saying?
- Where are the outliers?
- Where am I strong?
- Where am I weak?
- What actions do I need to take today?

- What items do I need to follow-up on in my next review?

That helped me stay organized and get back into the "data mindset" in my monthly review.

The dashboard was a major success. The next step is to find a way to build a more comprehensive dashboard that includes items such as my YouTube analytics, website analytics, mailing list analytics, fan-mail analytics, and expenses. Imagine a one-stop shop where all your business data is visualized so you can make better decisions, with the ability to jump into Excel to do deeper analysis if you want. That's my goal.

PRE-VIDEO AD

A technique I used in the past to improve my sales was placing a video ad in front of my videos promoting my books.

In 2018, I created a Scrivener versus Ulysses Cage Match video comparing the pros and cons of each app. By chance, I happened to see a video on YouTube by a mega-YouTuber who inserted a video ad just before his videos that advertised a product he was selling. He used stock videos, hip-hop music, and he narrated over the top of it.

I decided to do that with my book *Be a Writing Machine*. I found stock footage of happy, smiling people reading and writing, and I cut them together in a 30-second ad. Then I narrated the ad to jazzy hip-hop music.

It was one of the smartest things I ever did—by luck, the Scrivener versus Ulysses video did very well, with over 36,000 views at the time of this writing. That's 36,000 people who see the ad for *Be a Writing Machine*, with hundreds more seeing it every week. That ad sells a ridiculous amount of books for me.

For my book *150 Self-Publishing Questions*, I tried to rekindle some of that old magic, but I wanted to be more intentional.

I picked videos that had a higher chance of being picked up by the YouTube algorithm. I produced algorithm-targeted videos for 8-10 weeks and put a new ad for *150 Self-Publishing Questions* in each video. Again, I used footage of happy people having fun and celebrating, with a link to the book at the end.

My reasoning is that while my audience might get tired of the ads after a while, if just one of those ten videos is successful, I will pretty much have guaranteed traffic and income for the book. The ad alone will make the book profitable. If more than one video is successful, well...then it's a jackpot.

I pay a yearly fee for stock media, so technically, it costs me nothing to create these ads. It took about 30 minutes of my time.

That's marketing I can believe in!

HTML EMAIL SIGNATURE

A friend of mine is a saleswoman. She has an attractive email signature with her headshot, contact information, and a call to action to schedule a call with her. She is good at her job and always has a steady stream of sales appointments.

Since my role at ALLi is a sales role, I decided to do the same thing.

I paid a freelancer on Fiverr to create an HTML email signature with my author headshot, contact information, and a clickable button to schedule a call with me that links to my calendar scheduling app where they can make an appointment.

It cost me $30.

I love this idea because it looks professional, and it creates a strong first impression.

EMAIL TIME SERVICE

Companies evaluate their employees by how quickly they respond to customer requests. The company I work for prides itself on the fact that a customer could speak to a live representative in about ten seconds on average.

I've tried to implement time service in my response to fan-mail. Generally, I try to respond to all fan-mail within 48 hours. Most times, it's sooner than that. Other times, I fail miserably.

When readers submit my contact form, I set expectations that I will respond in 24-48 hours. Then I do it.

It's great marketing when a reader sends me a note and I respond right away. It usually catches them off-guard, in the best possible way.

I recognize that this is tougher to do as you become more successful, but I've always believed that it pays to treat your fans right.

SALES IN ACTION

I stumbled upon a tweet about a new community app for influencers.

Instead of using Facebook Groups (which I loathe), Discord, or Reddit, this app allows you to create a community with similar functionality under your own label. Your fans sign up for accounts, and they can create threads, answer questions, and engage with you through a sleek interface that reminds me of a mixture between Slack and Facebook Groups.

A long time ago, I chose not to create a member community because I don't have the time or energy to maintain one. Also, I don't have the personality for it. But I recognize that it's a smart way to communicate with fans and keep them engaged. If and when I become a full-time author, implementing one will be the first thing on my to-do list.

I also like the idea of a fan community I can control. Given the volatility of so many social media sites lately, white label communities are worth paying for.

Anyway, I signed up to be on the waitlist for the service, mainly out of curiosity. I received an automated email from the founders who said that they'd personally be in touch with me in a few months to schedule a 20-minute demo.

I thought, *Wow. That's totally not scalable.*

But it's a great sales technique. They're meeting with everyone so they can learn sales objections. They want to hear every possible no and the reason behind it so they can defeat those objections in the future. I bet by the time they meet with me, they're going to be very smooth.

It reminded me of the lesson I learned in the book *New Sales Simplified* by Mike Weinberg. I discussed it in Vol. 1 of this series. In that book, Weinberg discusses a proven three-step sales method:

1. Choose a target
2. Employ weapons of attack
3. Develop a plan

It seems to me that the app's founders are still on step zero. They know who their prospective audience is, but they want to refine their targets. They're meeting with anyone under the sun who will listen to them so they can figure out who to go after in automated marketing campaigns on Facebook, Google, and YouTube. They're probably pitching *hard* at the end of their sales calls too.

We'll see if the technique works, but so far, there are some big names promoting their platform.

It's always fun to see sales techniques that I learned about previously in real life.

A DIFFERENT KIND OF BOOK
LAUNCH VIDEO

I saw a prominent YouTuber do something different with a product launch.

He announced that he had a new product out, and he talked about the basic product information, how well it was doing, how many people had bought it so far. Then he read a few reviews and put them on the screen.

He ended with a call to action that told people where to find the product as well as offered a special coupon code.

I liked that he was casual about it. It wasn't a "buy my product" launch video. Instead, it was, "I've got this new product, here's what people are saying about it, and here's where you can find it if you're interested."

It inspired me to try a similar video on my YouTube channel and podcasts with *150 Self-Publishing Questions Answered*.

TOTAL SALES FAILURE

I missed an easy sale this quarter that cost me at least one hundred dollars.

A reader reached out to me about buying one of my books. He wanted to buy copies of my books for his students to read as part of a virtual event.

He sent me a message on Facebook asking if he could buy my books from me.

I don't check Facebook that often, so I didn't see the message until three days after he sent it to me. I replied and told him yes. But I made a critical mistake that lost the sale, and I was angry at myself for it. Maybe you can learn from me.

Perhaps the best way to illustrate how I failed is to read the following transcript between me and my imaginary sales mentor...

Mentor: Tell me about that direct sales interaction.

Me: A reader reached out and asked to buy my books directly from me.

Mentor: Directly? Ebook or paperback? Audio?

Me: I don't know.

Mentor: You didn't find out?

Me: We didn't get that far.

Mentor: I noticed that you didn't reply to him for three days. That's unusual for you. What happened?

Me: He messaged me on Facebook, and I don't check it often.

Mentor: That's understandable, and I have two thoughts about that. First, when you replied the first time, why didn't you take the conversation to email?

Me: I wasn't thinking.

Mentor: Why didn't you ask for his email address, or give him yours?

Me: I did.

Mentor: Ah, you *did*, didn't you? But you didn't ask for it until six days after his original message. You replied to him after three days, and when he replied again, you forgot about Facebook again and didn't reply for three more days.

Me: Correct.

Mentor: Your lead went cold.

Me: That's a simple way to put it.

Mentor: My second thought was whether there is a way for you to prevent this in the future, such as an automated reply that directs readers to your email address.

Me: I'll look into it.

Mentor: So much in sales is about speed and ease of doing business. You failed in both of those areas.

Anyway, I committed a couple cardinal sins of sales, which is uncharacteristic of me. I've never done sales through social media like that before, so I wasn't comfortable in the venue, and it showed. As a result, I missed out on *at least* one hundred dollars in sales—a transaction that would have taken me just a few minutes to do. Literally, all I had to do was get the guy's address, send him a PayPal invoice, ship him the books directly from Amazon KDP Print, and send him a Book Funnel link to the ebook.

Automation would have been my friend here. A Facebook chatbot could have directed the reader to my email inbox or to a direct sales portal on my site. Turns out that Facebook allows you to do this with just a few clicks. Wow...very embarrassing to reveal my lack of knowledge of Facebook's new features!

I fixed this problem by creating an automated reply in Facebook that tells readers I don't check Facebook often. I give my personal email address for them to contact me.

Long term, I'll need to think about the best way to implement direct sales onto my Facebook pages directly. I know it's possible, as I used to have an integration with Selz.com where readers could buy my books from my Facebook page. That was several years ago, and the technology was clunky. I'm sure it's better now.

I learned from this experience, and I'll try to do better next time.

AN EPIC RANT ABOUT LAZINESS, SLIPSHOD CRAFTSMANSHIP, AND CLARITY, AND WHY CLARITY IS THE CURRENCY OF SUCCESSFUL PEOPLE

Someone told me that they didn't like all the responsibilities of being an author.

They didn't want to market. They didn't want to be a businessperson. They didn't want to think about the future. All they wanted to do was write. Yet they wanted to self-publish a book and have a successful self-publishing career.

If you meet me in person, I'm not ordinarily a jerk, but I had to be a jerk to this person, particularly because they were asking me to look at the "brilliant" book they had created. The book wasn't brilliant, and this person had no sense of reality.

So I was brutally honest with them. The cover was awful, the editing was practically non-existent, and the story needed work (from what little of it I read in the first chapter). I told them in no uncertain terms that if they wanted to be a successful self-publisher, that they would have to quit complaining and learn how to take control of their career.

They were mortified.

"But why is my cover bad?" they asked.

I replied with a question: "What instructions did you give your cover designer?"

They told me what I suspected—they didn't give their designer any meaningful instruction about the genre of their book, the true target audience, or the correct symbolism.

Then I asked, "In ten seconds, tell me who the target audience of your book is."

They also told me exactly what I suspected they would say —everyone.

And then I asked, "So you don't know what a book cover in your genre should look like. You don't know who the target audience is. And you're asking me why the book is not successful?"

And then I gave them what I hope was helpful advice. I told them, "If you don't want to wear all the hats that are required to be a self-published writer, that's fine. But it means you're going to have to pay people to wear some of those hats for you. And if you don't understand how to give clarity to the people you hire, then you're toast."

Furthermore, the author wasted *my* time because they weren't *clear* in what they wanted from *me*.

Anyway, I'll stop being a jerk now.

So much in marketing is about providing clarity. Clarity to your cover designer, clarity to your target audience, clarity to your readers about what you want them to do when they're finished reading. If you can't provide clarity, you're screwed.

Clarity is about putting yourself in the other person's shoes and trying to anticipate their thoughts.

When you decide to be a self-published writer, you may not know it, but you're signing up to be a leader. That means you're in charge of your career, everything is your responsibility, and *the work of everyone you hire* is your responsibility. When they do a bad job, it's not a reflection on them—it's a reflection on you. And if *you* have chosen to abdicate all your responsibility because you don't want to wear all the hats that are required, don't waste other people's time complaining when you only have yourself to blame.

Everyone's situation is different. I recognize that as an influencer, I have to have some empathy. We all have certain limitations, especially when it comes to children, aging parents, illnesses, and more. I don't minimize that, because it's a big deal. But writing is the only profession in the world where people bring unrealistic expectations onto the first day of the job.

In the working world, if a company offered you a job, but the hours were nights and weekends, but you couldn't work nights and weekends because of family obligations, you wouldn't take the job.

Yet when some people become writers, they understand the job description, yet they don't want to adhere to it.

Kristine Kathryn Rusch published a blog post this quarter that I appreciated because the gist of it is so powerful. In sum, she says that we're living through a pandemic—one of the worst social and economic disasters in our lifetimes—and writers are complaining about the work they have to do. This profession is *nothing* compared to what grocery store workers, first responders, and medical professionals have to deal with every day during this crisis. They risk their lives, and we sit in a chair and make stuff up, probably in our pajamas.

I hope this chapter gives you some clarity about what's really important, and why it's important to have radical clarity about why you signed up for this job.

REPEATING YOURSELF ON PODCAST INTERVIEWS

I was on a podcast interview that was broadcast live. We were talking about one of my books. At the beginning of the show, I gave the name of the book as well as a link to find it on my website. I also gave the name and link at the end of the show.

However, there were people who joined the broadcast late. Those people kept asking for the link in the comments.

I learned that, on live shows, you can never say the name of your book and give the link too much—there's always going to be someone who misses it. But only saying it once or twice means you'll miss out on potential sales.

PRESS KIT: PAYING DIVIDENDS
SINCE 2014

I've had a press page on my website for years, mainly to attract public speaking events and improve my professionalism. You can view it at *www.authorlevelup.com/press*

The page highlights my speaking engagements in the past and shows potential venue organizers what they can expect if they have me as a guest at their event.

I also host a press kit on the page—it contains author bios in differing lengths, author headshots, book covers and descriptions for some of my best books, and so on. I engineered the press kit to make podcast interviewers' lives easier so that they don't have to hunt down information about me.

Interviewers *always* ask for at least a bio and a headshot. Always. By giving them a press kit that has these items baked in, it streamlines the interview process. When podcast hosts book time on my calendar using my calendaring app, the confirmation email contains a link to the press kit. I don't even have to *send* it anymore. My platform automates it!

Earlier this year, I was invited to speak at the annual Writer's Digest Conference. The editor-in-chief found my videos on YouTube and reached out. After we finalized the speaking terms, I sent her a copy of my press kit, and she said she could tell I've done this a few times. That's a great compliment coming from someone who organizes one of the largest events for writers in the United States.

When I receive compliments on the kit, I know it's working. You'd be shocked how much time venue organizers burn chasing down little things like author bios and headshots. Having all of this in one place improves my professionalism and scores big points, which increases the likelihood of being asked to speak at events again. It also makes organizers more likely to recommend me to others in their network. It's one of the smartest, earliest sales tools I implemented in my business. I didn't do many things right early in my career, but this was one of them.

On several occasions this quarter, I received compliments and kudos from podcast hosts and event organizers for making their marketing easier. That makes me proud, and also makes me think of ways to take my kit to the next level.

BECOME A TECHNOLOGY-DRIVEN WRITER

AMP FOR EMAIL

I saw an interesting post on Twitter where someone was talking about a revolutionary email they received from Google promoting the newest version of their Pixel Buds.

The email allowed people to click on a color palette and change the appearance of a photo of the earbuds. They could even add Pixel Buds to a shopping cart and purchase *directly from the email*. Read that last sentence again. People were shocked and curious how this could be done.

I found a copy of the email and everything people said was true. The email was marketing brilliance.

Turns out that the email was coded with Google AMP4Email.

Google's AMP is a web protocol that helps developers make pages optimized for mobile e-commerce. It uses dynamic content such as sliders, checkboxes, forms, and mobile-friendly designs and images. I didn't realize it was also for email. This explains why email marketing services allow you to upload HTML for your emails...

I then discovered that there are websites that dissect and analyze AMP-created emails as a way to help developers create beautiful, effective emails. One such website is www.really-goodemails.com.

Discovering this was like stumbling into a brand new world. This functionality redefines author email marketing. What if you sent out a dynamic email for your book launch instead of the same old text email? The only downside is that the new AMP4Email standard only works for about half of mobile users, but this number will increase over time.

As I think about the next iteration of my website, I plan to keep AMP4Email in mind so that I can synchronize the design between my site and my emails. Ultimately, once I adopt direct sales, it would be pretty cool to sell books directly from an email so that users never have to leave the email.

BE OPERATING SYSTEM-AGNOSTIC

I wonder how much time people of the world collectively spend arguing which operating system is better.

Windows, Mac OS, and Linux...

Instead of joining the conversation on which one you think is better, why not become platform-agnostic?

This year, I bought a new laptop and installed virtual machines on it. I have Windows, Mac OS, and Linux operating systems on the same machine. I'm used to Mac and Windows, but Linux is an interesting adventure for me.

Sometimes you need a tool that doesn't exist in your operating system. You can either settle for a subpar equivalent or do nothing. Personally, I'm tired of that.

I'm tired of owning a Mac and accepting gigantic trade-offs. Sure, Macs help me be more productive and I don't have to worry about viruses, but they're junk for data analysis and business intelligence. Windows computers can do much more and have more applications that can assist with more tasks, but Windows computers aren't built to last—they never truly were. Windows also has some odd quirks that I'm not a fan of.

Owning all three operating systems means that you can use

any tool you want. If you need a tool, just switch operating systems with the click of a button. It's like switching languages, like English to Spanish. Once you become fluent in another language, you don't think too hard about switching. You just do it.

Many people will probably resist this idea, and I understand that. It's not for everyone.

I'm simply just suggesting that the writer of the future needs every tool they can get—just as you don't want to be locked into exclusivity with Amazon's KDP Select, you shouldn't be locked into an operating system.

WRITING WITH GPT-3

On her blog, Joanna Penn shared a website of a researcher who played around with GPT-3, which is rumored to be the most powerful language model AI in existence right now.

The website shared the researcher's explorations with the GPT-3 beta, which can create text that is so convincing that the average person would never know it was written by an AI. The website shows experiments in poetry, horoscopes written in the style of Weird Al, Tom Swifties, and more. The experiments are exceedingly long, but they all illustrate one thing: GPT-3 is good. Really good.

I saw someone on Twitter remark that playing with it is like seeing the future. It certainly feels that way.

One of the takeaways for me was the following observation: "The first limit is that it remains hobbled by the limited context window. GPT-3 has no form of memory or recurrence, so it cannot see anything outside its limited...[to] (roughly, 500–1000 words). This means it cannot hope to write anything of any serious length, because the beginning will soon vanish over the event horizon, and it also limits its ability to engage in few-shot learning, for the same reason: the prompt+generation will quickly exceed the window length."

Very interesting. So the model can create convincing text, but it can't think. Or, at least, it doesn't seem like it can. The memory limitations are also interesting, and leads someone as old as me to think about floppy disks and CD storage. Those didn't have much memory either, but now, the amount of storage on a mere flash drive dwarfs even the biggest floppy disk capacities exponentially.

Another curious takeaway for me was a reaction to the experiment on Twitter that I think sums up how most average people feel about words written by AIs.

I paraphrase: "I don't think people will care. I prefer well-written stories by humans. I have no connection with an AI so therefore they can never write anything that has real feeling. I don't believe that AI writing will ever be interesting."

Those sound like words that will be laughed at in about ten to twenty years when this type of technology is the norm.

What does GPT-3 mean for indie writers?

I see something obvious. If GPT-3 creates text indistinguishable from a human, imagine what text from GPT-5 or GPT-6 will look like. It's almost as if there will be a real book industry, and then an "AI layer" on top of it where many consumers live. People will cross between the layers without even thinking.

Here's an inevitable scenario that's bound to happen, most likely in the realm of poetry or short works first. A publisher, a news organization, tech company, or a successful author is going to run an experiment. They're going to publish a book, possibly under a sham pen name. The book is going to sell ridiculously well. Then the publisher or author will reveal that they didn't write the book; an AI did. Readers will feel shocked, betrayed, angry, and sad. The publisher or author will have made an important point, and book retailers will amend their terms of service to require authors to disclose if a book is written by an AI. They might even build AI systems to detect AI-written books. Ultimately, legislators will institute laws to require disclosure if even one word in a book is AI-assisted, much like influencers have to disclose if a link is an affiliate link today.

It's not hard to imagine a future where a publisher will use a powerful AI to scan all the books in its catalogue to create something unique. Imagine a publishing executive who says one day, "What if we created a poet persona who was one-third Billy Collins, one-third Emily Dickinson, and one-third Maya Angelou, with a focus on social justice?" The AI model would read everything the three poets have ever done, as well as the entire corpus of tweets from Twitter and Instagram on social justice issues of the last fifteen years.

The publisher could do this because they hold the rights to the poets' work. In fact, traditional publishers are in the best position to do this because they don't have to worry about rights clearance. Publishers usually take every right under the sun. I doubt any poet signing a publishing contract in the last fifty years could have foreseen this type of rights licensing situation. Therefore, the publisher probably holds AI rights by default.

What ensues would be a new genre: designer poetry, where publishers spin new poetry collections based on work already published. Imagine the marketing on a collaboration between a hot new poet and Billy Collins. The publisher could make it look as if the two poets wrote the poems together. The work would introduce new generations to Collins' work and also be a vehicle for discovery; he would receive a royalty for every book sold, without having to do anything.

A lot of poets (and authors) would reject this technology and even sue over it, prompting novel discussions about copyright and moral rights in the age of AI. Does an author have the right to quash an AI derivative work of their books because they don't want to be associated with the technology? What if the AI writes content in your voice that you find morally reprehensible, or that is inconsistent with your author brand?

This is doable in the near future with poetry. Some could argue it's doable TODAY. For long-form fiction, the horizon seems further out.

The idea of "designer" books opens up a gigantic can of worms, one I won't discuss here. But where there are copyright infringement issues, one can also see immense opportunity. The technology isn't all bad.

Take Nora Roberts. She has written many, many books totaling millions of words. What if she created a new pen name based on her prior works? The name could be Nora.AI. All those fans who wanted to see more adventures from their favorite couple might get spinoff novels written by an AI in Nora's style. The work might need editing, but most of the heavy lifting would be done by the AI.

To the people that are thinking "No one would ever read that," consider this: society said the same thing about ebooks. Society also rejected the first iterations of the automobile, smartphone, cloud apps such as Google Docs, Uber, and so much more. Twenty years ago, would *anyone* have thought that opening rooms in your house to random strangers on vacation would have been a good idea? Of course not, but AirBnB is immensely popular now

I believe that the sentiment "people will never read works by AIs" will one day join statements like "no one will ever buy a phone without physical buttons" or "no one will accept rides from strangers using their personal cars as taxis." It's such a foreign paradigm shift for us, but it won't be for future generations and other cultures.

Imagine finding a writer that you absolutely love, and then

spinning that writer's work with another writer you love, creating a fun hybrid. Pay a small fee and you can create whatever fiction experience you want based on the two writers' works. You get entertainment and the writers (hopefully) get paid. You can even design the narrator of the audiobook, like a voice in the style of Morgan Freeman.

Your designer book becomes a fashion statement that you can share with the reading community, and that becomes a feedback loop for writers and publishers looking to create more content quickly using technology. Tastes will change so quickly that publishers will need AI to assist them in following trends.

This might even create a class of haves and have nots—writers who have big enough bodies of work to command an AI model (and therefore more opportunities) and authors who do not.

Anyway, this is very interesting technology that has the power to disrupt the way we consume content. It's hard not to see it having a big impact of some kind.

STREAMLINING, AUTOMATION, AND OUTSOURCING

Streamlining. Automation. Outsourcing.

These are the three most important words in the writer of the future's toolbox, and shockingly underrated and underappreciated today.

The biggest problem with the writing life as it exists right now is that it is highly manual.

You have to write your book. You have to edit it. You have to market it. You have to do just about everything. Tools exist to help lighten the burden, but even with those tools, I would estimate that the writing life is somewhere between 80-90% manual. **In order to remain competitive in tomorrow's world of publishing, whatever it may look like, I suggest that we'll need to be somewhere around 40-50% manual. That means that we'll need to figure out a way to streamline, automate, or outsource 40-50% of our work so that we remain focused on the activities that matter—writing, marketing, and connecting with readers.** Otherwise, it'll be too difficult for us to stay nimble because we'll drown in our own work.

Will the writer of the future be able to think a thought and then see a finished novel and an executed marketing plan? Probably not. But we should ask what we can do to make our jobs less manual.

Let me explain the importance of moving from manual to automated with a simple equation: Time equals money.

Let's tackle time first. You only have so much time in the day. If you're a full-time author, you have more time; if you're a part-time author, you have less. Regardless of how much time you have, it's a finite resource.

We can divide time into three different categories: productive time, unproductive time, and wasted time.

Productive time is anything that leads to profit. Profit means producing more books, book sales, or growing assets such as your mailing list, for example.

Unproductive time is anything that you shouldn't be doing but that you have to do. If you spend tons of time fixing formatting errors in Microsoft Word, that's unproductive time. You can't avoid it, and it *will* hopefully result in profit (in the form of a book you can sell), but it will take longer.

Wasted time is anything you shouldn't be doing that doesn't lead to profit. Providing customer service to help readers get ebooks onto their devices is not a profit-generating activity. Readers have already bought the book and you're just servicing them.

When looking at activities, we have four options.

1. We can continue to do the task with no changes.
2. We can streamline the task, making it possible to accomplish the desired outcome or a similar

outcome, but with less time and effort. Streamlining may also mean eliminating the task altogether.

3. We can automate the task, which means that all or parts of the task will be done by software.

4. We can outsource the task, which means we hire an assistant to accomplish it.

Most writers immediately jump to outsourcing. It's "glamorous" to have an assistant, but I believe that doing this can be an expensive if not fatal mistake. Outsourcing should be the last step, not the first.

Take the notorious example of calculating your sales each month. An author who publishes their books "wide" and on all book retail platforms will receive anywhere from five to ten sales reports each month, each in a different format. They may also receive affiliate income and income from miscellaneous sources such as PayPal and Patreon. It's hard for them to figure out how much money they made, and harder to discern trends in their sales data.

As authors start making more money, some may decide to hire a virtual assistant to help them.

When I did my sales reports manually, it took me four to five hours per month.

Let's say it takes five hours per month to do your sales reports. A good virtual assistant commands at least $40 an hour. That's $200 per month for five hours of work, or $2,400 per year. If that sounds expensive and you aren't making much money from your books, it is. But when you're making more money, you can spend money on these type of tasks. Twenty-four hundred dollars is more palatable to a more successful author, but...if you're a six-figure author and make $100,000 per year, the virtual assistant expense would represent 2.4% of your *gross* annual income on *data entry* that probably won't be 100% correct. Really?

Also consider that the price of virtual assistants will continue to rise. Sales report calculation is tedious work, and when done manually, leads to people cobbling together their own home-brew systems. If virtual assistants quit (and they will), you'll have to train new people, which means your systems will break over time, leading to more rework for you.

Here's how I handled it. I recognized that a virtual assistant has no business handling my sales data in its raw form. Instead, I asked if there was a way to automate my sales reports so that a computer could handle it, with me serving as a steward to make sure my data was handled correctly. No data entry.

I researched existing tools on the market, and in about three weeks, I found a novel way to chain Microsoft Excel macros, Microsoft Powershell, Microsoft Access, and Microsoft Power BI together so that I only had to spend approximately 30 minutes each month aggregating my sales reports. The software handles everything, and it's 100% accurate every time. With the click of a button, I can see how much money I'm making, my top-performing books, and a geographical map of where my book sales are happening.

It cost me approximately 100 hours to learn the ins and outs of the software and how to create the best system for me, which I recognize is more than most people would want to spend. I also had to learn basic coding. To put 100 hours into perspective, it takes me about 40 hours to write a novel, so my time was worth 2.5 novels.

Money-wise, it cost me $79 for virtual machine software, $139 for Windows, and $150 in consulting fees to hire a developer to help me with some difficult code. Overall, my hard cost was $368.

That $368 system saved 4.5 hours every single month,

increased the accuracy of my data entry, and gave me unfettered access to my sales data, which helped me make better informed decisions that drove more sales into my business. The system should last me at least a decade because I'm using everyday technology that is widely available and supported.

Sure, I had to sacrifice a few books to do it, when you consider that it was taking me 4-5 hours per month to aggregate my sales manually, I was wasting 1.5 books per year already.

Now, the next logical step in the process would be to outsource the task. I've already built a standardized system that is far easier to train an assistant to use instead of expecting them to do everything manually. If it takes me 30 minutes each month, it'll take an assistant around an hour, which is $40 per month, or $480 per year. That's 0.004% of a gross annual income of $100,000. Much, much better. Also, it's a better use of my assistant's time and I'll be more likely to retain them.

My lesson: don't outsource anything that you can't stream-line and automate first. You'll overpay, be less efficient, and spend more time on it than you intended. You can't automate everything, but when you learn about the existing tools out there, you'll be surprised at what you can do, and how cheap it is.

WHY CHINA IS SO MUCH BETTER AT AI

It occurred to me while studying AI that I wasn't paying enough attention to China.

I read an article in WIRED by Kai-Fu Lee, who is an international expert in artificial intelligence. He also wrote a great book called *AI Superpowers: China, Silicon Valley, and the New World Order*.

My key takeaways from the article were that while the biggest AI discoveries are happening in the United States, the most practical implementations are happening in China. A number of factors make this possible, namely speed and execution. China has a huge population to test new software and technology on, and its population is eager to accept new ways of doing things.

Chinese entrepreneurs are relentless too, adopting a fail fast and often model. They ideate much faster than entrepreneurs in the United States and are willing to accept losses because they can use the knowledge to succeed in their next opportunity. I thought this was particularly insightful. There were other cultural factors that Lee discussed in the article, and I recommend that you read it.

In general, it got me thinking about authors and ideating. What would it be like to fail fast and often as an author, at a breakneck pace? What could you learn? What might self-publishing in China look like? If language were no longer an issue between cultures and both US and Chinese authors sold books across the borders of their respective countries, in what ways would Chinese authors approach book sales and discoverability? It's all intriguing to think about.

LATEX

While researching book formatting, I stumbled upon a document preparation system called LaTex (pronounced "lah-teck").

LaTex is typically used for typesetting difficult scientific or technical documents, but it can be used for any kind of book.

LaTeX is similar to a programming language, but it handles mathematics, charts, graphs, bibliographies, and indexes more easily than ebook formatting apps. Wiley and Sons (a traditional publisher), for example, has been known to use LaTeX for some of their technical guides.

There are LaTeX marketplaces where you can find templates for certain types of books—journals, essays, scientific articles, resumes, curricula vitae, and paperback books. Browsing through the marketplaces, I couldn't help but think LaTeX would be a unique way to format a writing book, particularly one with a lot of figures and graphs. It would require the right content, of course. It would be foolish to use LaTeX for LaTeX's sake, but I now consider it a tool in my toolbox the next time I have an unusual book that needs special formatting.

THE POWER OF THE BROWSER

On my YouTube channel, I reviewed a browser-based writing app that allowed users to create outlines in their browser. It was easy-to-use and built using an unusual code engine. I published a *video highlighting the software.*

Over 1,100 subscribers watched the video in 48 hours. I thought that they would have some trepidations about a browser-based app.

They didn't. In fact, they welcomed it. The only user who expressed concerns used an antivirus program that cleared his browsing history every day, which would have erased any content he created in the app. That was an insightful comment.

I learned not to discount the power of browser-based writing apps. As long as it looks good on desktop and mobile, there is a segment of the community who will use it. Some people can only access the Internet through a mobile phone and may prefer to use a browser instead of a dedicated app.

EMAIL AUTOMATION AND FILTERING

During the second quarter of this year, my email inbox was out of control. I'm normally an inbox zero person, but once the coronavirus pandemic broke out, a pandemic also broke out in my inbox...

It got so bad, I was missing out on sales opportunities because companies were emailing me with special offers to sponsor my YouTube channel. It was an embarrassing few months for me, and I'm not proud of the amount of time it took to respond. I also took a dreadful amount of time to respond to fan-mail, which is unusual for me.

At work, I use Outlook, and I love the program's rule engine because it allows you to apply rules to emails immediately when they hit your inbox. You can eliminate emails from your inbox very easily by automation.

I realized that I should have been doing this with my writing emails—no idea why I never thought of it.

I used Gmail's filter feature to start assigning rules to emails that came into my inbox. Doing this, I eliminated approximately 20-30 regular monthly emails, which represents about 1% of the emails I get on a monthly basis, but every little bit helps.

For example, when I make a purchase, I don't need to see the receipt. I have Gmail tag the receipt email as an expense and put it in a dedicated folder; this way, I can simply review all of my receipts at the end of the month instead of having to address each one individually as they arrive in my inbox.

While I wished I could have automated more of my inbox, I can rest knowing that my emails are as automated as they can be. Now, scale is my biggest problem; I don't receive enough emails to hire someone to help me with them yet, but that's on the horizon.

Once I start receiving over 2,000 emails per month, it will probably be time to hire an assistant. That would be around 65-70 emails per day. I'm only halfway there right now.

In an ideal world, I would prefer not to spend much time in my email inbox unless it's for fan-mail, important business emails, or special items that need my attention. I make more money when I'm not chained to my inbox because I can create content. Email drives my day right now, for better or worse, and I'm committed to finding better ways to minimize it. I don't see a path to email freedom that doesn't involve hyper-automation and hiring an assistant, unfortunately.

When I hire that person, I won't have to waste their time with emails that they don't need to see, as my inbox will already be optimized. That makes me more efficient, saves me more money in the long run, and respects a future assistant's time and skills so that they can do their best work and hopefully enjoy doing it.

NATURAL LANGUAGE PROCESSING
AND WRITERS

I've been learning about natural language processing (NLP), which is a discipline in artificial intelligence. Let's see how well I can teach it...

You're reading text right now. Or you're listening to it if you bought the audiobook version of this book. A computer can't read or understand text; it can only understand code.

Computers do best when they can analyze structured data, which is data that has a consistent, standardized structure. The sales report you receive each month from various retailers is a good example of structured data; with only a few exceptions, the report format is exactly the same each month. A computer can take that and do things with it, such as compile a database.

However, when we talk, that's unstructured data. Everyone speaks differently, with a different speed, with a different accent, and so on. Everyone *writes* differently too. This is what we call natural language.

Natural language processing takes natural language and converts it into data that a computer can understand and then process.

The mobile assistant on your phone is perhaps the most

ubiquitous example of natural language processing that you use every day without thinking about it. It converts your speech into data in almost real-time in order to answer your requests. You've seen NLP at work in other places, such as dictating a novel through Dragon by Nuance, speaking to a chatbot on a website when you need technical support, in developmental editing AI apps like Fictionary, and even Grammarly. Grammarly in particular uses natural language processing paired with machine learning to learn at a bigger and faster scale by reading the words of users around the world.

Natural language processing is all around us, but it is lesser known to consumers because all the buzz right now is around machine learning, neural networks, and sentiment analysis.

I watched a *basic video on NLP* and thought it was interesting, but I didn't see any applications to my writing business. Then I stumbled on *another video* where a programmer was explaining a proof of concept he built that involved creating a rules engine with simple conditions. The user was able to add conditions through a nice interface, which affected the code on the backend. That got me thinking—gosh, it wouldn't it be nice if I could do that with grammar rules?

Imagine an app where you could program a rule like, "If the article 'a' appears before a plural noun or noun phrase, then highlight the noun with a comment that says 'check subject-verb agreement.'" That little idea led to a hunch that felt very similar to the one I felt before I discovered how to build my book database.

It turns out that the rules engine that programmer built was possible, and that what I was trying to do *was* natural language processing—I just hadn't connected the dots.

That was when I had the breakthrough idea—what if you could mix natural language processing with a programming language to create the engine that I envisioned?

The idea of dabbling with artificial intelligence scared the *hell* out of me. As I started researching the idea, I felt my anxiety growing. I thought, maybe for once I had taken on more than I could handle. The discomfort was very similar to what it feels like when you write the novel you don't think you're ready for yet. I've learned to greet that feeling instead of running away because you never know what will happen. Some of the most important experiences in my life happened because I said yes to opportunities that were way outside of my skill level at the time. I'll write about this in the "Writer of the Future" section because it's important.

Anyway, the next day, I learned the basics of the Java and Python programming languages by watching a bunch of coding videos at 2x speed. I watched so many videos and read so much technical documentation that my head hurt. Yet, still, I had that hunch. It wouldn't leave me.

I kept thinking, *It's not worth it for me to learn a programming language to build an app.* Sure, I could do it, but it would be a massive undertaking, and I wasn't a data scientist, so even if I could program something, there was no way I could build an AI model.

And then I thought, *Have other people done this work? Surely there have to be open-source models out there.*

That was when everything clicked. I found the Natural Language Toolkit, a development kit considered by many to be the best entryway into natural language processing. Many Python developers use it. The NLTK contains a bank of virtually every word in the English language, and it can break any sentence into parts of speech. Take the sentence "I like a ice cream sandwiches." NLTK would break down the sentence and assign "part of speech tags" that look like this:

I_NN (noun)
like_ VBP (verb, present tense)

a_DET (article, or determiner)

ice cream_JJ (adjective)

sandwiches_NNS (noun, plural)

You can probably see the grammatical error in the sentence. Now that NLTK has broken the sentence down into parts of speech that the computer can understand, we can now use the Python programming language to create a rule that says:

- Given that a subject and verb must agree,
- if determiner "a" precedes any plural noun or noun phrase,
- then in Microsoft Word, highlight the noun phrase, create a comment with the text "Check subject-verb agreement and check determiner"

The end result would alert me to a potential typo in the manuscript. The actual rule is far more technical than that, so I've oversimplified it for clarity's sake.

Microsoft Word's spell-checker would catch this error, but what if I could potentially program errors that Word's spell-checker or Grammarly would NOT catch?

I posed the concept to my community and asked if anyone had Python expertise. A loyal subscriber who is a Python developer reached out and offered to help me build a prototype with four rules. It worked amazingly well. The developer taught me how to maintain the prototype, as well as some pointers on how to create additional rules. Now all I have to do is learn a narrow use of Python instead of the entire language, and I can pay someone to check it for me.

This allows me to implement the following workflow:

1. Write a book
2. Send it to my editor

3. Turn a certain percentage of my editor's edits into if-then statements
4. Turn those if-then statements into rules
5. Run my personalized rules engine to catch any edits my editor would have corrected
6. Send my editor an objectively cleaner manuscript

I should point out that not every edit my editor recommends can be converted. Also, no rule will catch 100% of errors.

But the great thing about the engine is that I can feed all of my backlist manuscripts through it. The engine would house all of my correctable mistakes from my last 50 books. There's no way I can remember every single edit an editor makes. Also, I've had different editors over the years, some better than others. Also, sometimes editors miss errors. The rule engine serves as a last line of defense.

It's impossible to quantify the number of errors in a book, but let's pretend we can for a moment. Imagine that your work-in-progress has 100 errors. Your editor normally catches 90. What if the engine could catch 10 of the errors your editor would normally have to correct? That would produce a manuscript that is 11% cleaner. In theory, it *should* save your editor time and effort, which means they will return the manuscript to you faster. It might even save you a small amount of money. It would also *possibly* allow the editor to find some of the other 10 errors they might have missed since it's easier to find errors in a cleaner manuscript.

Also, consider some additional uses.

You could use the engine to enforce your own style guide to ensure that your book's style is consistent from book to book. For example, you might choose to handle ordered lists a certain way that you want your readers to instantly recognize.

You could also use the engine to make the book transition to audio better. You could train it to capture words that are diffi-cult for a narrator to pronounce such as "grasp." Or, if you use phrases like "if you're reading this," you could have the tool flag the phrase to remind you to remain format neutral. Ironically, this was an idea that I proposed in the first book of the *Indie Author Confidential* series.

Anyway, the lesson I learned was that when I follow my hunches, they lead me to interesting places. Because I followed my gut, dared to venture into scary territory, used my network, and kept asking questions, I created another game-changing tool that can help me in becoming a world-class content creator, a technology and data-driven writer. And all the prototype took was five hours and less than 100 lines of code. So much tech-nology is around us, and it's free or very affordable. You just have to be willing to search for it.

CALENDARING APP

I have conference calls with people in the publishing industry on a weekly, if not daily basis. I spend a lot of time going back and forth trying to negotiate the best time to meet. A lot of people I meet with live in the United Kingdom and Australia, which further complicates the problem.

A friend of mine recommended an automatic calendar service. Instead of going back and forth to find a "good time," he sends a link to his calendar, and the other person finds a time on it, and the service automatically creates a calendar invite for both parties. The app takes care of availability issues, time zones, and conference call links.

I resisted this for a long time, but I finally broke down and bought one. Man, was it a game-changer! I should have done it sooner. When I bought the service, the number of calls I booked increased overnight because I didn't have to worry about technical issues.

This service is now an essential part of my toolbox. I tested it out with podcast interviews. A prospective podcast host emailed me asking to be on their show, and I sent them the special link.

Within minutes, they grabbed time on my calendar. The service I bought also allows me to control the conversation further—the form captures what the podcast host wants to talk about, and the confirmation email contains a link to my press kit.

Once the booking is complete, I just forward the confirmation as a quick thank you and tell the host I look forward to speaking with them.

That's the power of technology, and it only costs me $80 per year. The return on investment from my combined podcast appearances is worth well more than that.

SOME THOUGHTS ON AUDIOBOOK PRODUCTION EFFICIENCY

On my birthday, August 13, I received an email from Audible that they had accepted my first personally-narrated audiobook, *150 Self-Publishing Questions Answered*, without any technical issues or recommendations. It was a technical victory for me.

Before I recorded the audiobook, I decided to take a gamble. I hired an engineer to create an "audio template" for me. He took a sample chapter from the book and mastered it to meet Audible's technical specifications. He then saved those specifications as a "template" in the audio editing app we both use, and sent the template to me. I then imported the template and used it for the rest of the chapters in the book. My hope was that the entire book would pass Audible's QA, and for an entire month, I wondered if my strategy would pay off. My gamble was that it would, and if that was true, then I essentially bypassed the need for mastering or hiring an audio engineer in the future because I could use the template for everything.

Audible approved the audio with no concerns. This means that I can now record an audiobook and edit it, and then master it and get it ready with the click of a button. Huge efficiency win for me.

Ideally, if I could get my process to the point where I record the audiobook, and then have someone else edit it, and then I can master and upload, that would be perfect, but it's not that easy.

For starters, when I record a section, I don't know if the recording is 100% perfect until I listen to it later. I may mispronounce a word, there may be an imperfection in the audio, or I might accidentally bump my booth when I speak. If any of these things happen, I have to rerecord the entire sentence. I often have to rerecord a batch of sentences from the previous session the next morning, which is inefficient in my opinion, but unavoidable at the moment.

The most efficient way for me to record an audiobook would be as follows:

- I record an audiobook with the cleanest takes possible, which takes approximately two times the full length of the audiobook.
- I pass the book to an "assistant," who edits out the breath sounds and extraneous noises, and then recommends which sentences to rerecord.
- I rerecord bad takes in one session, verify that no errors exist, and send the new audio back to the assistant.
- The assistant then applies the audio specification template and uploads the audio for my review.
- I then have to listen to the entire book to make sure the job was done correctly, which would take approximately two times the full length of the audiobook. Then I would upload it to audiobook retailers.

This is the cleanest and most efficient way that would save

me the most time. For a four-hour audiobook, it would take me approximately eight hours to record, around one to two hours of back-and-forth with the assistant so that I can answer their questions and provide direction, four hours to listen to the final product, with one to two hours' buffer to communicate corrections, and another four hours to export the audio files and prepare them for publication. Overall, my time spend per audiobook would be around 15 to 20 hours. Naturally, that number increases drastically as the audiobook length increases.

But in this case, the editing *alone* would take 20 hours if I did it myself, so this workflow would halve the amount of time it takes to produce a personally-narrated audiobook.

However, the method would cost money. I'd have to pay the assistant a rate per finished hour. The only way to keep expenses under control would be to pay less than $100 per finished hour or the project becomes far more difficult to make profitable quickly.

I would have paid a professional narrator *at least* one hundred and fifty dollars per finished hour for my nonfiction titles. That's $600 for a professionally-narrated title. My method would cost $400, which makes you ask what the point is narrating a book myself if, for $200 more, I can pay a professional narrator who will do a much better job. Of course, a book narrated by the author is a great selling point, but it has to make financial sense too!

This is an interesting economic problem that I didn't find a clear solution to at the time of this writing. Where I left it was that there is probably a "first magic number" for audio length, where, under, it makes sense for me to handle the project myself. There would be a "second magic number" where it makes sense for me to hire a narrator because it will require too much time to record. I don't know what the numbers are yet, but I'll continue to explore the issue as I create more audiobooks.

BEWARE WEB CONNECTIONS FOR GATHERING YOUR SALES

I'm seeing a few data services for writers pop up that promise to connect with Amazon to download your sales data for the purposes of helping you figure out how much money you're making. It requires your Amazon login credentials.

Be careful.

The companies are not bad—they're providing a good service for a good reason.

Amazon KDP's Terms of Service state: "4.3 Account Security. You are solely responsible for safeguarding and maintaining the confidentiality of your account username and password and are responsible for all activities that occur under your account, whether or not you have authorized the activities. You may not permit any third party to use the Program through your account and will not use the account of any third party. You agree to immediately notify Amazon of any unauthorized use of your username, password, or account."

This means that if you provide your login and password to a third party, and the third party uses that to log in to Amazon, you've violated the terms of service. Some service providers have received approval from Amazon to do this legitimately. Those are the ones you should use.

I stumbled across a fairly new service that grabs your Amazon sales data and prepares it into nice charts and graphs for you. However, their terms of service were horrifying. I paraphrase:

"We are not responsible for any violation of any retailer's terms of service, even if that violation is made aware to us. We make your data available to you. If your account is canceled, you bear the risk."

Really? You're asking people to pay an annual subscription for your service with the understanding that they're bearing the risk for a *service you are providing*?

This line of reasoning is best described as follows: "We're just helping you make sense of your data. These are your books and you have the right to aggregate their data as you so choose." Philosophically, the argument is correct, or at least it should be. Legally and contractually, however, it's inaccurate. Reread Amazon's terms. Just because you create metadata doesn't give you the right to do whatever you want with it...inside Amazon's ecosystem.

Most people are never going to read the terms of service. I'll let you reread the contract language above and draw your own conclusions about what you would do.

I'm writing a book right now called *The Author Income Problem*, and in it, I explain that web connections to retailers to download your sales data is a dangerous game that you shouldn't play.

BECOME A DATA-DRIVEN WRITER

EMAIL STATISTICS

I found a service that reads your email inbox and then provides a metric dashboard with important key performance indicators.

Here are my metrics for June 2020:

- I received 713 legitimate email messages and 487 spam messages
- Forty percent of my emails are spam
- I sent 217 messages to 87 *different* people
- My average response time is approximately 1.5 days
- Tuesdays are my heaviest email days, with an average of 10-17 emails per hour between the hours of 11AM and 3PM

As I reflect on those numbers, I'm proud of a 1.5 day time service. Ironically, I discovered this metric after I wrote the chapter on email time service. I'm proud that I am meeting the service levels that I promise on my contact form. Of course there are outliers, but I think I can be forgiven even for a three-day service time if I'm really busy, as long as my reader gets an adequate response to their email.

My email flow is a problem. Two emails at 10AM, 17 at 11AM, 15 at 12PM, and so on is a problem. I can't stop the emails from coming in, so there's nothing I can do about that. However, as I think about scaling in the future, knowing when my emails are the craziest is helpful information. Once I've automated my inbox to the optimum level, I'll have to hire an assistant to help me with email at some point. Giving them set times to check my email inbox is smart. If my average peak email times are Tuesday between 11AM and 3PM, I might have the assistant check my inbox at 11:30, 12:30, and 2:30PM, and then once or twice again throughout the day. If we can hit service levels during peak times, then non-peak service levels will be easier to maintain.

The only data the report didn't give me is *what* emails I received during the peak times. I can easily find that information, but it's more digging and analyzing than I want to do at this point. But when I'm ready, it would be helpful to know what percentage of the peak emails are fan-mail, sales emails, emails from my inner circle, newsletters, and so on.

EMAIL PARSING

Over the years, I've flirted with QuickBooks for taxes. I don't like it, but I always find myself reconsidering it for one major feature: the ability to send emails to a dedicated email address and have the information from that email show up as an expense without you having to do anything. The feature is amazing.

It's called "email parsing." It's when a system breaks an email into a series of data points and passes them into a database so that you can use them for something else.

Let's say that I purchase editing services from an editor, who sends me a receipt. An email parser will take the receipt email and break it down into:

- Name of the editor
- Email address of the editor
- Date of the transaction
- Amount
- Service rendered

The parser would then download the data into either an

Excel spreadsheet or an Access database. In this example, I might have a spreadsheet of my annual expenses, so the parser would create an entry with the expense for my accountant. All I have to do is send the spreadsheet to my accountant at the end of the year. No data entry on my part.

QuickBooks has this down to a science, and it's why a lot of people choose them. It's too bad the rest of the program is unappealing to me.

I wanted to find out if there was a way I could do email parsing on my own.

There are software-as-a-service providers (SaaS) and downloadable applications that help you do this. After about an hour of market research, I decided they were a little too expensive for me right now. Fifty dollars per month is not worth spending on a handful of emails you need parsed. My biggest need right now is parsing receipt emails so I can cut down on my accounting each month. It would save me about 30-45 minutes per month, which is about six to nine hours per year, or about 15-20% of the time it takes to produce a book.

As I grow my writing business, email parsing has other benefits that *will* be worth paying for. Imagine parsing all the emails you receive from fans to assess trends or get content ideas; or parsing the dates and times of when you receive emails to determine the best time to dedicate to responding; or, linking parsing to machine learning or a chatbot to generate automated responses to questions you receive most often (with your approval, of course). Maybe for those types of inquiries, you have an "assistant," who is really just a bot that answers the easy questions so you can focus on the harder ones. That technology already exists and will become cheaper over time.

I'm not suggesting you abandon your readers to a bot; I *am* suggesting that some people email you with the same old questions over again without bothering to do basic research. Rather than deleting their emails (which many authors probably do), perhaps we should give those people a lower level of customer service compared to someone who asks you a truly thoughtful question. But the key is that they'll still receive an answer they can use.

Anyway, I enjoyed my time learning about email parsing. It's knowledge I can use to drive efficiency in the future.

TELLING STORIES WITH DATA

I took a free data science course. It was a basic course that introduced the principles of data science to everyday people.

The instructor emphasized the power of storytelling when it comes to explaining data. You can have the most powerful data in the world, but if you put people to sleep, then it's useless.

The instructor gave a simple equation to illustrate the point: Story x Analysis = Value.

He offered some tips on better storytelling with data analysis that honestly helped me more with writing this book than it did with data analysis.

The big takeaway was to avoid egocentrism, which means assuming that everyone knows something. For example, I can't assume that everyone reading this series understands the business and data terms I use, so I'm careful to give basic explanations any time I mention something that might be obvious to me but not so obvious to you. I'm still working on getting better at that.

His conclusion was to remember that clients know very little or nothing about data; that's why they hire data scientists.

Readers pick up books about wizards because they don't know anything about wizards, or they're intrigued.

Just as avoiding egocentrism is helpful with nonfiction, it's also helpful in creating more engaging characters because you can have characters explain things about their lives that are obvious to the character but not so much to the reader.

Funny how I learned this from a data science course. Some things are universal.

SIMPSON'S PARADOX

Have you ever wondered how data can say one thing at the macro level but say something different at the micro level?

For example, I write fiction and nonfiction. Overall, my fiction sales are down somewhat. In looking at the big picture, you'd think that my fiction is on the decline. However, if you look at just the fiction sales, a few of my fiction titles are doing quite well each month.

This is called Simpson's Paradox, and it's a well-known phenomenon in statistics. In the free data science course I took, the instructor explained the often-used example of college admissions in the University of California-Berkeley, where admission results at the macro level showed that men were more likely to be admitted, but department-level statistics showed that women were accepted at higher rates into certain programs than others. In some departments, the acceptance rate for women was equal to or slightly higher than men.

Learning about the paradox was useful when looking at my sales data. It's a reminder to dig into your data and never take it at face value because there could be contradictions.

AGGREGATING ALL MY SALES REPORTS: LESSONS LEARNED

In aggregating all my sale reports into a database, I learned a lot about my book sales.

For example, I learned that 65% of my ebook sales come from the United States. That's probably a decent number compared to most authors since I am not exclusive to Amazon, but it's a long-term problem I'll need to address. I need to reduce my dependence on Amazon *and* ebooks.

I also learned that audio, for the first time ever, eclipsed my ebook sales. It is now my leading sales format. That validated my decision to jump into audiobooks. In fact, my foray into audio was right on time.

I learned that in Canada, the majority of my readers live in Ontario. Thanks, Kobo!

I learned that the Pareto Principle is real—about 20% of my books drive 80% of my income.

I learned that YouTube AdSense is a bright spot for me that continues to grow at a rate of about 10-15% on average per year.

I also learned how truly volatile affiliate income can be. Last year was my best year in affiliate sales ever; this year may be my worst ever. It's crazy how up-and-down affiliate income is. You can't rely on it.

I learned other little nuances that aren't worth explaining here because they would probably bore you.

The lesson is that your sales data will tell you a lot. You have to be willing to assemble the pieces and allow it to talk.

BULK UPLOADING

I discovered a book retailer that I do not sell books at: Streetlib. They reach a few retailers that my other ebook aggregators such as Smashwords, Draft2Digital, and PublishDrive do not.

I immediately thought, *I should get my books on StreetLib!*

And then I thought, *Wait. I have over 50 books.*

And then, *That would be a pain the neck, Michael.*

And then, *Do they have a bulk upload feature so I can upload multiple books at once?*

Sure enough, they do. They don't support ONIX, which is a metadata standard I discussed in the first book in this series (so read that if you have no idea what ONIX is), but they do support a spreadsheet that basically has the same fields as an ONIX submission. Populate the spreadsheet, upload your book files and covers in a certain order, and boom—StreetLib will publish all your books simultaneously. Imagine the joy of publishing 50 books this way!

I'm not exaggerating when I say that the issue of bulk upload keeps me awake at night. It's the single most important short-term problem all indies will have in the future.

I *cannot* afford to upload my books one-by-one to new

retailers anymore. I simply have too many books now. Individual uploading is time-consuming, expensive, and it leaves me prone to making simple mistakes with data entry, like mistyping a title or a price. Little things will always go wrong, no matter how diligent I am. Individual uploading is also inefficient and too expensive to pay a virtual assistant to do, not to mention a liability since that person has access to your retailer passwords and bank information, not to mention the power to wreak pure havoc if they don't know what they're doing.

I *need* automation that will help me with data entry. I would much rather populate fields with the one true incarnation of my data—my book database, where I house things like the titles, book descriptions, prices, and keywords for all of my books. I built my book database earlier in the year precisely to help me with this problem so I could have one place to house the correct information for my books so I could keep everything consistent.

With StreetLib, my first thought was that I could use my book database to populate *most* of the needed fields on their required spreadsheet, then manually fill in the ones I don't have stored, as the answers are likely to be the same for all of my books. I could use Excel's autofill feature to great effect here.

Unfortunately, unlike other retailers that offer bulk upload, StreetLib requires an ISBN for ebooks. I don't like that because I am not a proponent of ebook ISBNs. I believe they are an inefficient expense that grants almost no benefits in return.

In this case, I'd have to purchase ISBNs solely to get my books onto Streetlib, which does not justify the cost. I could also distribute to Ingram Spark, but only for new titles moving forward. It didn't feel right. If other new book retailers offer bulk upload but require ISBNs for ebooks, I'll reconsider, but for now, I'm not distributing to StreetLib any time soon.

But I did learn that ONIX metadata management software also allows you to export to Microsoft Excel. ONIX has many additional fields that are specific to the publishing industry, such as book type and watermarks. These fields are useless to indies, but you have to have an entry in the field. I noticed that some of the fields I didn't have in my book database that StreetLib required were part of the ONIX standard. In the future, when I'm ready to start bulk uploading, I can export the data I have in my book database into one spreadsheet and the data that I have in ONIX into another spreadsheet and then join them together in the order StreetLib requires.

This would reduce data entry and improve accuracy. It would also allow me to bulk upload with unparalleled speed and execution.

Imagine with me for a moment: a new book retailer with immense potential pops up tomorrow. Tomorrow night, I have all 50 of my books uploaded. The day after tomorrow, they're published. That should be the goal we all strive for. That's the very definition of nimble.

Overall, at the time of this writing, it will cost me about $100 for ONIX metadata management software, $575 for 100 ISBNs, and about 10-15 hours of my time to get everything set up (or, a few hundred to pay a consultant if I run into road-blocks). Then, moving forward, there would be no additional cost and the time spend would decrease drastically.

While I'm not ready to invest in this technology yet, I'm glad that I now have a plan on how to execute it. Sometimes, the plan is the most important thing.

THE DATA-DRIVEN EDITOR

I talk all the time about how being data-driven will be an increasingly important aspect of being a writer.

Until now, I had never considered the idea of a data-driven editor.

If you think about it, book editors have the same efficiency problems as writers. The more clients an editor takes on, the more money they make, but there's only so much time in the day. What if editors could use software to assist them in working faster and smarter? It's intriguing.

I happened upon a startup that uses natural language processing to assess your story's weaknesses. That's not terribly remarkable; there are at least a dozen companies that offer something similar in a slightly different flavor.

What made this particular company unique was that they marketed their software to editors too. That made me sit up and pay attention. If the software is good, that's a winning value add for the editor. It helps them work smarter and faster through a manuscript, and produce a better work product.

Of course, this does beg an interesting long-term question: if you have access to developmental editing software and it's good enough for your purposes, why hire a developmental editor?

Developmental editing will become commoditized. It'll be like your hometown insurance agent in the United States. Decades ago, people relied on their agent's expertise to insure their homes, autos, boats, and more. Now people are buying insurance off the Internet from insurance companies directly. Agents have to differentiate themselves with service and expertise, and they're fighting a losing battle.

I see a world, not very long from now, where authors buy AI software for developmental edits, and authors with more money pay for a developmental editor who provides expertise and service.

I also see a dynamic shift where new authors will buy software because it's cheaper, and more established authors will hire real editors, who will serve more as consultants at a higher cost, offering a blended mix of editing, market research, and data analysis, probably around a specialized genre. It's the only way developmental editors will survive. The role will become more holistic, encompassing several disciplines. That's my hunch.

Anyway, I think just as authors must master technology and data to be more successful, so must our service providers. Imagine book cover designers that use computer vision AI to help them design better covers, for example. It's a very exciting future to think about, especially as the cost of technology decreases and becomes more accessible to small businesses.

GRAMMARLY SECURITY FLAW

You can't go anywhere on the Internet without seeing a Grammarly ad. If you're an author, their marketing team will find you.

I like Grammarly. It's no substitute for an editor, but it *can* help you find additional errors that Microsoft Word's spellchecker can't, especially for fiction. In fact, *I published a video on my YouTube channel* where I stress-tested Grammarly's accuracy.

In 2018, a white hat hacker discovered a security flaw in Grammarly's browser edition. The hacker found that Grammarly was leaking every keystroke a user made in the browser, not just inside Grammarly. Bad guys could have stolen credit card information, private emails, and more. It was a major security flaw. (Note that it affected the browser edition only, not the desktop versions). Grammarly fixed the bug very quickly, and it doesn't appear that any accounts were breached. This is why white hat hackers exist—to help organizations find flaws before the black hat hackers do.

I didn't find out about the security flaw until now. It raised serious questions for me about the viability of cloud-based AI software and browser-based writing apps. These apps don't process your work locally on your computer; instead, they pass it to the cloud, where it gets processed along with the words of other users using the service. There are numerous advantages to doing this.

Sure, anything can be hacked, but...a bestselling writer would be foolish to use a browser-based extension to write their books that doesn't have a track record of security. I once watched a talk by John Grisham where he said he was terrified of hackers. He uses two computers; one that is connected to the Internet, and another that is not connected to the Internet that houses all his manuscripts. If someone of his stature were hacked, it would be catastrophic.

You don't have to be at John Grisham's level to be concerned about getting hacked. I believe it's a legitimate exposure any author faces.

In the articles that covered the Grammarly bug, one person commented that every programmer will face the day that their code is tested by hackers. For some, that day comes sooner than others. But when it does, everything is at stake. And customers and their data are the collateral.

Grammarly has a strong development team. I wonder how good development teams at startups of the future will be, especially with cloud-based services for writers, which will have fewer resources than other industries.

PUBLISHDRIVE ABACUS

I was encouraged this quarter to see PublishDrive announce additional functionality to its Abacus tool.

Abacus allows co-authors to see a visual split of their royalties. If I write a book with you, and I'm the publisher, I can upload your sales reports to Abacus and it'll tell me exactly how much I owe you. You can also log in and view how much money you're owed.

This quarter, PublishDrive announced support for Ingram-Spark, Draft2Digital, Kobo, Google, and Apple Books sales reports. This means that co-authors who are "wide" and not exclusive to Amazon can now avail of the service, which is great.

I'm not crazy about the pricing, but that's a personal preference and I understand that they've got to make money and recoup their costs.

I don't see why PublishDrive can't turn Abacus into a service for single authors. In other words, why wouldn't a single author be able to upload all their books and see instantly how much money they made? Charge an annual fee, and I predict that the service would take off. Knowing PublishDrive, it's probably in their plans. They've shown themselves to be shrewd innovators with data and technology.

Spotify announced this quarter that it is getting into the audiobook game by hiring several people to head up a new audiobook division.

I also found *this study in Canada* about audiobook listening habits. It said that 40% of listeners borrow audiobooks from a public library in both digital and physical formats.

Furthermore, the study said, "When we combine channels that have both physical and digital options, we find that Amazon (Audible and Amazon physical formats) tops the list with 51%, followed by the library at 48% offering physical and digital formats."

My head exploded when I read that. People still listen to physical audiobooks?

I wanted to know if this was just a Canada thing or if there was a similar trend in other countries.

I found *a study from the Audiobook Publishers Association* (*APA*) that painted a different picture. While I wasn't able to access the raw data to verify it, the study didn't say which markets it was based on. I have to assume it's the US.

The study indicates that in 2014, digital sales were 69%

(based on dollar amounts). In 2018, they were 91. Physical unit sales were 27 % in 2014, and 7.8 % in 2018. Other formats such as pre-loaded MP3 items, book and CD box sets were two percent in 2014 and 0.8 in 2018.

In any case, physical audiobook habits are declining (I presume in the US). Also, it's probably worth mentioning that the digital number is probably much higher than 91 percent due to the fact that most self-published books don't have ISBNs, so therefore they are probably not included in the study. It might be closer to 96 or 98 percent in my estimation. I don't know *anyone* in the United States who listens to physical audiobooks. My mom does check out pre-loaded MP3 cartridges from the library from time to time, but I always considered that an exception rather than a rule.

I can only imagine that digital listening has trended upward in the two years since the study. Unlike music, audiobooks cannot exist on vinyl records, so I believe that CD audiobooks will truly be extinct in about five to seven years...in the United States.

Both studies paint drastically different pictures of the US and Canada. It doesn't mean that either of the studies is wrong, though. If both studies are true and truly representative of the markets, the difference between the US and Canada is probably explained by Audible's near-monopoly of the US market. If Spotify enters the audiobook market, their international presence ensures that most major countries will also migrate to digital, mainly because Audible doesn't have much of a presence outside of the United States, UK, and Canada. The data above supports that listeners will adopt digital quickly.

The question I kept asking myself while researching was whether it made sense to explore producing CD versions of my audiobooks. If there are other countries like Canada, then perhaps it makes sense. However, the conundrum is that the only place I'd be able to sell CD audiobooks is Amazon, which probably defeats the purpose.

CDs strike me as awfully inconvenient to produce, and the format is fading away.

If physical audiobook sales are shrinking internationally, and continue to do so in light of the audiobook subscription market heating up, it would be a foolish move to create CD audiobooks. Very foolish. I decided not to pursue it, as it would be too time-consuming and expensive to do, and a financial loss for me if I got it wrong. As much as I want to reach new readers, this doesn't seem to be the way to do it.

BEAST MODE DATA

From August 1, 2020 to October 31, 2020, I decided to go into "beast mode."

In beast mode, I write a ridiculous amount of books in a short period of time. Because I didn't write as many books as I planned during the first half of the year due to the pandemic, I wanted to change that and ensure that I had a solid production year.

During the month of August alone, I wrote almost 100,000 words and three nonfiction books. That equates to around 3,200 words per day. For one week, I was writing 5,000 words per day without breaking a sweat. That's a record for me. One day, I wrote 10,000 words alone.

If I wrote 5,000 words per day for fiction (which is very, very rare), I would be brain-fried.

The experience was helpful data for me because it showed me what my new limits are. If I want to write a nonfiction book quickly, I can do it.

PROTECTING YOUR DATA

Someone wrote me desperate because they lost all their data. They didn't think their writing app could fail, but it did, and it took their precious manuscript along with it.

The encounter was a reminder for me to review my backup systems regularly, and I'm passing that reminder along to you. You can't make data-driven decisions or think about your books as data points if your data gets destroyed!

At a minimum, I recommend the following backup methods:

- Backup feature within your app. Most modern apps offer a feature that will auto-backup your work every few minutes. This isn't a bulletproof backup method, but you should still use it because it's free.
- Cloud backups. Dropbox, Google Drive, or iCloud allow you to sync your work across devices and save it in the cloud. The cloud also won't save you, but it's still worth using because if you don't sync other storage-intensive items such as music or movies,

your entire library will fit comfortably within the free plans of these apps.

- External hard drive. You can buy one for less than $100. Buy two. Back up your computer to the external hard drives nightly and disconnect the drives from your computer when not in use. I also use Apple's Time Machine feature if I need to go back in time to a certain version of a file.
- Portable USB hard drives. These are so cheap these days, it pays to own a handful of them. Back up your manuscripts on them, then keep them safe and separate. Keep one in the security deposit box of your bank, for example.
- Backup service. I use Backblaze. It backs up everything on my computer AND my external hard drives several times a day and stores them in the cloud, with the ability to see and access your backups over time. Backblaze is my final layer of defense. You can download your backups at any time, and they'll ship you a hard drive with all your data on it if you need it. Backblaze has saved me a number of times. There are other similar services to Backblaze, so do your homework on which service works best for you. If you like Backblaze, however, you can buy it at www.authorlevelup.-com/Backblaze (paid link).

Protect your data. If something happens and you lose everything, it can be devastating.

BECOME THE WRITER OF
THE FUTURE

VISUALIZING THE CRAFT OF WRITING

A question I've asked myself repeatedly over the last few years is how to visualize the craft of writing.

I've always believed that if you can visualize something, you can understand it.

Data analysts don't wade through raw spreadsheets unless they have to. They turn those spreadsheets into graphs and charts so that they can see what the data is saying.

Why do we as writers wade through words as a way to understand how to learn writing craft? The words are important, but is there another way to help us learn the craft?

I've experimented with numerous tactics over the last few years.

I wrote a lead magnet called *The Writing Craft Playbook*. I identify mega bestseller techniques and try to explain them with simple drawings. The book was received very well by my audience and doubled my mailing list.

I produced a series of videos on YouTube illustrating the IRAC method. IRAC stands for issue, rule, analysis, and conclusion. It's used in law schools to study cases and I amended the method for authors to study books. I used animated Power Point slides to convey the techniques I studied. That also worked, but I found that the videos were too long.

I'm mainly including this learning in the book as a way to challenge other people. Writing a book is not the only way to teach writing craft. We should start experimenting with other ways that help us to become masters of the craft.

USAGE-BASED WRITING APPS

Which team of writers are you on?

Team A *abhors* paying subscription fees for anything, let alone writing apps. These writers have a personal vendetta against anything with a subscription.

Team B supports subscription-based services but would like more for their money.

Why not join Team C, which is writers who ask for usage-based writing apps?

Is such a thing possible? It's hard to imagine writers being okay with an app that works much like the utility bills they pay at their homes.

In today's environment, I don't think so. But I do think cryptocurrencies could make it possible.

It really is the best of both worlds.

Developers need a steady stream of income to support their applications. If they charge a one-time fee, they'll eventually reach a saturation point, which means they have to keep upgrading the app and charging for new versions to make money. Subscriptions ease this burden by giving them more reliable income, but users are leery of subscriptions because incompetent developers in the past took people's money, only to give them stability updates.

What if you could pay based on how much you use your writing app? You pay based on writing hours, which is an approximation of when the app is open and actively being used.

If you only write one or two books per year, you'll pay less than someone who writes ten. Power users could opt to buy themselves out of usage rates by paying a multiple of the average fee.

What do you think?

I tend to be on Team D—the team that doesn't think this payment model will work any time soon. I think writers would resist it. But if economic, technological, and market forces change in the right direction, it's not hard to see how this could happen.

DOWN GOES THE EBOOK! UP GOES THE AUDIOBOOK!

The German-based publication Bookwire and The Digital Book Report produced a virtual conference this year called All About Audio. Jane Friedman covered the biggest insights in her biweekly newsletter "The Hotsheet."

The highlights were that the audio industry could be split into two industries: audio and podcasting. Both are growing at a rapid rate, fast enough that the audio industry is set to surpass the ebook industry by 2023. The report cited subscription services and binge listening as being on the rise. It also said that audio-first publications will become more prominent. It also indicated strong frontlist and backlist sales, with the majority of unit sales coming from frontlist titles and the majority of listening time coming from backlist titles.

Overall, a glowing report for audio and audiobook sales, which validated my decision to double down on audiobooks. By 2023, I'll have a significant amount of titles in audio, more than I do now.

I'M NOT A GURU. I'M A GGDP

One of my most important decisions when I decided to create nonfiction books was that I didn't want to be a "guru."

I had an embarrassing little streak for about a year or so where I held myself out as an "author business coach," but those days are long behind me.

I've always been wary of a perception in our community that self-publishing influencers aren't trying to help authors—they're making money off them.

In my experience in getting to know many influencers in our community, that's not true, but the perception exists because there are unscrupulous people who give everyone else a bad name.

Therefore, I've never held myself out as a guru. Gurus take your money and expect you to treat them like gods.

Instead, I've always said that I'm just a writer trying to figure everything out, and I share knowledge as I obtain it in hopes that it will help someone. Sure, I write books and try to build my authority in the space, but my authority will always be based on my experience, and my experience is uniquely my own, not a prescription for other people. If you want to study my path, cool—I'll give you plenty to study, much of it for free. When I do charge money, I'm reasonable.

I'm not a guru. I'm a GGDP—guy going down a path. That's it.

I've watched "gurus" in other industries rise and fall. I don't want that future. I prefer to be a working professional who keeps getting better with every project.

TERMS OF SERVICE ALERT

I received an email from Amazon with an invitation to add my podcasts to its upcoming Amazon Music and Audible podcasts program.

I always review terms of service prior to signing any agreement. This one had a red flag. Essentially, people believed the terms said that one must agree not to disparage Amazon or any of its products in order for Amazon to distribute the show. A lot of people were really upset about this, but that's not technically what the terms said. The terms said that the content must not contain advertisements or messaging that disparages Amazon.

The legal question is, what did Amazon mean by "messaging?"

In law, if something isn't defined in a contract, courts look to the word's everyday meaning. According to Merriam-Webster, message is defined as:

1: a communication in writing, in speech, or by signals
Please take this message for me to my friend.
2 : a messenger's mission
the girl will go on a message to the shop

— Cahir Healy

3 : an underlying theme or idea

the message is that it is time to change

— The Economist

According to Wordnik.com, message is defined as:

n. A usually short communication transmitted by words, signals, or other means from one person, station, or group to another.

n. The substance of such a communication; the point or points conveyed.

Dictionary.com states:

1: a communication containing some information, news, advice, request, or the like, sent by messenger, telephone, email, or other means.

2: an official communication, as from a chief executive to a legislative body:

The definition that all of these sources have in common is that a message is intended to be a short communication. Only in one sense is it defined in a way that could be construed as a podcast.

One must then ask: if Amazon intended to exclude shows that disparaged it, why didn't it explicitly do so? It could have said "no content is allowed that disparages Amazon or its products" or it could have instituted an approval process. It didn't do that.

This leads me to believe that Amazon is on the lookout for a very narrow type of problem—probably shows that are deathly critical of it, or one that is sponsored by a competitor, for example. That's not 100% certain, and they can of course enforce this clause however they deem necessary, but one must question the company's intent.

The invitation created a media firestorm for Amazon, so my

guess was that they would revise their contract language to clarify their intent. (They did shortly after I wrote this chapter, so I was right. More on that in a moment.)

The next thing I looked for was exclusivity. Fortunately, they didn't require exclusivity. All a podcast host has to do is cancel their distribution with two days' notice.

So I signed the agreement.

First, I read all terms before I sign any contract.

Second, I never sign anything that I can't abide by.

Third, I always try to put myself in the shoes of the other party. Amazon is going to make this service available on its Alexa devices; therefore, it follows that they don't want Alexa saying things that make Alexa look bad...it would be the equivalent of a Pepsi worker drinking Coke on the job.

Fourth, I rarely discuss Amazon anyway. I tend not to speak poorly of the provider of my biggest source of income. That's common sense.

Fifth, if I don't like it, I can stop distributing my podcasts to Amazon. If they don't like it, they can stop my podcast's distribution, but they can't stop the distribution of my books.

Are we kidding ourselves when we pretend to be outraged that Amazon can bring down the hammer on us for disparaging it? Amazon routinely cancels people from its platform for any reason anyway, often for things they didn't do. They take a "guilty until proven innocent approach" in all things they do. That's not criticism; it's truth.

So I didn't see a real problem at this time. That could always change, and if it does, I or they can opt out of the contract any time.

Shortly after I wrote this, Amazon removed the offending clause from the terms altogether, so I was right in my analysis.

With terms of service, there is always an element of risk.

You balance what you can afford to lose with the potential benefit, and the potential of getting in on Amazon's podcast launch makes a lot of sense with my audio strategy.

ONE COMMAND CENTER

The writer of the future needs a unified command center. Not a writing app, a formatting app, a spelling and grammar app, and the myriad other software we use.

My workflow today is as follows: I write my books in Scrivener, then export them to Microsoft Word so that my editor can edit using track changes. I review the editor's edits in Microsoft Word, run the manuscript through ProWritingAid, copy/paste the book back into Scrivener, then export to Vellum for formatting.

I despise the workflow, but it's the best we have right now.

It's unreasonable to expect one app to execute on the level of Scrivener, Microsoft Word, ProWritingAid, *and* Vellum, but it is reasonable to ask that the writing apps of the future work together seamlessly.

I'd like to write my novel in Scrivener and be able to send it to my editor, perhaps by granting the editor permission to edit my Scrivener file with tracked changes (if Scrivener ever supports that). Preferably, I should never have to leave my writing app for anything, even formatting.

The bestselling writing apps on the market are extremely

vulnerable for disruption. Writers just don't realize it because the writing app as we know it hasn't changed in forty years and we can't conceive of how it can possibly evolve.

If a new writing app functioned similar to how I describe the following narrative, it would render the current landscape of writing apps irrelevant. Let's call it Shapeshifter.

Shapeshifter is a writing app that offers an interchangeable interface that supports WYSIWIG (what you see is what you get) writing interface a la Microsoft Word, or a markdown experience like Ulysses. With one click, you can change its appearance and therefore its layout. It's two or three different writing apps in one. That's the app's headlining feature. It "shapeshifts" extremely well, molding itself to suit the writer instead of asking the writer to adapt to it.

The desktop version is available on Windows and Linux. Mac users were originally left out, but they quickly learned that they could run the app by installing Windows on their computers—a deliberate and intelligent choice on the developers' part that allowed them to seize the Windows market, which was ripe for a new, modern competitor. Given the benefits you're about to hear, Mac users will have no qualms about upgrading their computers to quickly abandon their current writing app. Ironically, the app is available on iOS, iPad OS, and Android, with good feature parity so that users can write on-the-go no matter their phone or tablet.

Shapeshifter is also available in the browser, with an optimized writing experience.

No matter where you are or what device you are using, Shapeshifter will shift to suit your preference.

If that were it, Shapeshifter would be remarkable. But here's what makes it the writing app of the future: out of the box, the app itself is not terribly robust. It has a few key features such as a word processor and the ability to import and export.

However, the app has way more features available; you purchase what you need. If you don't need a distraction-free mode, you don't have to pay for it. If you ever want it, you pay a one-time fee of $5. The app and its features are like LEGOs that you can snap together based on your preferences. Every writer's app will look different; in fact, writers are encouraged to share their "space," which is linked to a generous affiliate program that rewards them for every referral they make.

Shapeshifter is also the first writing app other than Microsoft Word to offer third-party developer integration. The app's in-house features are comparable to most other writing apps, and without any integrations, it looks rather vanilla. Third-party integrations are where the app shines. Developers can create new kinds of writing tools—outlining features, dictation support, macros, and integration with other apps, like voice assistants. All of these plugins help you become a better version of yourself. This also allows the app to stay at the forefront of advancements in operating systems.

Shapeshifter offers a Discord or a Reddit community where users can request new plugins and developers can create them. The app gathers a cult following that quickly becomes mainstream.

Now, let's talk about the biggest selling point: the price.

Shapeshifter's developers wanted to create an affordable writing app and avoid the ire of the community by switching pricing models. For a one-time fee of $30, you pay to own the app. The developers keep the prices low because you pay a la carte for additional features such as cloud syncing between mobile and desktop and WordPress blog integration, for example. You only pay for the features you'll actually use. Overall, you might pay around $200-300 over the lifetime of the app, more including plugins, which can range from a couple dollars to a few hundred dollars depending on the plugin.

And that's not all...

Shapeshifter is just one app in a suite of apps for writers. Shapeshifter Writer handles the writing. You see, the developers figured out that it's impossible to do everything well in one app, so they modeled their app suite after the Adobe Creative Cloud so that all their apps work together seamlessly.

Shapeshifter Writer is an app and marketplace for *writing*.

When it's time to edit, the writer can, with the click of a button, "shift" the app into Editor mode, which is technically a separate application in its own right that you can also purchase.

Editor is optimized for editing. Shapeshifter Editor is a pioneering editing app that is designed solely for back-and-forth between a writer and editor. Drawing inspiration from apps like Google Docs and Asana, a writer and editor can collaborate on a manuscript without the manuscript ever leaving the Editor ecosystem. All the author has to do is invite the editor to join a given project. The editor can edit the book in a browser and does not need to purchase the software, though doing so under an Editor's license will grant them unique benefits.

All edits that the author accepts in Editor get pushed to Writer so that the manuscript is in sync everywhere. The author can of course revert and rollback changes at any time.

Editor also supports third-party integration, such as Grammarly, ProWritingAid, and anything else a developer can dream of in the editing process. Editor would also encourage and support artificial intelligence plugins.

When it's time to format your manuscript, you can "shift" to Shapeshifter Formatter with the click of a button. With just one click and a smooth wizard, you can have a publish-ready ebook and print edition. It offers the power of Vellum but also third-party integration for formatting templates and special features such as indexes. You could even grant access to a formatter who could upload HTML that the app would accept. Changes you make in Formatter are automatically synced with Writer and Editor.

Formatter even integrates with book retailer APIs so you can publish without having to leave the app.

Shapeshifter's holy triumvirate of Writer, Editor, and Formatter succeeds because it streamlines the process of writing and helps writers do more in less time. It takes advantage of the fact that some writing apps go years without receiving updates as well as writers' frustration with subscription-based apps. It leverages the power of Adobe-smooth integration between the three apps, with the ease of use and customization of Reaper (a very popular sound recording app among musicians).

While the future of writing apps may look different than the narrative I've written, consider that writing apps as we know them haven't changed much in forty years as I mentioned earlier. With emerging technology, writers will have such a need to evolve that it will be a no-brainer if someone offers them the ability to move to the cutting edge of technology and writing.

ESTIMATED TIME OF FUTURE ARRIVAL

I read a great book on futurism called *The Signals Are Talking: Why Today's Fringe is Tomorrow's Mainstream* by Amy Webb. It's a great book that explains how a futurist thinks about problems.

One of the questions she addresses is "How do I know when a certain future will arrive?"

She explains the power of thinking about the future like a GPS.

Your GPS tells you your estimated time of arrival at your destination, but your ETA can change. You might hit a traffic jam, an accident, make a wrong turn, or even encounter better traffic than usual. Your GPS constantly recalculates your ETA.

Looking at future technology and trends, it's helpful to think of them in this way too.

For example, if we agree that AI audiobook narration will become mainstream at some point, what factors might accelerate its ETA, and what factors might slow its arrival?

Webb talks about the distinction between express lanes and roadblocks.

Let me give you what I think is a very timely example right

now that will probably become dated in a few years. You will at first wonder why I am mentioning this, but trust me.

At the time of this writing, Tik Tok is one of the fastest-growing social media apps in the world. Users love the ability to make short and entertaining videos, usually with fun music choices.

Tik Tok's parent company, ByteDance, is headquartered in China. During the 2020 election cycle in the United States, there were national security concerns that the Chinese government was using Tik Tok to potentially spy on Americans and influence the election. The concerns may or may not have been valid, but US federal and state officials began posturing and threatening to ban Tik Tok from the United States. Companies such as Amazon made true on the threat, banning the app from its company phones. ByteDance maintained that there was no communication with the Chinese government and that Tik Tok was established in the United States, outside of the Chinese government's purview.

Right around this same time in the summer of 2020, Byte-Dance also released a new mobile phone app called Tomato Smooth Listening (Fanqie Changting). Don't let the name distract you; it is an audiobook listening app that allows readers to listen to audiobooks narrated not by humans, but by AI. Yes, that's right—an audiobook app where AI narrators read the books, not humans.

When it comes to the future of artificial intelligence, it's hard not to see the biggest advancements coming out of China. They're far more technologically advanced than the rest of the world, as it has been a key focus of the Chinese government. When it comes to voice AI, the Chinese language is easier to program with natural language processing than English, for example.

If the United States were to ban Tik Tok, either for a short period of time or indefinitely, that would introduce a roadblock to the progress of AI audiobook narration *for the United States*, particularly if ByteDance's app were successful and caught on internationally.

More than likely, the app is a small step toward AI narration and not the watershed moment.

What else would have to be true in order for the future to arrive?

For starters, audiobook services would have to allow AI narration. Today, none of them do. Audible in particular explicitly states in its terms that audiobooks must be read by a human.

Is it possible that a competitor will spring up solely for AI narration? That's unlikely. What's more plausible is that Audible and the other audiobook retailers are already planning for this future. It wouldn't surprise me if they released their own voice library that users could choose from. They've already done this with Alexa, offering a Samuel L. Jackson voice. Or, they may offer the opportunity for existing narrators with a certain number of audiobook finished hours (say, 100) to transform their voices into a persona. Their persona would read a cheaper version of the audiobook that would appear next to the traditionally-narrated one.

There are many roadblocks that would have to be removed for AI narration to move into the figurative express lane so that it can reach us. But thinking about it in terms of an ETA is useful.

COMPLIANCE

There are certain things in the writing life that aren't writing, marketing, or business, yet we have to do them.

General Data Protection Regulation (GDPR) in the European Union is an example.

Adhering to GDPR isn't going to sell you any books, but it'll help you avoid legal trouble.

I call this area of the writing life "compliance." You must learn compliance to play nice and be a good industry citizen.

My law degree is a specialization of risk management and compliance. I deal with it every day in my insurance career.

The longer I am an author, the more I realize the importance of anticipating and responding to compliance items. Let me give you a few examples.

I received an email from YouTube advising that certain integrations with their application programming interface (API) would soon stop working. An API is like a plug-socket arrangement where developers can plug into a company's servers to download data. The developer agrees to abide by the company's protocols in exchange for the data. I used a WordPress plugin that used the YouTube API to display all my videos in a grid on my website so that first-time visitors could watch my channel, subscribe, and like my videos without having to leave my website. If the API didn't work, I'd have to find another solution. I had to figure out first if the announcement applied to me, and if it did, how to rectify the situation. If I did nothing and it affected me, I risked having a broken page on my site and therefore a poor visitor experience. That's how compliance works. You have to spend time, money, and effort to stay compliant or there are consequences.

That same week, I also received a notification that there had been a security breach at a website that I frequent. My password was reset out of abundance of caution. I had to sign in, change my password, verify that nothing unusual happened with my account, and then change my passwords at other websites that used the same breached password. If I didn't do that, I risked being hacked.

The next week, I discovered that my Amazon affiliate links on YouTube were not compliant with the Amazon Associates terms of service in light of new Federal Trade Commission changes that had taken effect in the United States over the past year. I had to amend my affiliate disclosure on all videos on my channel. Fortunately, I found a tool that could do it in a few minutes, but it cost me $20.

Compliance won't sell books, but if you don't keep up with the industry, you will almost certainly *lose* book sales. It's perhaps more useful to think about compliance as a way to keep your money.

A big lesson for me this year was to allocate a budget for compliance, even if it's small. A *lot* of little compliance issues hit my inbox this year—more than usual. At one point in the second quarter, I was receiving compliance-related emails every week. I had to stop what I was doing to investigate and rectify the issues.

That is one of the downsides to being a long-term indie.

Sometimes it feels like I'm playing a tennis match with the world to keep my books for sale. Little things can force my books out of print or cut off my revenue streams if I'm not vigilant.

Let me give you another example of how not staying vigilant will cost you. I used a site called Kit to showcase the gear I use for my YouTube videos. It allows you to use Amazon Associates affiliate links. Kit was acquired by Patreon, but Patreon couldn't acquire the domain Kit.com, so then they sold it to Genius Link. It's a long story...

Instead, Genius Link had to change the domain name to Kit.co, which rendered all of the Kit.com links invalid.

I knew about the domain issue and I followed the instructions that Kit recommended to convert my links. However, I missed the news that Kit got acquired *again*, and the instructions changed, so my links didn't get converted. I didn't find out about this until a year later, when all of my links were beyond broken. I lost a lot of affiliate income, more than I care to share with you. (I should also mention that I didn't have my sales report tool when this happened, so I didn't even know that the revenue stream was choked off. I just thought people were buying less affiliate items...That's how compliance wounds you. Sometimes you don't know you have a problem until it's too late.)

Hopefully, you will learn from my experience that compliance is important.

Moving forward, I've decided to allocate a couple hundred dollars annually for compliance-related expenses. It might include buying tools, consulting with an attorney specifically for an industry legal issue, or the cost to pay a developer to fix something on my various websites. If I don't use the money, it's a win, but if I need it, I'll have allocated money for it.

YOUR BRAND IS EVERYTHING

In July 2020, the self-publishing community was rocked by a report that Mark Dawson *bought 400 copies of his book to secure a top 10 spot on the Sunday* Times *bestseller list.*

The first instinct of most in the community was to comment on the ethics of what Dawson did and to weigh in on whether they supported or decried his behavior.

I like Mark. It's undeniable that he's made our community a better place. I certainly have learned a few things from him. After reviewing the practices of bulk buying, I can understand *why* he thought what he did was okay. I still think it was wrong —not illegal, but borderline unethical. I think Mark misjudged the consequences and optics of his decision—but we all do that from time to time.

But when the story broke, I paid more attention to how the community responded. I noticed three things in particular.

First, cancel culture is a continued problem in our community. If anyone makes one false step, they get canceled. Gone are the days of forgiveness and grace.

Everyone makes mistakes. Everyone. Some mistakes are worse than others.

I've been around long enough to remember another author by the name of John Locke, a bestselling author who earned his success (in part) by *buying fake reviews and engaging in other unethical behavior*. Dawson is no John Locke. Not by a long shot.

I believe people can and do change if they are forgiven and provided a chance to prove they can do better. Not everyone improves, but *everyone* should be given the chance to do so. No exceptions.

We've lost our ability to forgive as a society, and that trend continues to be true in the indie community.

Whatever you believe about Dawson's actions, they don't warrant being canceled, but a lot of people have done that to him.

Second, Dawson's behavior forced a number of organizations, podcast hosts, and websites affiliated with him to take a stance on the matter. Their discomfort in commenting on the matter was palpable. Dawson's actions affected the entire community by virtue of his influence. And Dawson's influence cannot be understated—he had achieved bestseller status, a vibrant community around his marketing philosophies, a popular podcast, an amazingly successful course platform, and deep connections to the key players in the indie community.

This was not the case with John Locke—everyone lined up against him.

Third, Dawson's behavior after the event broke left questions about whether he made the situation worse. I'm not going to comment on this because, again, I don't think it's important for the sake of this book.

I learned three things from this event.

First, everyone makes mistakes. It's important to have a contingency plan for when *you* do. If you think you're immune to cancel culture, cancel culture will come for you one day.

Also, this is another reason not to participate in cancel culture. It's cancer, and karma's a bitch. I've been saying this for years, and I'll keep saying it. This story only proves my point.

Second, if you're an influencer or have any kind of platform, you need a contingency plan on what to do when *someone connected to you* makes an ethical misstep like this. The community will look to you for a stance, and for guidance. Your contingency plan needs to include a statement that clearly defines where you stand and denounces bad behavior, written in a professional and short manner. Your plan should also include how you will sever ties with the person or company if the situation warrants it. Not all situations do. Sometimes there's money at stake and you have to make tough choices. When these things happen, you have to do *something* because you'll lose credibility if you don't. The other person will drag your brand down with theirs.

Third, a public relations plan would have helped Mark considerably. A simple, honest apology with a promise to do better never goes out of style. A plan for how to communicate with his audience and online course communities would have also spared him some of the wrath the community unleashed on him.

In 2018, Chris Syme wrote an obscure little book called *Crisis Management for Authors*. It's a short book on how to navigate online crises and protect your reputation as an author.

I bought the book shortly after launch, mainly to support her for writing a book like this that so many people would ignore. She clearly had this book on her heart. At the time of this writing, the book has seven reviews and an Amazon sales rank of 750,000, which means it's not selling well.

Now, all of a sudden, it's the most relevant book any author can buy. It still probably won't become a bestseller, but if you have the ears to hear its message, you'll be better off than most.

What makes this situation so difficult is that Dawson is not a shady, spammy nonfiction author trying to make a dollar off the backs of innocent authors. He is a skilled fiction author, marketer, and businessperson. His courses taught a generation of authors how to make profitable Facebook ads. There are writers who owe their full-time living to Mark Dawson and the skills he taught them.

This is a gentle reminder that no matter who you are, your brand is everything. It takes years to build it, and seconds to destroy it.

Anyway, I have updated my contingency plan accordingly.

SAY YES EVEN WHEN IT HURTS

In the Technology section when discussing my personalized rules engine, I went on a tangent about saying yes to opportunities and following your gut.

To call this a learning about becoming a writer of the future is a stretch, but my programming adventures got me thinking about a few times in my life where the course of my entire life changed because I said yes to something that seemed innocent at the time but became very, very important.

My high school had a community service requirement in order to graduate. As a teenager, I would have rather played video games or read books, but my mom found me an opportunity to volunteer with the American Red Cross YouthCorps. I had a bunch of opportunities I could have pursued, but I chose the Red Cross because the work seemed more important.

I remember showing up to the Red Cross headquarters on a rainy afternoon after school. I had no idea what to expect. I ended up stuffing envelopes for an hour, but I got along with the volunteer director, so I enjoyed chatting with her every week. The next week, another group of teenagers attended, and we stuffed envelopes together. We became great friends, and I ended up bringing some more of my friends in band to volunteer every Friday. One of those people was a quirky guy I'd just met who played saxophone with me in band—on those Friday-afternoon drives, we bonded and became best friends. We wrote music together, and that was the beginning of my songwriting stint. We'd volunteer at Red Cross, eat dinner at the Outback Steakhouse, and then go to my grandmother's basement and write music until midnight.

I logged 365 hours of volunteer work with the Red Cross over four years. I volunteered there so much that I ran into the CEO numerous times in the cafeteria. We hit it off, and because I represented the youth groups so well and because I could talk business (at the ripe old age of seventeen!), he invited me to formally join the Board of Directors of my local American Red Cross. Yes, you read that correctly. At seventeen years old, I sat in board meetings with millionaires, and I had voting rights. I gained a lot of business acumen by sitting in those meetings and being a keen observer of human behavior. Honestly, I learned more from seeing the nervous heads of department get grilled by difficult questions than I did anything else. I learned how to ask difficult questions and get to the heart of issues quickly, mostly by mimicking other board members. I carried this skill with me as I grew older. Being able to sniff out issues and real problems despite tons of background noise is one of my key skills; it served me well in corporate America, in law school, and in my writing life.

Anyway, I've gone down a long tangent to show that sometimes decisions that seem inconsequential can make a big difference in your life.

In college, I majored in English and Spanish. When I graduated, I wanted to be a writer. I assumed that I would never use my Spanish degree. I loved speaking the language, and traveling abroad to Costa Rica, Nicaragua, and Panama was one of my college highlights, but I wasn't fluent, and I didn't see how I would ever achieve fluency.

My first job out of college was as a claims adjuster. It was my job to determine who was at fault for car accidents. It was a brutal and exhausting job. The first week of the job, the associate director came to my desk and asked me to join him in a conference room. I thought I was going to get fired. He had a copy of my resume, and said that he noticed I spoke Spanish. He was starting a bilingual claims unit and he couldn't find anyone who was qualified to do the job. He asked if I was interested, and told me he'd give me a seven percent pay differential if I said yes.

Keep in mind that I wasn't fluent in Spanish at this point. I spoke Spanish like Tarzan, and my skill level was laughable at best. But I said yes on the spot.

I barely spoke Spanish, but now I had to become *fluent* in it. The first six weeks were really, really hard. Customers couldn't understand me, and I couldn't understand them. I was speaking Spanish all day, so much that my English was starting to suffer. True story.

Around six months, something clicked. Suddenly, I understood everything, and customers understood me. I was switching between English and Spanish without thinking. Customers were calling my boss to tell him how much they appreciated me. One customer told me, "Señor, you speak some strange Spanish, but I understand you, and I appreciate you helping me and my family in our difficult time."

I did so well in that job that I was promoted quickly, into progressively better jobs that now give me the flexibility to write. Learning how to become fluent in Spanish is one of the reasons I am able to learn quickly, particularly programming languages—which leads me to the personalized rules engine and having to learn Python.

All because I said yes to an opportunity that seemed insurmountable at the time.

My writing life is filled with decisions that seemed unimportant at the time: starting a YouTube channel, writing a book that mixed my philosophies on writing with coping with being abandoned by my biological father, and randomly pitching a speech idea to a conference organizer that got me in front of a crowd of 1,000 people...with a pitch that I pulled out of the air.

Anyway, I'm not suggesting to say yes to everything. That's never a good idea. But sometimes big opportunities come disguised as trivial decisions. One of the reasons I've been so successful in life is because I've opened myself to opportunities and connections that didn't seem important or that suit my "agenda" at the time.

You never know where life will lead you.

A SWOT ANALYSIS OF THE INDIE AUTHOR PROFESSION

What does the writer of the future look like, and what challenges do they face?

A few things have been clear to me for a few years.

First, Amazon, while committed to its KDP program, is not committed to *innovating* the platform. As of July 2020, the KDP dashboard hasn't changed much since the program's inception aside from some cosmetic changes and a couple of feature updates. The upload process and the amount of relative data you have access to have not changed. The same is generally true with the other book retailers.

Second, it's difficult for entrepreneurs to create products for writers. Indie authors are price-sensitive, and rightfully so given the amount of money they have to invest into their books. If a product doesn't fall within the two "sweet spots" of writing and marketing, it will die in our community. Indies will not buy it because they are so focused on writing and selling books. There are rare exceptions, such as Book Funnel and Vellum, but authors only pay for those because formatting and book delivery are such a pain in the ass that they're willing to do something about it. There are other pains in the ass that they're willing to live with, however, such as calculating their book sales.

The lack of innovation and entrepreneurial investment in the indie space means that indie authors are going to be in a lot of trouble in a few years. Our progress as a community is dependent on the breadcrumbs retailers give us, and our financial prudence disincentivizes people from starting new products and services outside of the usual sweet spots for fear of losing money. This is why I believe that so many indies search elsewhere for solutions to the problems they have, such as the platforms of digital marketers and other entrepreneurs whose advice is not always a good fit for what we do.

Traditional publishers haven't gotten around to adopting emerging technology yet, but I'll bet good money that the coronavirus pandemic has them reevaluating their business model. If they haven't started looking into automation and artificial intelligence as a way to sell more books, they will. Before COVID-19, there was no incentive for them to change their business models. Now, they can't afford NOT to.

It will take years for traditional publishers to get the technology right, but it'll happen. And when it does, do you think indies will be able to compete with them by doing the same things they're doing today? The cutting edge scrappiness that we've had for the last decade will become irrelevant.

Combine that with new generations of more tech-savvy writers, new generations of writers from developing countries who to date have never had a voice but will through the power of AI translation, cultural preferences in emerging superpowers such as China that may place less emphasis on western books, and an ever-shifting sociopolitical landscape...and you have a recipe for mass indie author extinction. Our world of publishing is going to look very different in 2030 and 2035.

My fear is that as emerging technology becomes prominent, it will be inapplicable or unaffordable for indies, such as artificial intelligence. If we can't adopt emerging tech, we'll be left behind. We'll find ourselves in the exact same position that traditional publishers were a decade ago—decrying new technology and romanticizing the way we do business.

That's why I believe that we have to start finding ways to adopt emerging technology *ourselves*, *right now*, because no one else is going to do it for us. Writing books and marketing those books is important, but we have to be careful not to focus on those tasks so much that the rest of the world passes us by.

If you want to innovate your business, you'll have to fight to make it happen, and you'll be alone.

And yes, that might mean learning an entirely new skill, such as the basics of a programming language. Or hiring someone to do it for you.

Like I said, don't expect book retailers or entrepreneurs to do it for you. Any change we get will likely be incremental, and the tools we get may not be the tools we truly need.

If you refuse to adapt and innovate, you will be left behind.

I recognize that I may sound alarmist. I hope I'm wrong. But history and human nature are good teachers. All industries become stagnant at some point, usually because of bad choices, lack of foresight, and the inability to accept change. Today's innovators are tomorrow's resistors. If you need examples, look no further than the American car manufacturing industry, the retail industry (what's left of it), and the cell phone industry prior to the advent of the iPhone. And of course, traditional publishers—but you knew I was going to say that.

There may very well be two writers of the future—those who adopt the skills and tech needed to compete in a new marketplace, and those who have to fight to survive because they didn't see the warning signs. The latter group will always be behind the curve, unable to catch up.

I choose to be in the first group.

IDEAS YOU CAN STEAL

THE NEUROSCIENCE OF WRITING AND READING

The science of reading is fascinating. More fascinating is the science of writing!

What is it in our brains that compels us to pick up the pen or sit down at the keyboard? What happens to our brains when we write? What happens to readers' brains when they read?

I am sure that there are scientists whose life work is studying the science of reading and writing. What might we learn from their research?

It would be interesting if someone with a degree in neuroscience wrote a book about it. Lisa Cron wrote two great books on the topic, but there's so much more to be explored.

What about biohacking and writing? What kind of futures might be possible there?

Or the most cutting edge research around reading and writing, particularly with e-readers, smartphones, and tablets?

There's a lot in this arena that has yet to be explored.

AUTHOR SERVICING CO-OP

In the Marketing section, I talked about the difference between sales and servicing and how, long-term, you need a way to draw a clean line between sales and service in your writing business. For most successful writers, that means hiring an assistant.

However, most writers can't afford a virtual assistant. It's asinine to even suggest it.

What if a group of authors at a similar career level pooled their resources as a co-op into a single or set of virtual assistants who worked on all of their behalf?

The going rate for a competent virtual assistant these days is around $40/hour, minimum. The good assistants command more than that. For full-time work, that would cost around $1,600 per week, $6,400 per month, or $76,800 per year. Those numbers don't include benefits, of course, but this would be a freelancing relationship.

If ten authors formed a co-op, they could each pay $7,680 per year for access to a reader concierge service. That's around $160 per week or $640 per month. Is it expensive? Yes, but it's cheaper than $6,400 per month.

The authors would have to agree on what types of emails

the assistant would handle and which ones would be forwarded to the respective author. I could see a service like this being very good at answering questions like:

- "What's the best series to start with?"
- "Is this book in paperback, or at Kobo, or at my local bookstore?"
- "Do you have a Patreon page?"
- "Would you like to be on my podcast?"

You know, the common questions. Authors could also ask for dedicated help with a book launch, or for basic proofreading or website maintenance.

The co-op could be a white label service; each author would set up a dedicated email for the assistant and have their contact form routed to them. The assistant would work through the writers' inbox several times a day, answering the questions they can and deferring to the authors for any they can't. From the readers' perspective, it would look like the author has a full-time assistant. The assistant would have to have impeccable customer service skills, of course, and go above and beyond for the reader.

The author could log in to the assistant's email address at any time to see the emails that have been handled.

Honestly, this could be an author services company that, as it gains more authors, hires more assistants and offers access to a service that was previously inaccessible to most authors.

There are virtual assistant "companies" on the market, but they cater to a generic audience. I've used them in the past, and the big challenge is training them to understand how an author business works. The value in a service like this is that it would be specifically for writers.

YOUR SELF-PUBLISHING ATTORNEY

Years ago, I secured a trademark for one of my series. I could have hired a local law firm to research the mark and file the applications, but instead, I hired an attorney over the Internet who specialized in trademarks. More specifically, trademarks were the *only* thing he did.

What made him more unique was that he charged flat fees for every service needed. I knew exactly what I was getting for run-of-the-mill trademark work. While I don't necessarily believe he was cheaper than the traditional alternative, it sure felt like it. I also appreciated his transparency. His business is booming, and he's an expert in trademark law.

Why don't we have more attorneys in the publishing space that do this? I can only count the number of attorneys I know who assist self-published writers on one hand, and all of them charge hourly.

It would be interesting if there was an attorney or law firm that provided flat fee services to authors.

They'd charge X amount to send a cease and desist letter for copyright infringement, X for publishing contract reviews based on how many pages are in the contract, and X for wills and X per hour to answer legal questions. They'd help you with copyright permission questions.

The more successful you become, the more legal questions you have, especially around taxes and running a business. Having been to law school, my experience is that local law firms that don't specialize in authors are generally bad fits for these types of questions. For example, my family law attorney screwed me something awful with how we structured my estate because they didn't understand writing businesses and copyright. It was an expensive mistake to fix.

Since authors are cost-conscious, the prospect of calling a lawyer and hoping you can afford their fees usually puts most authors off. It would be far better to charge flat rates and publish those on a website.

A service like this could bring in a steady stream of customers and likely be a pretty good way to make a living.

YOUR SELF-PUBLISHING ACCOUNTANT

If a flat-fee attorney for self-publishers is a good idea, then so is an accountant!

Fortunately, accountants are more plentiful. Many offer flat fees, and there are many who specialize in digital entrepreneurs. I don't know of any who specialize in self-published writers, though. That doesn't mean they don't exist.

If someone wanted to jump into this space, here's the can't-fail blueprint for success: write *the* definitive book on taxes and bookkeeping for self-published writers. Expand your audience to creatives if that makes sense. Start a YouTube channel with a weekly tax tip in 5-10 minutes or less. Promote the hell out of yourself—it wouldn't be hard because you would be the only one...

Next, publish your fees on your site and drive traffic through Google AdSense, Facebook, and YouTube, and double your ad spend leading up to tax time. Market to authors but let people know you specialize in self-publishing. Get yourself on all the major podcasts and YouTube channels. Partner with Your Self-Publishing Attorney to offer special consulting packages. Then, wait for the leads to come in.

The hard part about finding an accountant in publishing is making sure you select someone who has experience with authors who have many streams of income. Just because someone is a certified accountant doesn't mean they know how to handle *your* taxes.

When I first started publishing, I used an accountant friend. My first year of publishing was simple. Then, every year, I called her with more difficult questions.

"Hey, I got twenty 1099s this year."

"Hey, I'm hiring a video editor. What do I need to do?"

"Hey, I just accepted a part-time job from a company based in London. Am I good?"

"Hey, I may sign a film deal this year. How would I potentially handle a large payment?"

"Hey, I'd like to form a trust. Oh, and I'd also like to incorporate my business. How do I protect my assets?"

She gave up on me because my operations were so different from her typical clients, which were local brick and mortar businesses whose tax complexity was much simpler.

That's why, just as it's a good idea to hire a book cover designer and editor who have experience in your genre, it's also a good idea to hire an accountant who understands the writing profession.

TRACK YOUR BOOK WRITING TIME

I gave a podcast interview where the interviewer asked me how I stopped outlining.

I described how, with my book *Android Paradox*, I timed how long it took me to do everything: outlining, rough draft, subsequent drafts, revising, formatting, and working with my editor and cover designer. I knew how long it took me to create the novel down to the minute.

I took the data and put it into a chart. Outlining took me the most time by far. I asked why. It was due to the research.

Then I asked how outlining affected my draft.

I realized that my finished novel deviated from the outline a lot. In fact, near the end, I broke away from my outline entirely.

Then I asked the breakthrough question: if I was spending all this time outlining only to ignore it, why was I outlining?

I made a commitment to reduce the amount of time I spent outlining with my next novel. Eventually, I stopped doing it.

As I told that story on the podcast, I reconnected with my earlier self, where I was just trying to figure everything out. In retrospect, that one little experiment that I did on a whim for curiosity's sake—timing my novel—resulted in one of the biggest successes in learning how to be prolific.

I didn't abandon outlining until I was ready.

I often ask writers to figure out where their time is going. Most people *think* they know, but they actually don't.

So that's my idea: time yourself as you write your next book and see what you learn.

VISUALIZE YOUR TOOLBOX

What's in your writer toolbox?

Aside from our computers, most of the tools we use in our business are virtual.

I believe that learning how to command your toolbox is important. I've collected a lot of tools over the years, and I'm good at knowing when a certain tool is appropriate for a task. I'm always asking, "What tools do I already have that can help me execute what I'm trying to accomplish?"

For fun, I created a mind map that laid out all the tools I currently use in my business. Maybe this will be helpful for me in the future, but if anything, it was a helpful refresher to understand what I have in my box so I can be intentional about using the right tool at the right time.

There's nothing worse than executing something like a marketing campaign and realizing that you had a tool that could have helped you do it better. For example, last year, I sent out advanced review copies for one of my books. It was a pain to follow up and chase reviews. I forgot that Book Funnel had a feature called "Certified Mail" that handles all the administration for you. You enter the email addresses of your reviewers, a welcome message, a follow-up reminder, and a final reminder when the book is live. Book Funnel's system handles the rest. I used the feature with the book launch for *150 Self-Publishing Questions Answered*, and it made everything much smoother.

To convey the concept of visualizing your toolbox, I used a tool called Mindomo to create a mind map that visualized my tools. You can view it at *www.authorlevelup.com/writertoolbox*.

KNOWLEDGE TRANSFER PLATFORM

Indie authors have careers because they turn their imagination into income.

Ideas equal income. So does knowledge.

There are so many people out there that have knowledge but don't do anything with it beyond their own personal gain. For example, if you're a nuclear scientist, you're unlikely to talk about nuclear science outside of your own circles; otherwise, you'll bore people.

But there is a writer out there that needs to know about nuclear science. In fact, maybe their book revolves around it, and they need to learn about nuanced details that they can't find on the Internet.

What if there was a platform that connected interested people like writers with people who have subject matter expertise?

Need an astrophysicist to review your space opera to check for implausible science? Need a police officer to verify if the police procedure you wrote is accurate? Need a carpenter to verify that your general contractor character is using the right terminology when they're building a house?

This platform would put you in contact with people who have the expertise you need.

Imagine posting a job that explains what you need, and then experts bidding to win the work. You can review their profiles to see which person would be the best fit. You send them what you need, pay their fee, maybe jump on a quick conference call. You walk away with a book that is 100% more realistic and the expert gets paid for it.

There would be experts for everything from nuclear science to sewing, and the people wouldn't necessarily be world-renowned. It might be a mom who sews on weekends but is really passionate about it because her grandmother taught her how to do it. She might be your greatest asset in writing your cozy mystery novel about a heroine who likes to sew.

One of the hardest parts about writing is writing what you don't know. There's only so much you can research before you need help. It's not exactly easy to ask random people a bunch of questions. Personally, I always feel self-conscious about this. It would be much easier if there was a platform that facilitated it.

THE INDIE AUTHOR APPRENTICE

I received an email from one of my YouTube subscribers; he was in high school and decided he wanted to be a writer. He was going to college in the fall and wanted to know what he could do every day to accomplish his dream. Not only did the email make me feel old, it got me thinking about the next generation of self-published writers and how they will establish their careers.

It's 2020 as I write this chapter. The next generation of self-published writers are probably in elementary and middle school right now, so when they come of age in 2030, they're going to be completely different than us.

For starters, they'll be more tech and data savvy. The tools and processes we use today may seem barbaric to them, but they'll have a strong desire to know what they don't know. They'll have the power of optimism, but we'll have the power of wisdom and experience (in ten years, I'll be 43...not sure I'll have much wisdom, but I'll certainly have experience).

How do we foster and support the next generation?

I believe the age-old apprentice system could be helpful. In that system, a "master" takes on an "apprentice," and the apprentice does much of the work under the master's supervi-

sion. After a few years, the apprentice knows enough to establish their own trade.

What would a master-apprentice setup look like in a digital
world?

In ten to twenty years, self-publishing will be more viable
and mainstream than it is today—with more people jumping
into the industry, it's only a matter of time before more self-
published authors become successful, igniting more awareness
of it. I also think that college and MFA programs will continue
to embrace self-publishing as a viable option, which means that
future generations of young people will be exposed to it.

Imagine if a successful author who is making a living from
their writing hires an apprentice. The apprentice is a fledgling
but driven writer who wants to write books for a living. The
apprenticeship would be a part-time job (unless the writer can
afford to pay a full-time salary).

The apprentice serves the master author in every area of the
business. They watch as the master brainstorms and plans a
new book, they see the rough manuscript that the master
produces, help with edits, coordinate formatting and cover
design, assist the master with marketing, answer customer
service emails, maintain the master's website, moderate the
master's communities on places like Facebook, and other odd
jobs that come up in the life of an indie author. Their role
would serve the function of a general virtual assistant, and it
would give them exposure to all areas of running an author
business.

In exchange for the apprentice's time and effort, the master
would also build in time for the apprentice to work on their own
books, and the master would review and offer feedback. The
master would also meet with the apprentice regularly for
mentorship conversations.

The master would also grant the apprentice free use of

his/her tools as well any other members on the master's team, such as other virtual assistants. The master would show the apprentice the secret tools of the trade, such as the nuts and bolts on how to write spellbinding fiction, tax tips, and other items that the apprentice would never find elsewhere.

The master would use their status, privilege, and influence to help the apprentice begin their career on solid footing. The master might even allow the apprentice to publish books under the master's publishing company for a short period of time, with copyrights reverting back to the apprentice upon completion of the program.

The master would let his or her community know that they have an apprentice and make the apprentice highly visible in everything the master did. This way, the community would rally around the apprentice and support them when it's time for them to leave.

This method would give the apprentice a fast, paid exposure to every facet of the publishing business from someone they can trust. They would get hands-on experience from an author who's much further down the road, possibly the furthest down the road you can be. Imagine how much you would learn from Stephen King if he did a program like this, for example. Being able to pick his brain and sit with him behind closed doors would be immensely valuable for a hungry, ambitious writer.

The master would get part-time help at a cheaper rate and know that they're giving back to the community. Of course, the master would have to ensure that they pick the *right* apprentice, preferably an author in the genre they write, and someone who will follow through and get the most out of the relationship. Someone looking for a lazy way to start a career would not be a good fit for the program, and the master would have to be extremely selective and rigorous in searching for the right person.

If I am ever in a position to do it, this is precisely how I would mentor someone from the next generation. It would be better than a college education by far. If I become a bestselling author with a multi six or seven-figure income someday, give me one to two years with an apprentice, and I would love to see what we could do.

WRITE ABOUT YOUR CAREER EXPERIENCE

I believe that everyone has a writer's guide in them.

Writers always find themselves in situations where they need subject matter expertise. Maybe they need to put a firefighter on the page, but they don't know any firefighters.

What's the first thing a normal person would do if they wanted to learn about firefighting? They'd talk to a firefighter, of course. Or they'd do an Internet search and hope for the best.

But we writers are introverts. We'd much rather find a book about firefighting, preferably for authors by an author. A book titled *Into the Fire: The Writer's Guide to Getting Fire and Fire-fighters Right* would be the perfect book for them.

Is there a mass market potential? God no, but you could probably recoup your editing and cover costs, especially if you hire a cheap cover designer.

A book like this would be a lot easier to write than a novel, so you could write it quickly because you already know what needs to be written. A short 20,000- to 30,000-word book on the topic that teaches writers everything they need to know to write the subject matter realistically is underrated in my opinion.

A few years ago, I bought a writer's guide to the United States armed forces. It was very helpful as I wrote my space opera series *Galaxy Mavericks*.

I argue that there aren't enough subject matter books for writers on the market.

Even if you think your career so far is trivial, what's obvious to you is not obvious to a writer who wants to make their book better.

For example, one day, I plan to write a book on the insurance industry for writers. It's the least sexy book I can think of, but a writer somewhere, sometime is going to need to know how insurance companies operate and what the life of a claims adjuster or an insurance executive might look like. They'll need to get the details right. My book will be there for them.

Anyway, I'm not promising gold. I'm merely suggesting that you can cash in on your work experience, even if you hate your job. It'll do someone a lot of good.

LET'S HIRE A FUTURIST

I've been reading books by quantitative futurists this quarter. I'm interested in knowing how they think.

Did you know that companies hire futurists to help them project the future? For example, Royal Dutch Shell did this and incorporated futurism into its way of thinking. It helped them make record profit and avoid pitfalls that ensnared its competitors.

Wouldn't it be interesting if self-publishers as a community banded together and hired a futurist to review the publishing industry and trends outside the industry? The futurist could provide a report with scenarios of what the future of the self-published author would look like, with recommendations of what we need to start preparing for now.

Futurists have such a unique take on the world. They're not always right, but when they are, it's fascinating.

There are so many trends in the world right now that it's hard to know how they will converge and affect us. A futurist studies trends every day. They're more comfortable looking at them. Therefore, hiring one could be fruitful and productive for the industry.

Of course, this would probably be very expensive, but maybe someone could do a Kickstarter. Maybe it wouldn't be that hard for a futurist since we're such a small segment of the industry.

But in any case, tapping in to the mind of someone who has a good grip on the future could be very advantageous for self-published writers and help us stay nimble.

AUTHOR EFFICIENCY COACH

I don't hold myself out as a coach or a guru. I despise both of those words. Coaches and gurus think they have all the answers.

I don't. I'm still learning on my journey.

I've always rejected the idea of providing coaching services. It's lucrative, but I'm not the coaching type. I've taken on a handful of clients in the past couple years, but they approached me, and I only took on clients who were extremely driven. I don't offer my services to the public.

An idea I had, though, was coaching in an area that I'm good at—efficiency.

Michael La Ronn, Author Efficiency Coach? Doesn't have a good ring. But it's interesting. Call me up and let's talk about how efficient you are in your writing business—what tools do you use, what are your processes, and so on. It's an area that I'm uniquely qualified to coach.

But still, it doesn't get me excited. Someone else can steal it.

AUTHOR INSPIRATION, THE ALBUM?

I was reading an article about vinyl and how its comeback surprised everyone. Fifteen years ago, people couldn't give their records away fast enough. I used to go to record stores and I'd buy old vinyls for pennies on the dollar. Usually, the vinyl section would be in some dusty old room in the back that no one dared to explore.

Today, artists are releasing their albums in vinyl, and the vinyls are more expensive than CDs! The same albums I bought in the back room of a record store are worth quadruple what I paid for them fifteen years ago.

In a parenthetical aside in the article, the author asked an ill-informed question about why audiobooks aren't available in vinyl format.

Seriously?

Unless you want to buy a set of twenty vinyls, and you want to listen to audiobooks on a turntable, it's a bad idea.

That got me thinking what people *would* listen to on vinyl in the writing space. I remember listening to old comedy albums my dad and uncle used to collect. Richard Pryor, Bill Cosby, Pigmeat Markham...really good stuff, and perfect for listening in the background while you're making dinner, fixing up things around the house, etc. My great-grandfather used to play vinyls as background noise while he did projects around the house.

Anyway. Wouldn't it be cool if there was an album that consisted of successful writers giving their best writing advice in 5-7 minute-long tracks? Each author would tell their story in a personal way, like a storyteller at a festival. Each track would be like a piece of art, with a storyline, music, and maybe even sound effects—kind of like the first few episodes of my podcast, *The Writer's Journey*. The tone would be relaxed, slightly comical, and fun. That's the kind of content that would be perfect for a vinyl album. Almost like an audio documentary.

Actually, it would be perfect as an audiobook too.

CONTENT CREATED WHILE WRITING THIS BOOK

150 Self-Publishing Questions Answered (Book)

This book was written in a partnership between Michael and The Alliance of Independent Authors (ALLi, a nonprofit organization for self-published writers), and it answers the most common self-publishing questions in a conversational question and answer format. The audiobook is narrated by Michael!

Buy your copy at www.authorlevelup.com/150

Author Level Up YouTube Channel - Highlights

Watch at youtube.com/authorlevelup.

The Ultimate Guide to Self-Publishing vs. Traditional Publishing - 2020

. . .

Copyright for Authors (playlist)

Interviews & Appearances

Draft2Digital Live with Michael La Ronn: Michael sits down with D2D's director of marketing Kevin Tumlinson to talk about writing, life and productivity.

Remaining Relevant with Michael La Ronn (The Fearless Storyteller Podcast): With host Ethan Freckleton, Michael talks writing fiction, writer's block, and beating self-doubt so you can develop staying power with your author career.

Mental Models for Writers with Michael La Ronn (Twitter Chat): In this Twitter chat for the Alliance of Independent Authors, Michael talks about the power of mental models and how you can utilize them to advance your writing career.

VOLUME THREE

INDIE AUTHOR CONFIDENTIAL

Secrets No One Will Tell You About Being a Writer

VOL. 3

M.L. RONN

INTRODUCTION

This volume covers the fourth quarter of 2020—the year to end all years.

I don't know about you, but I'll be glad to see the end of this year. It was my best year ever for sales, but it was emotionally difficult. I'm looking forward to seeing what 2021 brings.

Volume 2 of this series covered my efforts to improve my author infrastructure so that I could have a more stable business heading into 2021, as well as the start of my "Beast Mode" challenge, where my goal was to write as many books as humanly possible.

This volume is decidedly more marketing focused. I harvested a lot of opportunities that I planted for myself in Volumes 1 and 2. I wanted to finish 2020 strong.

In fact, my "challenge" for the fourth quarter was "Amnesia Mode." What if I woke up one morning, knew nothing about marketing, and had to learn it all over again? I tried to challenge the marketing knowledge I already knew to see if I could push myself to another level.

. . .

My Core Strategic Priorities

As a refresher, my mission is to create content that entertains and/or educates my audience, preferably both, while staying nimble.

I do this by focusing on five strategic priorities:

1. Become a world-class content creator
2. Become a world-class marketer
3. Become a technology-driven writer
4. Become a data-driven writer
5. Become the writer of the future

I believe these five priorities are the most important for me to have a long-term sustainable career.

What's in This Volume

In the previous volume, I discussed my "Beast Mode" Challenge. In this volume, I'll share what worked, and a very real and unfortunate price I paid for writing so many books in a short amount of time.

I share my journeys into "Amnesia Mode" and some important marketing actions that helped me make a lot more money this quarter.

I also stumbled upon the rare opportunity to give a TED Talk, and I had to prepare a pitch. To use the cliché, I pitched like my life depended on it. I'll find out the results by the time I publish the next volume.

Last time, I described natural language processing and how

I believe I can use it to create a tool to help me catch errors that my editor has made in the past BEFORE I send them to her. I made some more progress in that area.

I also took a new job in the corporate world, one that forces me to use Microsoft Excel at a master level every day. That has done wonders for my data analysis adventures.

I also detail my 2021 strategy and how I plan to start the year strong. I share all of my tactics in nitty-gritty detail. Hopefully, you'll find something useful in it.

And, as always, I came up with some pretty unique and interesting ideas for you to steal too.

There's plenty to explore, and hopefully, this book will inspire you to think differently about your writing business.

Thanks for reading this very experimental series. My sincerest hope is that it helps you in some way.

M.L. Ronn
Des Moines, Iowa
December 5, 2020

BECOME A WORLD-CLASS
CONTENT CREATOR

SETTING AS AN ECOSYSTEM

I'll start off this volume with a craft lesson.

I am a big fan of British-Canadian thriller author Arthur Hailey. Hailey is lesser known today, but he was a household name in the 60s and 70s, with one of his books, *Airport,* made into a 1970 major motion picture with Burt Lancaster and Dean Martin, among other stars.

Hailey's books focus on events taking place in a single location. *Airport* takes place in an airport, featuring employees of the airline industry. *Hotel* is a thriller with events taking place almost entirely inside a historic hotel in New Orleans, Louisiana, with the hotel's assistant manager as the hero. *The Moneychangers* takes place in a bank, with bank employees as the heroes. I love the branding and consistency. Hailey is an amazing storyteller too, using the five senses and other mega bestseller techniques to keep you hooked. To this day, I'm amazed at how an author could make *airports* interesting!

Something I learned from Hailey is the concept of setting as an ecosystem. He is masterful at switching between POVs of various workers in the setting. *Hotel,* for example, follows the assistant manager, the bellhop manager, several guests in the hotel, and other employees who work behind the scenes in the hotel. You really get a sense of the place, and that all of the characters are playing their part in the ecosystem.

Most settings are not this prominent, but it would be a fun opportunity to write a story similar to Hailey's where the setting is so front and center. This could especially be fun in a science fiction and fantasy setting.

BOOKS AS PRESENTATIONS OR COURSES

I released eight nonfiction books this year.

I did a talk around my book *Mental Models for Writers*, and it went well and led to decent book sales afterward.

I also did another talk around my book *Be a Writing Machine*, where I took the main ideas from the book and turned them into a talk.

Then I had the idea to structure my future talks around my books. I can easily turn most of my writing books into a talk if I wanted to.

I may start declining speech requests unless I can tie it to a book for a couple of reasons:

- It's easier for me to prepare the talk because I already know the material.
- The talk is better received.
- I have a clear call to action at the end, which is to buy one of my books, which attendees usually do.

It's just an idea at this point, but the more I think about it, the more I like it. It could mean fewer speaking engagements, though.

VIRTUAL EVENTS

I don't often receive speaking invitations, but because of the pandemic, I received more speaking invitations than ever.

I suppose it's because I don't have much of an international reputation yet, so I'm easier to book. I couldn't do many in-person events because of my full-time job anyway.

But I did three speaking events this year. I enjoyed them. Two of them asked me to submit a pre-recorded presentation, which I collaborated on with my video editor. One was a live talk.

I love public speaking, mostly because I enjoy hearing from people and listening to their questions. I always come away with more from Q&A than the talk itself.

I do wonder if virtual events are here to stay. It's hard to imagine many venues going back to big in-person events—not the way they used to. The speaking industry has changed irrevocably as a result of COVID-19. I believe in-person conferences will be smaller, *and* online. I also believe that in-person events won't have the same intimacy and closeness that they used to. There will be a day when people look back on speakers speaking to arenas of thousands of people and remark how those were the good old days.

Anyway, I spent a lot of time preparing for the talks I did this year, and I welcomed the opportunity.

Dedicating a video editor to the talks was above and beyond, and a little unusual—most speakers would never do something like this. They'd just turn on their webcams and speak. Quite frankly, my videos probably stuck out in an odd way compared to other speakers at the virtual venues. But I see this as a resume builder, so if I do a good job with my virtual talks, I can send 10-minute segments to potential venues in the future and give them a *really good* representation of what I would be like in-person. I can also build a "portfolio" of talks. Hell, I could even record generic talks and *license* them to virtual events, and then create bonuses specifically tailored for the venue's audience...wow, I better stop before I give too many secrets away...

That's the way I believe things are going. I could have one pricing structure for venues that want to book me for prerecorded virtual events, another structure for talks that require me to present live, and another for in-person events. Each requires a certain amount of time, money, and resources.

BEAST MODE LESSONS

In Volume 2 of this series, I discussed my Beast Mode Challenge and I promised to share how it went.

On August 1st, 2020, I set a goal to write as many books as humanly possible until October 31, 2020. The main reason was because I hadn't published much during the early days of the pandemic, and because my sales had increased, I wanted to sustain the increase.

I wrote seven books:

- Indie Author Confidential, Volumes 1-2: Secrets No One Tells You About Being a Writer
- 250+ Writing Tips, Vol. 1: A Comprehensive Guide to Writing, Publishing, and Marketing Your Book
- The Reader's Bill of Rights: A Manifesto on How to Treat Readers Right
- The Indie Author Atlas: Your Guide to the Five Continents of the Writing World
- The Indie Author Bestiary: An Epic Guide to Slaying the Beasts of the Writing World

- The Author Income Problem: Track Your Sales Without Pulling Your Hair Out

You can find all of the books at www.authorlevelup.com/ books

More results:

- I wrote around 220,000 words.
- I blogged my daily word counts, and my audience loved it so much that I continued blogging after the challenge.
- I did a livestream "writing sprint" on YouTube that was so successful, I continued doing it on a monthly basis.
- In August, I managed to keep writing, even when a powerful derecho storm knocked out power to the entire state of Iowa for a week. In fact, I wrote over 100,000 words in August *alone*.
- I kept momentum on a family trip to my hometown that lasted three days, writing while on the road.
- I had to prepare for and teach four insurance classes during Beast Mode, which takes an extraordinary amount of time and effort.
- My back went out at one point, laying me up for about a week...but not my word count.
- I compiled the finished books into an omnibus called the *Beast Mode Collection* that I offered as a limited edition directly on my website.

I don't share my results to brag, but to show you what is possible when you pour your entire soul into a challenge. I would have never achieved these results in 2014 when I started publishing. But I've come far enough that I have a handle on craft, productivity, time management, and the emotional aspect of being a writer. Many writers would get trapped in their own heads during a challenge like this, especially if they did it in public. They'd be too worried about failing publicly. Me? I don't care. I win whether I lose or fail, and that mindset is one of my hidden secrets to success.

For me, a challenge is just a game. It exists for me to test my limits and break past barriers I wasn't aware were there. It's fun entertainment for me, fun entertainment for my audience, and I share transparently whether I win or lose. Then I take the lessons I learn, roll them into my next project, and keep leveling up.

The funny part? There's always someone better than you. Sure, I wrote seven books in three months, which is more than some authors write in several *years*...but right after I finished the challenge, long-time prolific author Dean Wesley Smith announced that he was going to "write his age"—publish 70 books in an entire year. Yes, you read that correctly. I have a sneaking suspicion that Dean will make my Beast Mode look like the amateur hour at a comedy club. That's master craftsmanship at a completely different level, especially because he's doing it with novels.

No matter how hard you push yourself, there are always new levels of learning.

THE PRICE OF BEAST MODE

I paid a hidden price for my Beast Mode challenge: focusing only on writing for 90 days meant that I neglected marketing and other areas of my business.

I knew this would happen, but I underestimated the extent to which it would hurt.

After all, I'm a part-time writer. I have to spend my time deliberately. Most days, I have to decide between writing and marketing. I can survive a week without marketing, but three months is problematic.

Some of my Amazon Ads switched off without me realizing it for a few days, resulting in lost income. My email inbox grew out of control and emails went unanswered. I missed sales opportunities, and at least one direct sales order of about $100 because the lead went cold.

I'm not complaining. I put myself in this situation. But when I think about other authors who do the same thing for months if not years, it could be a major reason why people don't sell more books.

For most of us, writing is safe. It's comfortable. Marketing is hard. When we do less of it, we make less money.

I do very little marketing in my business, and that's by design. I've managed to do pretty well for myself by focusing on organic growth and portfolio volume. It's not a strategy for the faint of heart. But when I stopped doing the little marketing I usually do, it hurt for a while.

The good news is that the seven books I wrote during Beast Mode started generating income immediately, so in a way, the sacrifice was worth it because I more than doubled the size of my nonfiction portfolio. But this chapter is a reminder that we pay a price for every decision we make in the writing life. Not all decisions have such happy consequences.

FICTIONALIZING THE REAL WORLD

I like to take chances when I write. For most of my books, I begin with an idea that can roughly be described as "this will either be awesome or it will end in flames." That's the only qualification for every book I've ever written. The result is that I have some books that don't "hit," but the ones that do usually do pretty well.

In the early days of my YouTube channel, I offered a lead magnet for my email newsletter called "The Indie Author Roadmap." I outlined the different things that an author needs to learn to start their writing business. It had a decent conversion rate, driving around 100 signups one year, maybe more. That's a low number by most marketing standards, but pretty good if you consider that I did almost nothing to promote it.

Over time, the lead magnet became outdated, so I retired it.

This year, I mentioned it in a video and people in my audience said they wanted to see me bring it back. There's no shortage of things to learn, and the landscape has changed a lot since 2015.

I played around with the idea of updating the PDF and making it available to people for free, but as I combed through it,

I realized that a PDF full of bullet points was...boring. It worked in 2015, but I owed a better product to my audience in 2020.

One day, I had a weird idea: what if I took all of the things that a writer needs to learn to be successful and turned them into fictional vacation destinations? What would the locales be like? What if I could reimagine the writing world as a fictional world?

The result was The Indie Author Atlas: Your Guide to the Five Continents of the Writing World. It's written in the style of a *Lonely Planet* travel guide with an imaginative and humorous tone.

Since the writing life can overwhelm you with all the things you have to learn, I tried to make the act of learning fun.

Each continent represents an area of the writing life: The Commonwealth of Craft, Marketstan, the twin utopias of Technology and Data, the Sacred Lands of Distribution, and the Kingdom of Business. Each continent has many cities and tourist attractions within, each with their own chapter that suggests what you need to learn without beating you over the head about it. I used a fictional narrative to frame concepts in ways that you might not think about.

For example, the first place in the Commonwealth of Craft you visit is the Dreadwood Nature Preserve, a shadowy woodscape where your psychological shadow tries to ruin your vacation. It's hardly a vacation destination, but I can't think of a better way to illustrate how fear and self-doubt ruin our travels in this beautiful writing world.

Once you escape from Dreadwood, you arrive at the Learning Lodge, a western-style lodge just outside the dangerous woods built by an elderly couple who want to help writers learn. The lodge is a place of refuge and rest, and while there, you learn "what you need to learn."

With the book, I also had the idea to commission custom

illustrated maps of each of the continents. I hired a designer whose style I loved, and she helped me take the atlas to the next level. This was a gigantic financial risk, but I believed it was worth it to realize my vision.

It's too soon to report on sales, so we'll see how the book does. But regardless of the result, I created a piece of art that I am proud of.

TRANSFORMING THE EMOTIONAL PROBLEMS OF THE WRITING WORLD INTO MONSTERS

I had another idea for a writing book that fell into the "this will either be awesome or will end in flames" territory.

I talk frequently about fear, self-doubt, and other emotional challenges in the writing life. Sometimes battling them is like battling a monster that shows up unexpectedly during a writing session.

This was right around the time I was writing *The Indie Author Atlas*, and I thought, "What if I took the emotional problems of the writing world, turned them into mythical beasts, and taught writers how to slay them?"

The result was The Indie Author Bestiary: An Epic Quest Against the Beasts of the Writing World. It is inspired by medieval bestiaries and *Shadow of the Colossus* (a classic PlayStation game).

I studied medieval bestiaries for structure and I drew from Middle Age lore. The book features 21 beasts, which symbolizes perfection and maturity in Christianity.

But unlike a typical bestiary, which explains the existence of the beast through a folk tale, I made this one a narrative told through the second person, but with a twist...

You are a knight wandering in the dangerous writing world. In the first chapter, you encounter Michael La Ronn, who is also an elder, more experienced knight. Michael takes you in and trains you how to fight. Then something dastardly happens, and you and Michael ride off to do battle with the 21 beasts who have gathered at a sinister tower. A beast resides on each story of the tower, and you and Michael climb and fight your way to the top.

You do battle with fear, self-doubt, the inferiority complex, and more—all envisioned as nightmarish, cunning monsters whose only purpose is to destroy you. The battles are equally physical and psychological.

Technically, Michael narrates the story, speaking to you, the hero. So when Michael is around, he handles the narrative. But at times, he exits the stage, and the narrative shifts to pure second person POV.

The book was the most technically complicated nonfiction I've ever written. I followed my subconscious, even though it was not easy. How do you handle things like the five senses when another character is telling the story, but the viewpoint is through the second person POV? How do you handle narrative shifts? How do you handle descriptions of things?

The book was great fun. Not only was it entertaining to write myself into a book for a change, it was challenging to push the boundaries of my storytelling ability. I hope others find the book entertaining and instructive.

I even commissioned a medieval self-portrait of myself as a knight with a dragon companion. I had way too much fun producing this book.

TURNING A PODCAST INTO A BOOK

Since July 2019, I have hosted a podcast called "Writing Tip of the Day." Every Monday through Friday, I share a writing tip in five minutes or less.

I started the show primarily as an Amazon Alexa Flash Briefing because I wanted to be an early mover in the smart speaker market. The show receives a modest amount of downloads every day, though not anything spectacular by any means. But the listeners who love it *really* love it because it's no-frills, no bullshit, and you can binge it. A lot of people start their workday with it.

I also syndicate the show to podcast networks such as Apple, Stitcher, and Spotify.

I had an idea to take the first year of the show and repurpose it into a book to bring in more listeners to the show. I called it the 250+ Writing Tips series.

I took the tips and reimagined them onto the written page. It would have been easy to use audio transcripts of the show, but that's the cheap and lazy way to do it. I wrote every chapter myself, often expanding on the original tip and adding even more value.

The book consists of short chapters organized by different areas of the writing life. The series hook is that it's the most comprehensive writing omnibus on the market.

When I'm done with the second year of Writing Tip of the Day, I will spin those tips in Volume 2, and so on.

Imagine an omnibus called 1000+ *Writing Tips*, full of unique and interesting tips you won't find anywhere else. I engineered the series to have "one-click" potential—if someone likes the first book, they'll buy the whole series in one click.

So far, Volume 1 is available, but I believe the series has immense long-term potential. It'll take at least two or three years for me to see the return on the investment, but when I do, it will have been worth it.

Also, I probably won't continue "Writing Tip of the Day" forever. When I pull the podcast down in the future, it will be nice to have memorialized the content in book form.

THE AUDIOBOOK PRODUCTION PROBLEM

Earlier in the year, I recorded my first audiobook. It was a fantastic experience.

However, I am now suffering from the consequences of recording your own audiobook: it's extraordinarily time-consuming. Even with shortcuts.

I'm not complaining, though. Just explaining why.

Let's say that I have a four-hour audiobook.

I have to record the book, which takes around five to six hours since I make mistakes.

Then I have to edit the audio I recorded, which takes another five to six hours. This includes re-recording sentences here and there.

That's twelve hours to record a four-hour audiobook. And honestly, it takes more time than that when you factor in exporting the audio, uploading it, and dealing with QA issues.

To give you some context, it takes me approximately forty hours to write a novel. Therefore, an audiobook takes approximately a third of the time it would take me to write a novel. Consider that I can write around five to seven writing books per year and you can see the problem: I can't record audiobooks fast enough.

I've experimented with unusual ideas to solve this problem. The first is developing a "magic number" for length. If an audiobook is under the magic number, then I do everything myself. If it's above that number, I hire an engineer to do the editing and mastering so that I only have to do the recording. But that route has its problems, namely cost. The main reason I recorded my own audiobooks was because of the profit margin. Even if it takes twelve hours, there's no expense other than my time. Whatever I would pay an engineer is usually equivalent to what I'd pay a professional narrator. Economically and time-wise, it doesn't make sense.

The second idea is hiring a recording studio to help me record the book. But again, cost. And I'm not convinced that executing on the highest possible quality is worth it for a short audiobook. Readers are listening for the information. They don't care, as long as the audio quality is *good enough*. A thirty-hour audiobook? Different story. But most of my writing books are short.

I'm betting on the fact that audiobooks narrated by the author are a unique selling point. And I believe that. But I have to avoid making unwise decisions with my time.

So the verdict is that I will continue to record audiobooks, but I've accepted that my pace will be slower for a while.

ASSISTANT FOR A DAY

Writer's Digest asked me to speak at their Annual Writer's Digest Conference this year. What an honor to speak at the conference sponsored by the writing magazine I used to read as a kid!

The conference was virtual this year due to the pandemic. *Writer's Digest* hired a conference platform called Intrado to facilitate the speaker sessions. Intrado was like Zoom on steroids. Each speaker received their own dedicated audiovisual engineer as well as a *Writer's Digest* staff member on-call if needed.

Intrado had another feature that was cool in theory, but problematic in execution: a chat box as well as a question and answer box. The chat box needs no explanation—it existed solely for viewers to engage with each other during the chat.

However, the question and answer box were more complicated. Viewers could ask questions and then the questions would flow through to me while I was speaking. I could then approve questions and organize them based on high, medium, and low priority.

There was only one problem: I was expected to monitor the chat *and* manage the questions in real-time while I gave the talk.

Nope. Just thinking about that gives me chills even to this day. This was my biggest speaking engagement of the year and I was determined not to screw it up, especially since it was going to end up on YouTube.

So I hired a virtual assistant on Upwork for one day only. She only had three jobs:

- Monitor the chat and post links to my YouTube channel and the book I covered in the talk if people asked for them. (My experience with live events is that people join late and sometimes miss the opening of the talk, or they ask for links that you give—even if you repeat it multiple times.)
- Organize the viewer questions so that I could answer them when I arrived at the Q&A session at the end.
- Export the questions to a Word document for me so I could study them after the event and give me a report of what people said in the chat.

I needed her to do those things so I could focus on giving the talk. I also didn't want there to be awkwardness as I transitioned from the talk to the Q&A.

And guess what? Everything went smoothly! The assistant was phenomenal and she went above and beyond what I asked her to do.

Sure, I had to spend a portion of my speaker fee to pay her, but it was worth it. The talk went so well that it led to future opportunities to work with *Writer's Digest*, which is a win. Money well-spent, in my opinion.

AMNESIA MODE

I discussed previously the cost of my Beast Mode challenge. Since I neglected my marketing, I decided to make that my next challenge from November 1st to January 15th.

I called it "Amnesia Mode."

I pretended that I fell down and hit my head and forgot everything I knew about marketing.

What could I learn? What would change in my business if I approached every marketing concept again with the eyes of a newbie who knew nothing?

This challenge was far more balanced than Beast Mode, since I wrote books during it.

While the challenge is still ongoing at the time of this writing, it has been a hit with my audience. Many of the people who follow me are always looking for ways to sell more books and they appreciate transparency.

Every day on my blog, I share a lesson learned and a lesson executed.

A lesson learned is usually from a book I'm reading or marketing course I purchased.

A lesson executed is when I take action. I cover exactly what I did, play-by-play.

My hope is that Amnesia Mode will expand my mind to new opportunities, help me stay current with new marketing trends, and improve my sales.

If I improve my sales, others can follow what I did. If I don't, others will know what possibly didn't work, and why. Win-win.

I'll share the results of Amnesia Mode in the next volume of this series.

PITCHING FOR A TED TALK

I've always dreamt of giving a TED talk. It's a public speaker's paradise: you share your biggest idea in front of an enthusiastic, thoughtful crowd, and watch the idea spread all over the globe.

I watch TED Talks frequently. I even bought a couple books a few years ago about how to land and deliver one just in case I ever found myself in the position...

My understanding was that you had to know someone who knew someone in order to get selected. As such, I had written off the possibility of giving a talk until way into the future.

Imagine my surprise when I discovered on LinkedIn that TEDx was coming to Des Moines, Iowa where I live, and they were accepting applications for local speakers!

My head almost exploded. This was the opportunity of a lifetime.

So many thoughts raced through my mind.

"Can I apply?"

"*Should* I apply?"

"Would they even accept me?"

"I'm not credentialed or sophisticated enough to be a TED speaker."

"I don't fit the TED mold."

"What would I even talk about?"

I almost talked myself out of applying, honestly. I wasn't sure that they'd be interested in anything I had to say.

But then I realized that applying for a talk would be the ultimate test of my marketing skills at this point in time, especially since I was in the middle of my Amnesia Mode challenge. I would likely be an underdog in the applicant pool, so I'd have to create a pitch that was superior in every way.

The deadline was quickly approaching, so I gave myself an eight-hour deadline to come up with a talk and submit the application. No excuses, no procrastination. I would do it, be done, and move on with my life. Like going to the grocery store and buying toothpaste. That was the only way I could mentally address the task without dwelling on it and spending days or weeks preparing an idea.

I blocked four hours to think about the topic. I didn't want to get up on stage and talk about writing. That's too niche for TED audiences. When I think of TED talks, I imagine highly credible speakers talking about highly specific topics that have broad appeal. Writing a book doesn't fit that mold, so I had to think broader. I focused instead about being a creative. I found a topic from an old autoresponder I wrote that resonated with my audience, and I made that the basis for the talk. If selected, it might be the only talk that ever originated from an autoresponder.

Then I used a method that worked well for me in the past: the 3-Minute Rule by Brant Pinvidic. The gist of the method is that you start with an idea and follow a guided pattern to grow it into a pitch that is three minutes or less. It contains all the details the decision-makers need to know while also addressing their potential objections. This is the method that Pinvidic (a

TV executive) used to pitch some of the most famous shows on TV.

Developing the pitch took me about two hours.

With two hours left, it was time to fill out the application. I had to provide a three-sentence description of the talk as well as record a three- to five-minute video explaining the talk and why I wanted to do it.

Ironically, I made a pitch video that was exactly three minutes long using a mixture of Pinvidic's guidance, basic sales tactics such as a strong closing, and my prior YouTube experience. I filmed the audition on my DSLR in the same way that I record my YouTube videos, with good sound and lighting. I finished with about thirty minutes to spare.

We'll see what happens. If I land the talk, it will be purely because my pitch was on-point. I don't know anyone on the selection panel and they don't know me, so I don't have any connections to rely on. If I don't land it, who knows—maybe my pitch was ineffective or maybe the committee already had people picked out. It doesn't matter.

Regardless, I'm pretty proud that I applied. It was also great content for my community. I wrote about the experience in a newsletter, talked about it on *The Writer's Journey* podcast, and I dedicated this chapter to it!

A major weakness that a lot of writers have today is marketing themselves. I don't pretend to be good at it, but I'm willing to try and improve. The process of pitching a TED talk is really no different than pitching a short story to a literary magazine or a book to listeners during a podcast interview. The results may be different, but the steps are the same. It would be pretty cool to share the exact steps I followed if I land the talk. Maybe it could help a few folks.

BECOME A WORLD-CLASS MARKETER

LUNCHCLUB

So much in marketing is about relationships and your network.

I received an invitation to join Lunchclub.AI, a platform that uses artificial intelligence to match people together for networking meetings. You create a profile, tell the platform what type of people you're interested in meeting, link it with your calendar, and the next day, you receive email introductions with people you're going to meet. The platform handles the scheduling and the Zoom calls. All you have to do is show up and talk to people.

I was skeptical of the service at first, but now I'm one of its biggest fans.

In the first few weeks of the service, I talked to so many interesting people:

- An award-winning poet (a very *acclaimed* poet, actually)
- A money coach
- A freelance marketing director who works with big brands

- A yoga instructor who moonlights in using the power of AI to drive lifestyle design

All of the conversations were insanely interesting. I learned something from each person.

We just chatted about our careers and followed the conversation down interesting paths. Most of the conversations ended with a "feel free to reach out any time if you have questions about X." And that's fine, since that's how most networking conversations in real life end.

I don't have any expectations about Lunchclub, but maybe one day some of these connections I'm making will come in handy.

THE HOLY DUO OF MARKETING: THE BOOK DESCRIPTION AND OPENING CHAPTER

I was browsing Amazon for bestselling self-published books to see how their book descriptions were worded. I noticed something that seems obvious now, but somehow, I missed it for years.

I looked at books with at least 100 reviews. Without exception for the dozen or so books I studied, if you read the book description, it matches the first page of the story. The book description serves as a primer. The first page delivers.

For example, the book description might say "Now I have to figure out why a vampire is in my backyard trying to kill me." The first page of the book will be the hero in their backyard, fighting a vampire.

It's helpful to think of the book description and the opening chapter as an interlocking unit. What one starts, the other finishes.

REPURPOSED SPEAKING ENGAGEMENTS

I was invited to several speaking engagements this year. Due to the pandemic, the events were cancelled in-person and moved online. This meant that I either had to pre-record a video of my speech or livestream it.

In each case, I asked if the venue planned to upload the speeches to YouTube. One of them told me no. No????!!

Opportunity, opportunity, opportunity!

They told me I was welcome to upload the talk to my channel after the event was over. I told them I'd give them 60 days as a courtesy. Additionally, the speaking agreement does not take the copyright or place any limitations on what I can do with the talk, so the copyright is mine, baby!

(See, this is why it pays to understand copyright. I was able to anticipate this before signing the contract.)

The venue got (hopefully) a good talk from me.

I got to repurpose the content and post to my YouTube channel, which is quality content for my audience. YouTube also favors longer videos, so the ad revenue is better. It also boosts my credibility.

Everyone wins.

This is why I'm always careful to ask about repurposing the talk before I do the event.

CUSTOMER SERVICE IS A CONSCIOUSNESS

I listened to a great podcast interview where the interviewee was talking about her first job as a waitress. She described how she learned to tell what customers wanted, and how waitressing is the embodiment of the golden rule: treat others how *they* want to be treated.

For example, some patrons don't want to chat with a waitress. They just want to eat. Other patrons are a little *too* chatty. It's the waitress's job to figure out what each person wants and balance their interests accordingly.

She then said something that clicked with me: "Customer service is a consciousness."

Some people have that consciousness, and others don't. For example, an Internet tech came to my house once to help me with a bad Wi-Fi signal. We ended up making small talk, and he gave me some extra tips on how to maintain a good signal. This was the third time the Internet company had been at my house in six months. The other techs tried to fix the problem as soon as they could and didn't explain very much to me. This guy took the time to help and teach me to fix the problem myself so that I didn't have to call again. He also told me that one of his favorite parts about the job was working with the elderly. He said that it was time-consuming working with them, but they were always grateful for the help.

That's the customer service "consciousness." The tech had it.

Let me give you an example of someone who didn't have it. I upgraded my cell phone, an ordeal that took three hours because I had to buy and activate new phones for me, my wife, *and* my in-laws. The sales representative at the store was a young woman who just graduated high school. She was friendly enough, and we didn't have any problems in the store.

The next day, I received an unexpected charge on my bill. I couldn't figure out what it was, so I called the corporate headquarters. They told me that the "discount" the sales representative promised me wasn't actually a discount. I had to pay in full first and then it would post to my account in 90 days (or something like that—I'm still not sure I understood what the hell they told me). Really? Why didn't the sales representative tell me that when I was in the store? She had to have known as this is a routine sale the store runs, and she told me she had been working there for about two years. She didn't have the customer service consciousness. A better salesperson would have explained the billing problem in the store; otherwise, there's a high chance customers will return angry, and that's bad for business.

In the customer service world, this is called the "first time final" problem. Companies grade their representatives on how well they handled an encounter by gauging if the customer has to call back within a certain time period. Again, this is part of the consciousness.

What does this have to do with writers?

Whether you like it or not, you're in the customer service business.

Customer service needs arise in the following areas of the writing life:

- Prospective readers want to know which book in a series they should read first, or which *series* to read first. Your website had better offer that information; if not, readers will email you to ask the question directly, or they'll find another author who makes the buying process easier for them.
- When readers buy your book directly and need to sideload it onto their device.
- When readers email you with a question.
- When readers mention you on social media.

Those are just a few. There are more. When readers engage, are you ready?

Think of customer service as occurring in three phases: needs the customer has before they become a customer, needs the customer has when they're using your product, and needs when something goes wrong.

How are you serving your readers, and how can you develop the customer service "consciousness"?

WE KNOW WHY YOU'RE HERE

When I upgraded my phone this year, the cell phone store didn't have a good selection of accessories.

When I got home, I did a quick Internet search, and I stumbled across a well-known company that is known for making quality accessories for mobile phones.

When I clicked on the home page, the first thing on the top of the page was the newest iPhone and an assortment of accessories, with language that said something like "Looking for a case for your shiny new phone?"

Wow. That's some killer salesmanship!

They knew exactly why I was there and they read my mind; they knew that my cell phone store didn't have a good selection, and they capitalized on that.

Did I buy from their website? You betcha.

I thought about how I could accomplish something like this in my writing business. When done wrong, this sort of thing can be obnoxious.

An easy idea was to do it after speaking events, where I send people to a landing page on my site with the logo of the event and a headline that calls back to something I said in the talk. I'd offer one of my books on sale with a coupon code if they buy directly from me. I might also curate content from my YouTube channel or podcast that complements my talk and design the page in a simple but attractive layout.

Just an idea, but something I'd like to try in the future.

UPDATING BACK MATTER

I discovered an inconsistency in the back matter of my writing books.

One book had a sample of the next book in the series. Another had a buy link to the next book in the series. One didn't have a call to action at all!

Not good.

I standardized my back matter so that the elements appear in the same order every time.

I created a page called "Read Next" that has the cover of the next book in the series, some sales copy, and a link.

This way, no matter what book you're reading from me, the ending experience is the same.

I'm paying special attention to the interior consistency of my books. Long-term, I want readers to have the same general experience from cover to cover, no matter what book they're reading.

THE MARKETING METRICS THAT MATTER

Marketing is all about metrics and analytics. You can drown in numbers if you're not careful, and it's easy to focus on numbers that don't actually drive growth.

What are the key performance indicators (KPIs) for an author? In other words, if you filtered everything down to a few key numbers that tell you how your business is performing, what would they be?

In the previous volume, I listed my sales metrics. I've updated them. Here they are:

- **Net Units Sold**: The total number of books I have sold, with refunds subtracted.
- **Income**: How much money I make from my books and other revenue sources.
- **Revenue Stream Mix**: A breakdown of how much I make across different retailers, geographies, and across different channels such as fiction versus nonfiction.

- **Expenses**: How much money I have spent in the business.
- **Yearly Cost**: How much it costs per year to run the business.
- **Profit**: Revenue minus expenses.
- **Leverage Ratio**: How well-funded the business is. How much money is in the bank account versus the yearly cost? If I have $100 in the bank account and it costs $1000 to run the business, that's a leverage ratio of 0.10 (100 divided by 1000), which is pretty bad. I'm too leveraged and it means I have to borrow from my personal savings to pay expenses. On the other hand, if I have $1200 in the bank and it costs $1000 to run the business for the next year, that's a leverage ratio of 1.2 (1200 divided by 1000), which is better. It means that if something unforeseen happened, I'd have enough cash on-hand to last me the next year, plus a little extra. The higher the leverage ratio, the better.

I can also view the metrics above:

- Year over year or month or over month
- For any given time period

Over the years, I've stopped tracking a lot of marketing metrics. Numbers like website analytics, link tracking, number of reviews, and review averages don't tell me very much about the vitality of the business.

Ultimately, it boils down to how much money is coming in, how much money is going out, which products are driving the growth, which expenses are driving your spending, and how insulated the business is from shock.

I settled on these numbers this quarter because I am planning on building a visual dashboard that shows me this data automatically.

VIDEO TRAILER ADVERTISING A COURSE

I happened upon a YouTube channel for writers. The YouTuber sold writing craft courses. She created a one-minute trailer for each course, explaining what the course was, why it was important, and an intriguing example tip that demonstrated what you would learn.

The trailers were a free and smart way to promote the courses. While the videos didn't have many views, that wasn't the point. The YouTuber made the videos to make prospective buyers (me) *aware* that the course existed. I ended up buying one of them because it covered something I had been wanting to learn for a long time. If it hadn't been for the video, I might have missed it.

I made a mental note of the technique so I could try it when I create my next course.

FACEBOOK LESSON LEARNED

In the last volume, I wrote about a sales failure involving Facebook and a delayed response on my part that cost me a big sale. I wrote about how I fixed the problem so it wouldn't happen.

Sure enough, someone else messaged me on Facebook with a basic question. I received an immediate notification and responded right away. The reader then started a conversation with me and asked if I would be willing to sell them signed paperbacks of my *Galaxy Mavericks* series. Galaxy Mavericks is nine books with an average paperback price of $10. Do the math.

KA-CHING!

That's how you fix problems on your platform and stop sales from leaking through. A simple two-minute fix on Facebook a few months ago made all the difference here.

DIRECT SALES INTEGRATION

I finally got around to implementing direct ebook sales on authorlevelup.com.

I used to have it, but I wasn't happy with the provider, so I removed the option. Plus, it didn't sell well anyway.

I integrated with Payhip, which is a great service that makes it easy for readers to buy quickly. You can also do coupon codes.

Within 48 hours of integrating direct sales onto my website, I started seeing sales. Nothing substantial, but small revenue streams add up into mighty rivers over time.

I'll eventually install Payhip on michaellaronn.com too, but I'm waiting to see if there are any issues with the service. So far, it's working well.

At the end of my Beast Mode challenge, I packaged all the books I wrote into a single book and sold it only on my website, which helped bring in some additional income that I wasn't expecting.

Now I need to figure out how to do direct audio and paperback sales. There are two providers I am sourcing right now, but I don't like that you can't sell ebooks, audiobooks, and paperbacks all from one retailer. You can *in theory*, but it's not the best customer experience right now. I'll discuss this later in the book.

P.A.S.T.O.R-ING YOUR CUSTOMERS

I read *Copy That Sells* by Ray Edwards. Ray is an acclaimed copywriter who has worked with many big-name clients.

I've read a lot of copywriting books, but Ray's book clicked with me. Suddenly I understood copywriting on a completely different level.

A major takeaway from the book was Ray's P.A.S.T.O.R method of copywriting, a technique he uses to write sales letters that "shepherds" prospective customers from awareness to paying customer. Through the method, you focus on the following elements:

Focus on the **p**erson, pain, problem.

Amplify the problem.

Tell the **s**tory of the target person, explain the solution and the system they can follow.

Tell the story of **t**ransformation and use testimonials.

Make an **o**ffer.

Anticipate the customer's **r**esponse to the offer.

Do those things, and you will increase your chance of pastoring them into your flock.

I'll admit that Ray's method wasn't helpful for fiction marketing, but I found it invaluable for email newsletters and other sales techniques. It's a smart way of thinking about your customers.

LIFE'S A SQUEEZE

I read a copywriting book by an advertising legend. At the end of the book, there was a call to action to download a special offer.

I clicked the link and it took me to an outdated squeeze page that made me question if the author still maintained it. (A squeeze page is a landing page intended solely to convince visitors to take an action, such as joining a mailing list.)

In fact, the page was *so* out-of-touch that I decided not to download the offer.

I immediately checked my squeeze pages to see how they'd aged. I made some minor tweaks to them that should make them timeless.

Definitely not a mistake I want to make. This particular writer should have known better.

BECOME A TECHNOLOGY-DRIVEN WRITER

TECHNOLOGY IS THE KEY

When I talk about technology, I often hear people say that it's too complicated or that they don't have time to learn. After all, so many of us are just focused on writing next book.

I get it.

And I would understand resistance even more if people had to pay big money to download new apps and services to accomplish the kind of automation I am referring to.

But almost all of the tools we can use to automate portions of our writing business *are already on our computers*. We just aren't aware of them, or don't know how to use them to their true potential.

So much technology is literally at our fingertips.

There's a great movie called *Defending Your Life* with Albert Brooks. In one scene, the hero goes to the afterlife, where he meets several people, each of whom has unlocked more percentage of their brain than the average person. Technology is like that—you can unlock more of your computer's processing power, get more value out of the apps and services you already use, all at little or no cost.

My ultimate goal is to create a writing business that practically runs itself. I'd like to spend as little time as possible doing nonessential tasks.

The more time I spend writing and marketing and the less time I spend doing clerical tasks the better. Using automation to help me with that directly translates into revenue; for many of the tasks I am automating, most people would either not do them or hire an assistant at an expensive hourly rate.

Let's just say for the sake of easy math that I hired an assistant full-time to do clerical tasks for me without any automation. And let's say that it's a good assistant, commanding at least $30/hour or more.

That's $1,200 per week, or around $60,000 per year.

For easy math, let's say that I could automate around 50% of the tasks that the assistant could do. That cuts my costs down to $600 per week, or about $30,000 per year. I can then take that $30,000 per year I saved and invest in more activities that will bring in money. For example, my Amazon Ads are very profitable. What if I took that extra $30,000, put it into ads and turned it into $50,000?

Or what if I could use that extra income to pay off my house and therefore reduce hardship when my income decreases?

Or invest in a startup in the writing space? Or keep it in the bank for a rainy day?

Or...?

The margin between what I can automate versus outsource is what I call the "margin of opportunity." It will allow me to do things that others can't. It's a strategic advantage.

Combine the "margin of opportunity" with:

- A well-capitalized business with enough in savings to deal with surprises;
- A low overhead expense load; and

- A *profit* that pays a living wage;

And you have a recipe for amazing innovation and growth.

Now that I *really* have your attention, I repeat: you can take steps to achieve this today using the *tools that are already on your computer.*

Don't believe me?

Microsoft Excel allows you to automate data entry and data analysis.

Microsoft Word also offers macros, and you can use free macros off the Internet to help you catch more spelling and grammar errors than its spell checker can.

Microsoft Powershell, Applescripts, and Apple Automator allow you to automate routine tasks on your computer.

Programs like Apple Time Machine allow you to back up your work automatically.

Your email client allows you create filters or email rules to manage the flow of your emails.

Free apps like Calendly allow people to grab time on your calendar, eliminating "scheduling" emails between you and another person.

Formatting apps such as Vellum allow you to create better formatted books in less time.

Some writing apps allow direct integration with WordPress so you can blog directly from your app without having to sign in to WordPress.

Spell checker apps like ProWritingAid and Grammarly check your manuscript for additional spelling errors that you might have otherwise missed.

Social media scheduling apps allow you to schedule posting content well into the future. Almost all of them have free plans that are more than enough for most authors.

Again, all of this is free. What would your writing business look like if you optimized your time accordingly? How much time and money would you save, and could you invest that time and money back into your business in ways that support your mission and drive growth?

ZAPIER IS FOR AUTOMATION

Zapier is a web service that helps you automate routine tasks by linking other web services together.

For example, if you have a Mailchimp mailing list, you might want to download your subscriber information into a spreadsheet on Google Sheets. You can create an automation task so that every time you receive a new subscriber, Zapier will download that information into Google Sheets. You never have to get involved other than to make sure that the automation is working.

I've been aware of Zapier for a while, but I didn't understand how powerful it was until now.

I'm playing around with a few ideas to help me automate areas of the business that are less essential.

For example, bookkeeping. It's necessary, but it's not an "essential" task that *I* should be doing. I have an accountant who handles that for me, but he uses Quickbooks, which I despise because it doesn't offer the flexibility that I prefer when I'm digging through my expenses. I like to categorize my expenses based on more obvious terms, such as editing, marketing, continuing education, and so on.

My idea is to create a Frankenstein automation sequence that follows these steps:

- In Gmail, create filters for every expense receipt I receive so that new expenses get marked as "read" and moved into a dedicated folder.
- Once an expense receipt hits my inbox, Gmail moves the receipt into the folder.
- Zapier (which is connected to Gmail) then identifies the expense type and "parses" the email, looking for the date, company name, item name (if possible), and the price.
- Zapier then passes the "parsed" data fields to Google Sheets, where I have a spreadsheet that corresponds with the data fields, as well as a category column with an IF formula that tags each expense as a certain category depending on what the data says.
- Zapier moves the original email into another folder that lets me know that the expense was parsed.
- Once per month, a calendar reminder hits my inbox. I go to Google Sheets, verify the expenses, and fix any data that didn't pass through correctly. Inevitably, there will be some issues here and there.

I currently spend around one hour to 90 minutes preparing my expenses each month. I already set up Gmail filters a few months ago as part of a separate project, so that's done. I just need to create the "zaps" in Zapier, which would take me about 30 minutes to configure.

I believe that automating this activity would save me around 40 to 80 minutes each month. That means I would reduce my time spend to around 10 to 20 minutes. That's the very definition of efficiency because I can spend the time I save doing other things in the business that drive revenue and growth.

FOLLOW-UP ON PERSONAL THANK YOU VIDEOS

In Volume 1 of this series, I wrote how I started using the app Bonjoro to send personal thank you videos to people who buy my courses.

I implemented direct ebook sales on my website this quarter, and I added thank you videos into the workflow when someone buys a book directly from me.

I received the following response from a reader:

"THANKS so much for the personalized 'thank you' video!

"I was pleasantly shocked to hear my name (yes, you pronounced it correctly--LOL) along with your offer to answer questions about the material in your book collection.

"What a classy thing to do! I truly appreciate it and I'll be sure to reach out if I have any questions."

Just a sign that the technique works, and when it does, it works amazingly well.

I still don't advertise that I do this except for writing about it in the *Indie Author Confidential* series. It's a neat little surprise.

I checked my Bonjoro dashboard for analytics because I was curious what kind of data they provide. Of all the video messages I've sent:

- 93% were opened
- 100% of the opened messages were watched
- 43% replied

Solid numbers. It's good to know that the messages aren't going into people's spam filters and that people aren't having any trouble watching the videos.

I'll keep doing this until it becomes logistically impossible. And even then, I may keep doing it in some capacity.

MORE EXCEL ADVENTURES

I took a new job that challenged me in ways I've never been challenged before. It involves a *lot* of data and analytics, to the point where I have to be a numbers person. That's a scary proposition for someone who struggles with basic arithmetic and has no statistical background. But hey, I'm up to the challenge. It's good for me, and I can port the lessons I learn into my writing business, so it's a win-win.

The more time I spend in Microsoft Excel, the more I believe it is the most powerful application ever created. No other application I can think of even comes close to the sheer power and breadth of services that Excel provides. Not by a long shot.

However, Excel has a marketing problem. Too many people (myself included) think it's an app for numbers people. It certainly does have functions that automate math, but it's not a numbers app at its core.

Excel is a *logic* application. It offers tools you think critically about problems and answer questions you have about your data. "Numbers" are only a small part of the experience.

I actually think a lot of writers who are scared of Excel

could do pretty well at it if there were better resources out there on how to use Excel for your writing business. Excel is ultimately about using logic to think critically—writers do that every day with their stories. We're good problem solvers.

But Excel and (most) writers don't mix. Almost every writer I've ever talked to is terrified of it.

Anyway, I gained experience with the following features that I believe could be game-changers for writers.

Pivot tables are essential Excel learning. I read an article online that said it is estimated 90% of Excel users don't know how to use them. Considering I didn't know how to use one until about six months ago, and almost no one I know even knows what they are, I consider that an accurate statement. They're not hard to learn, but you do have to watch a few YouTube videos and play around with them for a while before it clicks.

I use pivot tables and pivot charts to help me gain insights into my sales. I also use them to help me cut through the noise of certain reports. For example, my AMS Ad search terms report is a pain to read. Put it into a pivot table and it becomes instantly more readable.

Believe it or not, you can throw your monthly sales reports into pivot tables too.

I learned a ton of other things about Excel in doing this new job. I'd bore you if I shared them, but it got me thinking about a way to make Excel easier for writers so they could unlock some more of the benefits.

FIXED MY INTERNET CONNECTION

In Volume 2 of this series, I recounted how my second interview with Joanna Penn for "The Creative Penn Podcast" went awry because my WiFi decided to go on vacation when we started recording. I swore that this would never happen again, so I wanted to follow up on my progress.

I hired an electrician to install ethernet ports in my studio so that I can connect my computer to hard Internet when I'm working from home and doing speaking interviews. This way, I (hopefully) will not have to worry about dropped connections.

I also had the Internet company come over and fix some things at the house that were causing signal issues. I should be all set now.

This is a win because it improves my professionalism. Yet, this professionalism is invisible. No one ever thinks "I'm glad Michael has a good Internet connection" when they're interviewing me. But they think the opposite the moment my signal drops. My goal is to never have a dropped signal ever again with any speaking engagement. Will that be possible? Probably not—things always happen outside of my control, but at least I know I'm doing all I can on my end.

The work in my studio was also tax-deductible, so another win.

Since installing the ethernet ports, I have done approximately seven podcast interviews and three speaking engagements. No signal drops for any of them.

I'd call that a huge level up.

TYPO REPORTER

My friend Kevin Tumlinson has a cool way to catch typos in his work. In the back matter of his books, he includes a link to a page that encourages readers to contact him if they find a typo. The page includes a form that readers fill out to help him identify the error.

He also thanks readers who catch typos in his future books on the acknowledgments page.

This is a smart idea if you're on a budget but want some additional support with proofreading. It's smart, even if you hire multiple editors. While not something I plan to implement personally, I wanted to pass the idea along.

DAILY PROMPT

I received an email from the developer of an iOS app for writers called Daily Prompt. The app is designed to help writers beat writer's block by giving them daily inspiration and writing prompts. I featured the app on my YouTube channel.

Each day, the developer curates beautiful and thought-provoking images that are designed to stimulate your imagination. There are also daily written prompts.

I love the idea. It reminds me ten years ago when I was a beginning writer and a friend and I would come up with writing prompts each week to write stories to. Many weeks, we struggled with ideas. An app like this would have been great for that.

Daily Prompt is well-designed with a noble purpose. But most importantly, it offers a free version and is quite affordable. I can't think of a better way to use technology to solve an age-old problem.

If you'd like to check it out, you can do so through my paid link at http://www.authorlevelup.com/dailyprompt. I only receive a commission if you buy the paid plan.

SALES COPY BUILDER

One of my biggest problems with book descriptions is that I wait until the last minute to write them. As a result, they sometimes read like afterthoughts, which hurts my sales and creates rework for me later. Sometimes the descriptions are decent; other times they're terrible. I don't like that inconsistency. I want to create a description that is the same level of quality every time—preferably one that converts!

Another problem I have with book descriptions is that I write them so infrequently that I forget the best copywriting methods. Even if I publish seven books in a year, that's only seven days out of the year that I'm writing a book description, which isn't enough to build muscle memory quickly.

I need a structure that can help me remember the steps.

During my Amnesia Mode challenge, I reread books by authors whose methods are most popular for fiction: Bryan Cohen, Libbie Hawker, Dean Wesley Smith, and a few others.

I created a simple spreadsheet that I call my "Sales Copy Builder." It helps me snap the different elements of book descriptions together like LEGOs so I can build high-converting book descriptions in less time, with no consistency gaps.

Here's a screenshot of what this looks like for fiction:

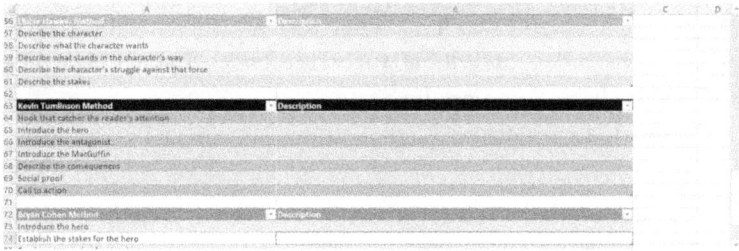

	A				C	D
56	Libbie Hawker Method	Description				
57	Describe the character					
58	Describe what the character wants					
59	Describe what stands in the character's way					
60	Describe the character's struggle against that force					
61	Describe the stakes					
62						
63	Kevin Tumlinson Method	Description				
64	Hook that catches the reader's attention					
65	Introduce the hero					
66	Introduce the antagonist					
67	Introduce the MacGuffin					
68	Describe the consequences					
69	Social proof					
70	Call to action					
71						
72	Bryan Cohen Method	Description				
73	Introduce the hero					
74	Establish the stakes for the hero					

I broke each method into a series of steps, with each step representing a paragraph in Column A. In Column B, I write my book description. When I'm done, I simply copy all the cells in Column B and they copy over like magic into wherever I need them to go. When I'm done, I created a quick macro that erases all the content with the click of a button.

Here's what this looks like for nonfiction:

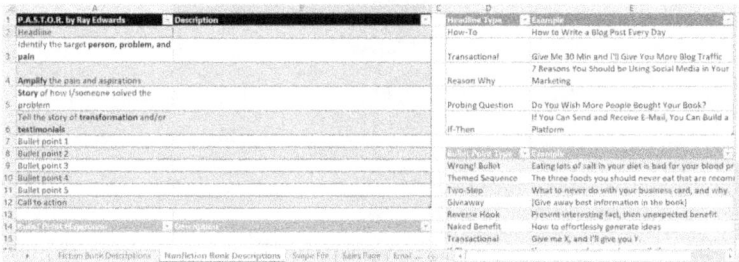

	A	B	C	D	E
1	P.A.S.T.O.R. by Ray Edwards	Description		Headline Type	Example
2	Headline			How-To	How to Write a Blog Post Every Day
3	Identify the target person, problem, and pain			Transactional	Give Me 30 Min and I'll Give You More Blog Traffic
4	Amplify the pain and aspirations			Reason Why	7 Reasons You Should be Using Social Media in Your Marketing
5	Story of how I/someone solved the problem			Probing Question	Do You Wish More People Bought Your Book?
6	Tell the story of transformation and/or testimonials			If-Then	If You Can Send and Receive E-Mail, You Can Build a Platform
7	Bullet point 1				
8	Bullet point 2			Bullet Point Type	Example
9	Bullet point 3			Wrong! Bullet	Eating lots of salt in your diet is bad for your blood pr
10	Bullet point 4			Themed Sequence	The three foods you should never eat that are recomm
11	Bullet point 5			Two-Step	What to never do with your business card, and why.
12	Call to action			Giveaway	[Give away best information in the book]
13				Reverse Hook	Present interesting fact, then unexpected benefit
14				Naked Benefit	How to effortlessly generate ideas
15				Transactional	Give me X, and I'll give you Y.

Fiction Book Descriptions | Nonfiction Book Descriptions | Sample File | Sales Page | Email ...

Nonfiction is different. In this screenshot, I have Ray Edwards's method laid out, but I also have some help documentation on the right to jog my memory. It's easy to forget that there are different types of headlines and even bullet points, for example. It's helpful to have that information on-hand in the same screen so I can refer to it.

This spreadsheet took me 45 minutes to create and it has

been a game changer. It improved my book descriptions overnight—not only were they more consistent, they didn't have anything missing. Even better, I can use the tool to write *several different book descriptions* at the same time! Then I can pick and choose lines that work best.

I also have a tab for email newsletters, since I write those monthly.

I also included a tab for a swipe file. I have collected clever marketing phrases and "money words" over the years, so I dumped them onto this tab so I can pull it up if I need some inspiration.

In my opinion, this is a perfect albeit unusual use case of how you can use existing apps and technology on your computer to help you execute better.

BROKEN WEBSITE

Once or twice a year, an element on my website breaks. Because I patrol my website properties so infrequently, I may not find out about the break until some time has passed.

Recently, a reader wrote me to tell me that my book pages were broken. I found the issue and fixed it, but I have no idea how long my website was malfunctioning, and that's scary.

Every time this happens, I tell myself I need a new website, but I can usually fix the issue to where it doesn't happen again. It's one of the downsides to WordPress. I minimize my plugins, but even then I have problems.

I set a reminder to patrol my website once every other month to catch errors earlier. I don't like to do that. A website should run itself with minimal interaction if needed.

But I do need a new website, which brings me to the next chapter...

PREPARING FOR A NEW WEBSITE

I need a new website, but I've been putting it off. I'll probably keep putting it off for a few more years. The only problem with that is that it will be more expensive the longer I wait.

I've published over 50 books. Each book has its own dedicated page on my sites. That's at least 50 pages that I would have to populate on a new website, or pay someone to do for me. Very, very expensive.

I also need better functionality on my site, as it has fallen behind the times. I've done all the little tweaks I can do at this point.

The nice part about author websites is that readers don't really care what they look like; they just care about finding the books they care about, and maybe learning a little about you in the process. So no one is going to come to my house and verbally berate me because my website is a little outdated.

However, this has given me the opportunity to think carefully about how I want to design my next website, and what types of functionality I want to have on it.

My first wishlist item is a professional design that suits my brand. I'm also desperate for a better sales experience. I need my website to be a "consummate salesperson," selling books at an even higher converting rate than it does now, all while I sleep.

My second wishlist item is to be up-to-date with all the latest web standards.

My third wishlist item is integration with a SQL server to solve the book page problem. I'd like to maintain a server that stores "one version of the truth"—all of my book metadata such as title, book description, book cover, links to retailers, and so on. This server would integrate with the website and communicate with it whenever I have a new change. For example, if I publish a new book, I'd update the SQL server, and then, within minutes, I'd have a new page on my site with all of the book's metadata laid out in accordance with how my designer designed the book pages to look. This way, all the book pages have a consistent look and feel, are always up-to-date, require zero maintenance, and could handle any amount of books I throw at it. While this might take some time and money for a programmer to create, it would save me time and maintenance costs over the life of the website.

My fourth wishlist item is smoother integration for eCommerce so I can create a better buying experience for readers who wish to purchase books from me directly.

My fifth wishlist item is a tool that can get the right book to the right readers at the right time. I have a simple tool on michaellaronn.com called Book Wizard. Book Wizard asks site users a series of questions and then recommends a book based on their answers. I envision something like this but on steroids. Ideally, it might even recommend books to a user based on their demographics or where they are coming from. Ideally, I would have back-end analytics that tell me which of my books are getting recommended most often and which ones are receiving clicks.

My sixth wishlist item is some kind of "break" detection. I want a notification when my website is not operating as intended. I also want a monthly report of broken links. I shouldn't have to find out from one of my readers that the site is broken or not functioning properly.

And lastly, I need to remain cognizant of emerging technology like AI-narrated audiobooks, cryptocurrencies, audiobook direct sales and delivery, artificial intelligence, and so much more. Those will play a prominent role in the future of author websites too.

At a minimum, even if I can't achieve *all* of these wishlist items, I need a website that is flexible enough to accommodate them in the future.

Will this be expensive? Yes...which is why I'm putting it off...

But if I can pull it off and execute it on a high level, it'll pay for itself over a few years.

In the meantime, I'll keep dreaming and saving.

BOOK BRUSH COVER DESIGNER

Book Brush is a web-based service that allows you to create professional marketing graphics for your book without having to use Photoshop.

Book Brush just released a new feature in their app suite called the Cover Designer. You can now design book covers in the app for ebook, paperback, and audio.

I've featured Book Brush on my YouTube channel, and I've done private webinars with them for my audience. I'm a big fan of the tool and I want more people to know about it.

The cover designer is a game changer. It allows authors who previously couldn't design their covers to do so with a small learning curve compared to Photoshop. The best part about it is that you can design a paperback and audio cover with no hassle. Just click a button and it automatically sets up the proper dimensions.

As they keep adding functionality, Book Brush could become the watershed tool that finally allows authors to create professional book covers at a fraction of the cost and in a fraction of the time. Is it a replacement for a cover designer? Probably not, but if you're tight on money, it's a great alternative until you can afford something better.

Don't sleep on Book Brush. They're going to be a lot bigger than they are currently.

LOGISTICAL PROBLEMS WITH FORMATTING

I still haven't released the paperback version of my book *150 Self-Publishing Questions Answered*. I wrote it with The Alliance of Independent Authors (ALLi).

The book is supposed to have a neat feature that is a hybrid between a glossary and an index called a "glindex."

Originally, as ALLi and I were producing the book, we thought that it would be as simple as sending the Vellum file to the indexer to add the "glindex" into it. Boy, were we wrong.

Five months later, and we're still working through the best way to do it. Normally, I would have just published the paperback without the glindex, but this is an important element for ALLi to get right.

I learned far more about book typesetting than I ever thought I would. Book indexers have a certain way of speaking, and they're not always the easiest to follow.

I'm confident we'll get it done, but suffice to say that indexes are way more complicated than they seem. There's a reason why there are indexers who make a living doing this stuff.

Oh, things you learn when you've been doing this a long time...

BECOME A DATA-DRIVEN WRITER

GLOBAL LINK LOCALIZATION
UPDATE

In Volume 1 of this series, I discussed how I implemented a link localization service. In the author context, link localization is when a link directs readers to the proper Amazon store depending on their country. This is helpful because you don't have to worry about sending people to Amazon.com and them not being able to buy anything there because they live in another country. It's also helpful because you can improve your Amazon Associates income.

Anyway, I wanted to report on how that is going.

Since implementing link localization in the second quarter of 2020, I have received over 1,000 clicks on my localized links, which have redirected readers in 64 countries. Only 46% of that traffic was from the United States, which in my opinion is a solid number, as it shows my traffic is not overly dependent on the United States, which is a trap a lot of US authors fall into.

I watched my non-US Amazon affiliate income grow approximately 1200%. While the starting numbers were quite small, I'll take any increase I can get! I'm also starting to see Amazon Associates income from Australia, Canada, and

Europe—that's never happened for me in the eight years I've been publishing.

The investment has already paid for itself, and it hasn't even been a year yet. Probably one of the best ROI decisions I've made this year.

This is a win for the following reasons:

- I am doing the right thing for readers around the world and creating a better buying experience for them.
- I am increasing my international reach.
- I am increasing my affiliate income, which is small, but small streams add up to mighty rivers.

Anyway, I wanted to make sure I provided an update, as I consider it another level up.

MY DATA SPIDEY SENSE IS TINGLING...

In Volume 2 of this series, I talked about Natural Language Processing (NLP) and an idea to use it to catch corrections that my editor has made in the past, as a way for me to send her cleaner manuscripts. My goal is to stop as many repeat mistakes as possible in order to reduce my long-term editing costs. It also frees up my editor to focus on more important items in the book. Plus, it just respects her time.

Every author's process for editing is different, but in my opinion, here are all of the steps that an author could follow if they wanted to ensure their book was as error-free as possible:

1. Author self-edits to catch obvious errors.
2. Author uses built-in writing app spellchecker to catch errors.
3. Author uses Microsoft Word spell-checker (if it's not their primary writing app).
4. Author uses an advanced spelling and grammar checker like Grammarly or ProWritingAid.
5. Author uses beta readers to catch more errors.
6. Author uses a professional copyeditor.

7. Author uses a professional proofreader.
8. Author may use Word, ProWritingAid, or Grammarly (again).
9. Author may use a "typo squad" to help them catch errors after they publish the book, giving readers a way to report typos.

Here's my problem with the process: it's redundant even if you don't follow all of the steps, and it's not terribly effective. What about repeat mistakes that your editor catches? That's not contemplated in the steps. Therefore, you're doomed to follow the same process over and over again without any incremental improvements other than what you can *remember* to fix next time.

I can't remember what I ate for dinner last night, so there's no way I can remember what grammatical errors I made in my last book...

That's where this project comes in. Spell-checkers only get me so far. I want to create a system that "learns" my style and gets better with every book I write. And I want it to proactively catch errors that my editor would have caught.

I have been taking baby steps toward working on this project. This quarter, I took a few more.

The first step is to figure out some way to "capture" my editor's edits so that I can translate as many of them into if-then statements as possible. If you can turn something into an if-then statement, then you can (potentially) turn it into a command that a computer can understand, assuming the computer can understand the variables.

Granted, I can't do this with all the editor's edits, but if I could turn a handful of them into if-then statements that a Microsoft Word *macro* or an NLP engine can capture, it would make a gigantic difference in the internal consistency of my books.

In order to do this, I need to stop thinking about my manuscript as a series of words, but instead, a series of data points.

When I uncover opportunities like this, I can't stop thinking about them. I am relentlessly curious. I dig, dig, dig until I find a strand of yarn. Then I pull on that strand, and the whole problem unravels.

After much searching, I found a random website on the Internet around 3AM one night. It advertised a free Microsoft Word add-in that allows you to extract data from your manuscript—most importantly, tracked changes. You can export all of your editor's tracked changes (and comments) to a table in a separate Word document.

This was the strand of yarn I was looking for—I just didn't realize it would be this easy.

Let me show you some images how it works. This is how the tracked changes table looks:

And here is how the acronym table looks:

Acronym	Definition	Page
ALL		40
COVID		11
EPUB		14
FOREVER		34
GDPR		17
NOT		45
NWA		7
SEO		7
TRUST		41
USGA		44
YOU		41
YOUR		38

Most people would yawn at this. Why is this even important? Because if you can create a table, then you can copy AND paste it into Microsoft Excel, where it is much more workable.

I pasted my edits table into Excel and added additional columns to help me tag and categorize the different types of edits.

Once in Excel, I added to the table, summarizing my lesson learned and where I thought it could be addressed by a Word macro or NLP:

And here's the last part of the table that contains some *rough* if-then statements:

If	Then
If a preposition is followed by noun phrase that includes a proper noun	Insert comment: Check for dropped article between the two nodes
If words "my current" exist	Insert comment: Verify "my." Editor flagged the words "my current" in past and replaced them with "the current"
Macro/if "notice/noticed that" exists ... AI if VERB precedes "that	Insert comment: "Check "that" Include link to a "that" resource"
"Writers' conferences" exists	Replace with "writer's' conferences"
"bill of rights" or "Bill of rights" or "bill of Rights" exists	Replace with "Bill of Rights"
"Constitution" or "Constitutions" are capitalized	Lower case them with a comment: "Unless it is the United States Constitution, constitution should be lowercase."
If a comma precedes the word "too"	Delete the comma as a tracked change.
Say/Says/Said/Ask/Asks/Asked/Shout/Shouts/Shouted/Yell/Yells/Yelled is not succeeded by a comma or a period	Insert comment: "Check dialogue construction. Introducing dialogue after a said-type phrase should always be done with a comma."

And some more if-then statements:

If	Then
If dialogue opens with a lowercase character and dialogue is NOT preceded by Say/Says/Said/Ask/Asks/Asked/Shout/Shouts/Shouted/Yell/Yells/Yelled + comma	Replace first letter of the dialogue with a capital letter.
preposition is followed by a plural noun	Insert comment: Check for dropped article
If a less than two commas exists in a sentence, the sentence does not contain a simple list of items, and the word there is only one instance of the word "and"	Insert comment: Consider adding commas for clarity, particularly before in the final phrase.
the word "but" is preceded by plural noun	Insert comment: Consider adding a comma before "but" for clarity.
The words "at first" are not followed by a comma, period, or semi-colon	Insert comment: Consider adding a comma after "at first" for clarity.

Please note that the rules on this table are specific to my writing only, not a declaration of how *you* should write your books. These are errors that my editor has caught that I agreed with. Some of them are purely stylistic.

Ultimately, I need to figure out:

1. How many errors I can program into Microsoft Word macros (which, in my opinion, can serve as another layer of grammar checking that Word's grammar checker can't do).
2. How many errors are leftover that can be programmed into an NLP engine.

3. How many errors are exclusively in my editor's realm.

So if you think about the editing process as a sieve:

1. The errors that spelling and grammar checkers can catch are big rocks that the sieve catches.
2. The errors that my editor catches are small rocks.
3. The errors my macros catch are fine particles that the sieve catches.
4. The errors my NLP engine catches are even finer particles that the sieve catches.
5. The errors that the writing apps, my editor and I miss are the grains of sand that flow through the sieve.

I want my editing sieve to catch as much as possible. The macro and NLP system adds an additional layer of protection.

In analyzing the first ten pages of one of my writing books, I found repeat mistakes of one of my biggest frustrations: dropped articles. I don't know an app that can catch them. The human eye frequently misses them because the brain pretends they're there. Even editors miss them all the time. Readers miss them too, but when they catch them...it's embarrassing.

In just two examples in the sample book I reviewed, the dropped article followed a preposition and came before a plural noun. For example: "Even her coworkers teased her about [the] novels she carried..."

Another time, the dropped article followed a preposition and came before a proper noun phrase:

"I worked at [a] Fortune 100 insurance company."

The rules of the English language dictate that prepositions and articles accompany each other frequently. If I want to catch a dropped article, I should start with the preposition and the following noun. They might offer clues for how to teach my system to predict situations for when an article might be dropped. I won't be able to catch them all, but by God, if I can catch a few...

This process also raises some philosophical questions about natural language processing: Can NLP identify rhetorical devices such as anaphoras? I'd love the ability for a program to spot common rhetorical devices such as anaphoras and help me identify if I'm not using them correctly. (Martin Luther King Jr.'s "I Have a Dream" speech is the most famous anaphora ever. He repeats "I have a dream" over and over—that's the anaphora.)

Also, can natural language processing detect proper noun phrases? Take "Fortune 100 insurance company." If you extract the proper noun from that sentence, Word only recognizes "Fortune." It doesn't understand "Fortune 100" unless you add it to the program's dictionary. And it doesn't understand the relationship between "Fortune 100" and "insurance company." Because of this, it can't detect subject-verb agreement, which explains why it missed the dropped article.

Yeah, this stuff is complicated. But it's fascinating.

Sure, I don't have time to code or create Word macros...I'm a writer after all. But I'm handy enough that I can create a prototype. Then I can pay someone to build what I need.

Word macros aren't difficult. You just have to understand how they work. I can easily do those myself after an hour or two of YouTube videos.

I don't know how much time and effort an NLP system would require. That's a big question mark that I'll learn as I continue on this journey. If it's too expensive, I can still pay someone to create a system based on my top ten or twenty offenders—that would still make a big difference. Either way, if I can figure this out, I don't see a scenario where I don't win in some way.

I've written so many books that I can probably find almost all of the programmable repeat mistakes by combing my existing work. After that, it's just adding a few new edits here and there with each new book.

Also, this system is retroactive. I can run my old manuscripts through it and catch previously missed errors, so that's an extra benefit too.

I believe that writers need to maximize the mileage out of the tools they have. Many are not, mainly because they don't know what their tools can do. No one (except me) wakes up in the morning and says, "I bet Microsoft Word macros can help me solve problems!" Nope. The very idea of Microsoft Word macros puts most writers to sleep. It's boring, too technical, and they can't see the benefit.

That's fine. While everyone else sleeps, I'll keep finding my strands of yarn...

AMAZON ADS HYPOTHESIS LOG

I've been focusing on Amazon Ads intensely this quarter. In fact, I have doubled my spending and created double the amount of my normal ads.

I do pretty well at Amazon Ads, so I can afford it. I haven't lost money as a whole on my ads since March. I want to see if I can double my income.

In my opinion, the hardest part about Amazon Ads is that it's hard to remember what you did or when you made a change.

I used to keep a journal of changes, but it didn't work because I didn't understand the ad data well.

Now I am much better at interpreting the ad data and I know what to do in almost every situation since I've been successful for almost a year now.

I need to get better about making hypotheses around the data and following up on them. You know, the responsible thing to do.

I started tracking my hypotheses, like "If I raise the budget for my automatic ads, then I should see more impressions within a week." Then, a week later, I check the hypothesis and go validate it.

This gives me a long-term look at the decisions I made.

It's a small but important step to help me make more data-driven decisions.

THE ADULTERATED DATA PROBLEM

Earlier this year, when I created my sales database, I arrived at a crossroads: did I want my database to contain *all* of my sales data or just the highlights?

The most important fields on any sales report are the date, title, marketplace or country, (net) units sold, and income. However, many retailers include unique fields that may be specific to the retailer, but not that useful to the author, such as book IDs. Kobo in particular includes a battery of cost of goods sold (COGS) and Value-Added Tax (VAT) fields that I honestly don't care about. Are these fields worth storing in the sales database?

I believe they are. In fact, I believe that you should store your reports as close as possible to the original format. You never know what you may need later.

Storing everything means you are storing what I call unadulterated data. You don't make any changes to it. The pros are that you keep everything in case you need it later and you also have some peace of mind. The con is that your database will be bigger over time and you're storing data you may never need.

You can choose to adulterate your sales data, which means that you only keep what you need and discard the rest. The pros are that you can focus on what's important and your database will be smaller. The con is that if you ever need the discarded data later, you won't have access to it. You'll have to refer to your raw sales reports to get the data you need, which is inconvenient.

Trackerbox, the popular (and only) sales tracking tool, operates under the adulterated data framework. It's one of the app's biggest drawbacks in my opinion.

Anyway, you may not find anything in this chapter useful in your career right now, but know that you'll need this knowledge someday.

DATA STEWARDSHIP

Most writers I know are terrified of Microsoft Excel. Whenever they open a spreadsheet, their foreheads get clammy, their hands sweat, their eyes glaze over, and fear paralyzes their brain from even doing the simplest arithmetic. I call it "spreadsheet-itis." Hundreds of thousands of writers suffer from it each year, but it's curable.

I used to be no different. I used to use spreadsheets in such a primitive manner that even the worst data analyst would have laughed me out of a room and blacklisted me from ever using Excel again.

I used to track all of my book royalties manually. I'd look at my various sales reports each month and I'd type in the amounts I made into a summary spreadsheet. It was so painful and agonizing that by the time I finished the data entry, I didn't want to *analyze* the data I spent so long entering. Plus, I made a ton of mistakes.

I invested in some Excel courses. It took a while, but I finally learned that I was doing everything backwards.

If you identified with anything I just wrote, then you have a *data entry* problem.

People hear the word data and tense up, but data is not scary. Data is objective and easy to understand. Getting to clean data is the difficult part, but only if you're uninitiated. And you can get yourself initiated by an hour or two's worth of videos on YouTube.

Data entry, on the other hand, is death. Few writers can tolerate it, and I suspect it's why most writers don't even bother tracking their sales.

Instead, we need to think of ourselves as data stewards. Instead of taking rows of data and manually moving them from Point A to Point B, we should instead let tools like Excel do the heavy lifting. Our job is to simply ensure the safe passage of the data.

When you think about data in this way, your approach changes. You start managing it at the highest levels instead of digging into minutia. And you can finally make decisions that will impact your writing business in a positive way.

The next time you're staring down a gruesome spreadsheet, or heaven forbid trying to get data from Point A to Point B, remember that you're a steward, and that avenues were designed to do the heavy lifting for you. If you invested your time and energy into discovering those avenues, how might your author business change for the better?

PRESTOZON

I discovered Prestozon, a service that helps you manage Amazon Ads using the power of artificial intelligence and machine learning. Prestozon helps you optimize your ads by giving you a better dashboard and deeper data analysis tools to make better decisions.

Prestozon intrigued me because I have said for the past year that I believe AI can run ads better than authors in the long-term. There are so many transactions per day across the entire industry of authors using ad platforms that an AI-assisted ad tool could optimize ads insanely well, and even aid with discoverability by finding links between books that authors wouldn't have thought of.

Well, the tool predated my idea, and it seems to be gaining attention and popularity. I haven't signed up for Prestozon because it uses a completely different methodology than I do to gauge the effectiveness of Amazon Ads. To use it would mean that I would have to change my entire approach, something I'm not ready to do yet.

I spent an evening watching their in-depth tutorial videos,

and I liked what I saw. If enough authors use the platform, it will get better.

If you need some help managing your Amazon Ads, check Prestozon out.

EMAIL WHILE WORKING FROM HOME DATA

I found an app that monitors my email inbox statistics. The service sent me a neat little report about how my email habits had changed since the beginning of the COVID-19 pandemic.

I sent 99% more emails during lockdown.

My response rate was identical compared to pre-COVID-19 times.

And I received 11% more emails.

Interesting data. Despite being in a lockdown, I still continued to respond to emails quickly despite receiving more emails overall.

Those emails aren't just "emails." They're questions from readers, amazing fan-mail, speaking opportunities, and so much more. But they're *relationships* first and foremost, and there is always a person on the other side of an email. It's cool to know that I'm continuing to keep my promises on my website around email service time.

THE POINT OF EXCEL

I don't consider myself to be an Excel expert, but my skills with the app are far better now than they were a year ago. I've invested a lot of time and energy into learning it. It also helped that I took a job late in the year where I spend five to six hours in Excel every day. That job was a blessing in disguise in my journey to become a data-driven writer...especially when you consider that my Excel skills before taking the job were the equivalent of a person who types with two fingers.

Anyway, that's why I am discussing Excel a lot in this volume. Learning it is an essential skill for any author who wants to become data-driven. I realized just how much I was missing when I finally understood how to use it. So many authors are terrified of spreadsheets, yet understanding how to use them correctly is one way to unlock opportunities in your writing life because you can see issues in your data. Act on those issues, and you'll make more money.

Many people think of Excel as a math tool, or a data analysis tool. Neither of those descriptions are true. Excel is a *logic* tool. You use the tools that Excel provides to apply logic to a problem so that you can solve it.

And in my experience, writers *excel* at logic (pun fully intended). We're masters of using logic to persuade and entertain people, but in the realm of spreadsheets, we don't know how to use that skill.

The more time I spend in Excel, the more I realize how little time I need to be spending there.

Excel masters don't spend hours in spreadsheets unless it's their job or they're building a tool. They open a spreadsheet, ask the right questions, get to the heart of the data, make a decision, and then get out. And they do it quickly. In minutes.

In fact, my goal with using Excel for my writing business is to make data-driven decisions in five minutes or less.

Why did my sales dip last month?

What's my best performing Amazon ad campaign, and what customer search terms are driving it?

What is my bestselling audiobook in the United Kingdom?

I need to be able to dive into Excel and answer these questions quickly. I'm nowhere near my goal of five minutes or less yet, but I can imagine how powerful my data skills will be when I get there!

That's a good goal for any writer to have. The less time you spend in a spreadsheet, the more you can write and market.

INTERFACING WITH THE
AMAZON API

An application programming interface (API) is a way for programmers to access data on a server without hacking or data scraping. In Amazon's case, they offer access to their backend data for developers to integrate the Amazon shopping experience directly into a website. There are many other ways to use the Amazon API.

I encountered a tool on YouTube that allows you to connect with the Amazon API directly from Microsoft Excel. You can enter an ASIN, and it will pull the data from Amazon into your spreadsheet. Very cool.

Some potential use cases:

- You could use this tool to pull in all the sales ranks for your book onto one spreadsheet so that you didn't have to check each book individually. Just refresh the spreadsheet.
- Amazon Advertising search term reports often give you ASINs for the books that your ads are being served on; in order to find the product information, you have to go to Amazon and search for the ASIN.

Imagine entering a bunch of ASINs in bulk, and in a few clicks getting the product information populated next to them in Excel.

- You could pull all the books in a category to get market intelligence, such as average price. There are better tools for this, though.

I won't share the app, as I'm ultimately not sure if this tool is a *sanctioned* use of the API. But I love the fact that it streamlines research and allows you to pull the data into the app you're already using.

I did not use the app because it requires an Amazon Seller account, which I do not have right now. But this is the future. Few people know that Excel can connect to APIs.

SPARKLINES

I discovered Microsoft Excel's Sparklines feature this quarter.

Sparklines are mini charts that fit within one cell but summarize data from another cell range.

Sparklines are useful on dashboards because they save space.

Most experienced Excel users know about Sparklines, but it was a neat discovery for me, especially as I think about creating a visual dashboard for my sales database.

CUSTOM DATA TYPES IN EXCEL

Excel offers a "data type" feature that, until now, has been limited. You could create cells with financial stock and geography data that updated in real-time. You could also add additional data without leaving Excel because *all* of the data attributes are contained in one cell.

If that sounds complicated, it's because it's not an easy concept to explain in writing. It makes more sense when you see it in action.

The Excel team released a new feature called "custom data types" that lets users create their own data sets to reference dynamically in a cell.

I've been waiting for this feature for a while. I have an idea to create custom data types for my books and their metadata.

Maybe I want to do a comparison in my sales database on how well books priced at $3.99 sell compared to $4.99. If I stored all of my book metadata as custom data, then I could overlay that on top of my sales database pivot.

I could also use the custom data set as the storage point for my book metadata rather than housing it in a separate database, making it easier and more portable.

URBAN FANTASY BOOK AND PARANORMAL ROMANCE BOOK DATABASE

In 2019, I created a tool called The Urban Fantasy and Paranormal Romance Book Database with my author friends John P. Logsdon and Ben Zackheim. The goal was to create a database of urban fantasy and paranormal romance that readers could search based on what they like to read.

Goodreads is a poor reading management tool. It does a lot of things right, but it's difficult to find anything on Goodreads beyond the subgenre level.

Yet, if you look at most urban fantasy books, the first thing that the book cover makes clear is what type of supernatural character the hero is.

What if you wanted to look for books where the hero was a werewolf?

What about a treasure hunter?

Good luck finding that on Goodreads. Listopia is where you would start, as that allows users to compile lists of books based on themes. But anyone can add books to a list, and the result is lists that aren't helpful.

Also, book discovery on Goodreads isn't useful. Despite the

website having an extremely complicated algorithm that was a pioneer ten years ago, it hasn't improved much since then.

That brings us back to urban fantasy. Goodreads isn't set up for how most urban fantasy and paranormal romance readers browse.

The Urban Fantasy and Paranormal Romance Book Database contains series in a giant database that you can filter and sort by:

- Series Name
- Author
- Protagonist Gender
- Protagonist Supernatural Type (Vampire, Werewolf, Necromancer, and so on)
- Protagonist Profession
- Setting
- Subgenre (of urban fantasy or paranormal romance)
- Publishing Type (traditional or self-published)
- Young Adult
- Paranormal Romance
- LGBTQ
- Reverse Harem
- Adult Language

So let's say for example that you wanted to find all of the non-paranormal romance wizard books by self-published authors. In a few clicks, you would have a list of series meeting those parameters, with links to the series on Amazon or the author's website.

Even better, anyone can add series to the database. If you're an urban fantasy or paranormal romance author, you can add your new series to it, so it's free marketing.

If you're a hardcore reader, you can bookmark it and use it for endless new reads.

Everyone wins.

As of this writing, here are some fun statistics:

- The database contains 315 series by 469 different authors
- The gender breakdown for protagonists is 68% female, 31% male, and 0.21% transgender.
- Most people would expect vampire heroes to dominate in the database; however, they only represent 7% of the books in the database.
- The top five most represented supernatural heroes are: witches, mages, faeries (fae), and most surprisingly, heroes with *no supernatural powers at all.*
- Seven percent feature LGBTQ protagonists.
- Students and cashiers were among the most represented professions.
- Sixty percent of the titles in the database were self-published.

I'll stop there. How cool is that data? I created the database so we could aggregate data about the urban fantasy genre. Sure, the database is still small, but readers are adding books to it regularly, and maybe one day it can encompass several thousand books and become *the* definitive resource for authors and readers in the genre.

The database has been helpful in my marketing efforts since my main genre moving forward will be urban fantasy.

BECOME THE WRITER OF
THE FUTURE

2021 STRATEGY

Every October, I design my strategy for the coming year. I do it in October so that I'm done before the holidays. November and December pass at light-speed, and I don't like planning for the year in January after it has already started.

This year, I decided to share my author strategy publicly. You can view the interactive mindmap at www.authorlevelup.-com/2021strategy. I did this so that other people can see it and use it to think about their strategy.

The author community as a whole doesn't always do a good job of thinking long-term, so I'd like to try to influence that.

My mission as an author is to entertain and/or educate the niches that I serve, and to remain nimble.

Nimbleness is important. In a rapidly-changing publishing landscape where the future of traditional publishing is uncertain, indie authors' ability to pivot is an underrated asset. It's how we win, *and* how we stay relevant for decades to come.

Any good mission must be supported with strategic pillars.

You already know the five pillars of my author business because they comprise the structure of this book:

1. Become a world-class content creator
2. Become a world-class marketer
3. Become a technology-driven writer
4. Become a data-driven writer
5. Become the writer of the future

If I had to distill each strategic pillar into an essence, they would be:

1. Become a world-class content creator by developing a diverse and deep portfolio of work of the highest possible quality.
2. Become a world-class marketer by mastering the current tools on the market to improve my profit while simultaneously reducing my expenses and tax liability.
3. Become a technology-driven writer by creating technology-assisted writing business that helps me create world-class content and sell more products.
4. Become a data-driven writer by becoming a master of analyzing my author business data to unlock new opportunities hidden in plain sight.
5. Become the writer of the future by staying up-to-date with the industry, looking to the future, protecting the business, and making smart investments that will pay off in five to ten years.

Those are the high-level details. My strategy itself is far more tactical and analytical, so check it out if you're interested.

For me, 2021 will be the year when things finally converge: the years I spent learning and improving my craft, the investments in profitable advertising, mastering technology and using it in unique ways to streamline and automate my business, learning data analysis, studying the future, and most importantly, running a profitable author business.

Will I become a mega bestseller? No.

But many of the things I've invested in the last few years are starting to bear fruit, and I believe that I'll be able to start harvesting some of that fruit as early as 2021.

If you'd like to learn in greater detail how I will be carrying out my strategy, be sure to check out the interactive mindmap at www.authorlevelup.com/2021strategy.

I also recorded an hour-long livestream about my strategy in greater detail. Watch it at www.authorlevelup.com/2021strategyvideo.

DEVELOPING A READER FIRST MENTALITY

This quarter, I published a book called The Reader's Bill of Rights: A Manifesto on How to Treat Your Readers Right.

In one of the chapters, I talk about fan-mail.

When you become a bestselling writer, you receive a ton of emails. I bet someone like George R.R. Martin receives hundreds if not thousands of emails every day. There's no way you can keep up with that amount.

But what if you could? What if someone at George R.R. Martin's level committed to providing a response to every reader that emailed them or sent them fan-mail?

Authors at that level have the least amount of time, but they're in the best position to address this problem. For example, there are systems that can read an email for sentiment analysis using artificial intelligence. That could divide the emails into "positive" and "negative," much like reviews on Amazon.

A certain percentage of the negative emails don't deserve a response—maybe they're laced with profanity, contain death threats, or something else that loses the sender the privilege of a dignified response. These emails can be handled by an assistant who can verify whether the sorting is correct. If so, with one click, the assistant can send these people a generic, standardized response. The author doesn't need to see these emails, and assistants who handle them should have access to mental health resources if needed.

For the negative emails that are constructive and productive, the assistant could scan them for certain keywords to determine which ones are the most important. The assistant could handle the majority of them, with the rest going to the author. The key criteria, in my opinion, would be whether the email will hurt the author's production or emotional mindset, or whether the email is part of a bigger trend that the author should know about. If the answer is yes, then the assistant handles the email and reports any trend findings to the author. Any leftover emails go into the author's queue.

For the positive emails, those can be segmented too. Some positive emails don't need a personal response. They might be a "just wanted to say thank you and keep up the good work" type email, or a "just an FYI, but..." Those can be addressed with a different standardized form letter, maybe with a coupon or a bonus short story or something.

There might also be positive emails that are best handled by an assistant, such as "what book should I read first?" or "when will the website be updated?"

All other positive emails are squarely in the author's realm. If someone sends an email about how the author's book changes their life, they deserve a response from the author, not the assistant. In my opinion, it doesn't matter how long it takes, as long as the author sets expectations properly on the contact form page of the website. Whatever the author promises is what the author should deliver. I bet that readers wouldn't even mind an absurd timeline like one or two years.

Imagine what readers would say if a mega bestselling author did this, and if they received a thoughtful response to their fan mail. First, their heads would explode. Second, they'd buy *more* of that author's books. Third, they'd tell their friends.

What an amazing opportunity for a big-name author to make long-lasting impacts on their fans, and even more money in the process.

Would it be possible to respond to every email? Of course not. Fans know that. But if someone sends you a thoughtful email praising you and telling you about the impact your work has had on them, that's a super fan. Most readers don't do that. Super fans deserve the best because they'll stick with an author for a long, long time.

Any investment in assistants or software would pay for itself.

But, as I say frequently, I'm an alien. I don't think like most people. Most people look for ways to minimize their contact with fans as they become more successful. A classic example of this is creating a forum or Facebook group and then only popping in once or twice a year.

But I believe that your link with your fans is vital. The more you stay in contact with them, the more information they'll give you about how to keep them happy. And if you do it right, you can do this without ever compromising your art.

THE EMPLOYEES OF THE WRITER
OF THE FUTURE

In a moment of weakness, I was watching some YouTube videos of Kim Kardashian.

It's amazing how many people follow her around on a daily basis. Assistants, makeup artists, and so on.

It got me thinking about a silly idea: if I was a filthy rich multi-millionaire author on the level of Stephen King or Nora Roberts, what would my staff look like? I doubt I'd have people following me around, except if I traveled to writing events, but I would definitely have a team, as I couldn't do it alone.

And yes, this chapter will be vain, but don't pretend that you haven't had these daydreams!

Let's assume that I continued the same activities I am doing today. Writing like crazy, YouTubing, podcasting, public speaking, and so on. I'd be doing them on a bigger scale.

First, I would need a chief of staff or operations manager. Entrepreneur and virtual assistant expert Chris Ducker calls this a "general virtual assistant"—someone who manages the details of the day-to-day operations. For example, they would manage my other assistants, manage my calendar, control the flow of certain information to me such as fan-mail trends, control *access* to me, handle some of my personal affairs, and so on. My chief of staff would need to be someone I can trust, probably someone who has the opposite personality type of me. They need to be a whip-cracker, and, to use the famous legal expression, have an iron fist in a velvet glove. (Trust me that I can exhibit those qualities too, but I'll be spending my time doing other things, remember.)

Next, I would have a dedicated customer service assistant. This person's job would be to keep my readers happy and delight them in other small and unexpected ways. A professional, cheerful attitude with a sales mentality is required. I have extremely high standards. This person would monitor my email inbox and triage it accordingly (see my chapter on fan-mail earlier in this book). They would handle refunds, ensure that readers who purchase products directly from me have a delightful experience, handling small problems before they become big ones. All roads would lead to my customer service person first, which is what makes this such an important position. They would be my secret weapon.

Next, I would need an audiovisual team—someone to edit my videos and someone to edit my podcasts. If I traveled to a speaking event, preferably my video editor would travel with me and film my speech and my interactions with readers, and maybe even content I might conduct for my YouTube channel on location. This person's sole job would be to make sure that I always look good and to capture as much content that we can repurpose later on the website, blog, YouTube channel, and more.

I would also need a marketing assistant. This person would, *under my direct supervision*, manage ad campaigns, handle social media posts, design promotional materials, and find ways to market my existing catalogue. This person would *never* have access to any of my financial information. That's very, very important. So many authors are happy to give away access to their bank account or wave their hands and let their assistant handle their financial affairs. Nope. Not with me.

And lastly, I would contract with a few individuals who wouldn't be full-time employees, but they would provide regular services:

- An editor, proofreader, and cover designer who would prioritize my work. My chief of staff would coordinate them and prepare my books for publication according to my standards, with me having the final say.
- An intellectual property attorney on retainer to handle lawsuits (since mega bestsellers get sued all the time). The attorney would also advise me on urgent legal matters as they come up, like Hollywood contracts, for example. The attorney would also handle occasional copyright infringement situations where someone is infringing on my IP and I need to stop it.
- An accountant.
- A financial advisor and a tax attorney, as I would be making purchases and investments in the name of the business for tax purposes.
- A bodyguard, if necessary.
- An IT security expert on retainer who would help me secure my network and the computers of employees working for me. As a mega bestseller, I would be a target for cyber attacks and ransomware attacks. The expert would help me minimize vulnerabilities and ensure that my work and products are always available, always protected, and that I can restore them if needed. They would also

ensure that my employees don't inadvertently
expose my networks. Not an easy job.

Subtract the salaries of all these wonderful folks from my
annual salary and I'd still have money to burn!

As for me and my daily activities, I would need all these
people because my days would be spent:

- Sharpening my overall author strategy and vision
- Writing like a madman
- Engaging with my fans
- Traveling and making public appearances
- Finding new revenue streams
- Negotiating licensing agreements
- Managing the financials of the business
- Developing relationships with fellow authors and key players in the industry
- Managing my staff

What a daydream! Maybe some day it will happen.

WHAT'S YOUR MAGIC NUMBER?

I'm nowhere near making a full-time living for my work, but I thought about what it would take for me to go full-time in a perfect world. How much money would I need to make? In other words, what's the "magic number?"

I thought about this one day. I added up:

- my average monthly business expenses with a padding of ten percent to account for growth, since my expenses increase from time to time.
- my average household expenses with a padding of ten percent.
- my average "contingency" expenses (leaking toilets, car trouble, home improvements, and so on).

The sum of those three items is my magic number, but it's not that easy.

How much money would I need in my business and personal savings accounts as a cushion? I'd need at least eighteen month's worth of expenses, and honestly, that's not enough.

The writing life is cyclical. Sometimes you have high

months and then you have low months. How do I factor that into the equation?

And what about how I want the business to *look* when I go full-time? Ideally, many of the projects and investments I'm making right now would streamline, automate, and outsource many tasks that I'm doing manually today. My hope would be that the business would be as optimized as I can make it, possibly with an assistant in place helping me run some of the day-to-day operations. Me stepping into a full-time role is the last piece of the puzzle, an accelerant that will help grow sales even more.

Of course, life is never perfect. It's not that easy. Few people get to command their destinies on their own terms. A lot of people are forced to go full-time before they're ready because life happens. That could very well be my situation too. But I believe it pays dividends to *think* about your future because it can inform your decision-making.

TRACKABLE EXPENSES AND ROI

Every writer has expenses. They're vital to running an author business.

But a question I've been asking lately is "how is my spending supporting my strategy, and how can I spend in a way that drives revenue?"

While logging my expenses, I've started to assign return on investments to them. This isn't possible with everything, but I wanted to know how many of my expenses for the year directly resulted in revenue that was more than the expense itself. Then, in theory, I could subtract those expenses from my overall expense amount, which would give me an adjusted expense amount that more accurately reflected what my "true" expenses were for the year. It would also potentially clue me in to how much I'm "wasting" each year—i.e. an expense that I cannot directly tie to revenue.

A few examples:

- I hired my video editor to edit my video for a virtual speaking event this quarter. The amount of books during the event offset the amount I paid him so that I made a small profit from the event. Many of the comments viewers made during the event were around my video production, so I can assume that the gamble paid off and netted more sales than if I hadn't hired him. Thus, I can subtract a week's worth of video editing expenses from my overall expense amount.

- I hired an illustrator to create maps for my book *The Indie Author Atlas*. After I signed off on the work, I found a typo that I accidentally missed. I would have had to hire her again, which would have cost approximately $25. Earlier this year, I purchased an app called Affinity Publisher, which surprisingly, allowed me to edit the source file of the map in question. Affinity cost me $25. I originally thought that Affinity would have been a "dud" purchase because my needs changed after I bought it, but it paid for itself.

Those are two examples. They're minor, but my hypothesis was that if I did this exercise on all of my expenses for the year, I bet I could find savings. And I did.

This type of thought exercise works best with operational expenses. It's not as helpful when looking at your production or marketing expenses, because that requires different, longer term thinking. Some of your books might not turn a profit for a few years, if ever. But what about an app that you purchase a one-time license for?

Some other ways to think about this:

- How can equipment and applications you buy for your writing business pay for themselves?

- Do the subscriptions you pay for on an annual basis pay for themselves? If they don't, what other justification can you make? Maybe they save you time or improve your reader experience. That's valid too. If you can't find a justification, can you cut the expense?
- What percentage of your expenses can you quantify with hard dollars? Knowing that you can't do this for everything, is there a "right" number?

To make this more concrete, let's use a common author example.

Most authors purchase a subscription to an email marketing service. Let's say you pay $100 per year. How would you tie revenue to this expense? Easy. When you launch a book and send an email to your fans, look at how much you make within 48 hours after you send the email. Over the course of the year, is that number more or less than $100? If you're a new author, it'll probably be less—so don't cut it. Just understand the number, as it would be unwise to stop email marketing just because you have a small audience. But if you're a more experienced author, it's smart to know how much revenue your email platform drives for you each year. It also helps you justify upgrades. For example, I had to upgrade my email service this year, which cost me around $75 extra per year. Since I know how much money my emails drive each year on average, I knew I could afford it.

Let's show how this can make a big difference in how you view your expenses each year. Assume that you spend $5,000 this year for writing expenses. Your budget is $4,500, which means you overspent by $500. Not good, right?

What if you were able to show that $250 of your expenses paid for themselves and/or drove more money than you spent?

First, subtract the $250 from your total expenses. You now have a $250 overage.

So if you look at your total amount for the year, you would have exceeded your budget by 11% ($5,000 divided by $4,500).

But if you use the adjusted amount instead, you only exceed your budget by 5% ($4,750 divided by $4,500). So you're still over for the year, but by a little less.

What if your average adjusted expenses resulted in a 5% difference each year? What if the next year you were more cost conscious, coming in at around $4,600 in total expenses? You'd go from a 2% overage to a 97% underage.

What if you had a year where you came in under budget already? Well, then a 5% difference would show an even *better* performance.

It's great if you "stumble" into this number, but what would happen if you became more intentional about it? What if you could improve this number?

It's an interesting thought exercise because it forces you to quantify your expenses with hard dollars, which can at times be painful, especially in the beginning of your career when you don't know what you should be buying.

If you did this exercise, what would the difference between *your* total expenses and *your* "true" expenses be?

I like this exercise because it stacks up with other "invisible" numbers in your writing business.

For me, business is revenue minus expenses, which equals profit.

Increase your revenue by diversifying your revenue streams, improving your marketing, and expanding your portfolio.

Spend strategically in a way that increases your revenue and helps your expenses pay for themselves as much as possible.

Find areas in your writing business where technology and data can help you streamline, automate, and outsource your daily tasks, which reduces your expenses further (and possibly increases your revenue).

Reduce your tax liability to increase the amount of profit you keep every year.

All of these tactics work together to help you maximize the impact of your art and run a sustainable business.

DEALING WITH CRITICISM

Gary Vaynerchuk did a great video on criticism on his YouTube channel. A young woman was telling him about her struggles with self-doubt. She struggled because other women told her that she was inadequate and not capable enough to follow her dream. She had developed a sizable Instagram following but never felt like she was good enough to have the success that she built.

Gary told her that she needs to think about her body like armor. That armor blocks bad criticism, but it also blocks the really good criticism too. He mentioned how someone replying with a comment like "you're the best" is a quick sugar high. We crave those comments, and because we allow ourselves to be open to *those*, that also lets in the really bad comments. The solution he offered was to take less stock in the really positive comments. Read them, appreciate them, and move on. Don't fall for the sugar high. By doing that, the really negative comments would affect her less.

I found it to be sound advice, and definitely true for me. I'm just passing it along.

PROCRASTINATION AS STRESS RELIEF

I subscribe to Mel Robbins's YouTube channel. I like her worldview and her positivity. I also think her type of vulnerability is most similar to mine.

Mel answered a question in one of her videos about how to deal with procrastination. She called procrastination a form of stress relief.

I used to call procrastination a lot of things. Stress relief wasn't one of them. But it makes sense when you think about it.

We procrastinate because putting off the task we need to do feels good in the short term, even though it's painful in the long-term. In some cases, procrastination can be helpful, particularly if we need to come up with a creative solution to an idea. But for reasons we all know, it can also be harmful.

I have had many times this year where I've put things off, even though I knew I needed to do them. For example, at the time I'm writing this chapter, I should have finished this book and sent it to my editor by now. But I kept putting it off because I chased other things that were more important to me at the time.

I'm not advocating for people to procrastinate to feel better. But understanding the emotion is key to learning how to defeat it.

TALENT + ENDURABILITY = SUCCESS

I was listening to a podcast and the guest (a very successful career writer in the literary genre) said something interesting.

She said that there are a lot of writers in the world with talent. Sometimes they waste their talent. Sometimes they don't realize they have talent and self-destruct, or do things that squander their gift. Sometimes they make bad life decisions. Or they're just impatient, or they can't handle rejection and uncertainty.

She gave a simple equation. Talent + endurability = success.

Not everyone has talent, but you can work on it. As Dean Wesley Smith says, talent is just a measure of a writer's skill at a point in time.

Anyway, the writer continued with an explanation of endurability. Endurability is more than resilience. It's the ability to keep going even though others tell you that your work isn't good; it's the ability to keep walking in the dark and leading without followers.

I'm paraphrasing her, but I believe the quote below is mostly right (I typed it as I was listening, so forgive me): endurability is about good habits, patience, discipline, ability to shrug off rejection, the ability to not be self-destructive, the ability to not get in one's own way, to make good lifestyle choices, to not become a drug addict or an alcoholic...to persist and to honor one's gift, and to understand that to have a gift is a precious thing, and to nurture it, give it the time and space that it needs, and not give in to the demands of the rest of the world, which does not exist to nurture your gift."

Wow. I'll just leave that there for you to digest.

WRITERS AS WHALES

When I finished my Beast Mode challenge, I started my Amnesia Mode challenge. Re-learning marketing after such a prolific period of writing felt weird, like I was out of my element.

It reminded me of a whale.

When I'm writing, I'm in the water. I'm feeding on plankton, exploring the world, and communicating with other "writer whales." It's where I love to be.

But I can't breathe underwater. I have to come up to the surface for air. Air gives me life. And that air is marketing. Without it, I can spend as much time in the water as I want, but my explorations and feeding sessions won't bear any fruit.

Yet, if I spend too much time out of the water, I'll die. So it's a delicate balance.

What's your balance? For me, I tend to spend too much time in the water and I don't come up for air nearly as much as I should. If I don't change that, it'll be hard to become a true writer of the future. Some writers are too scared to go into the water and stay near the surface. They're marketing geniuses, but their craft is shallow.

How might thinking of yourself as a whale change your perspective in how you approach writing craft and marketing?

ACX RETURNS CONTROVERSY

ACX caused controversy this year when they announced that Audible customers could refund or exchange an audiobook up to a year after purchase. The refund would come from the author's royalties.

The backlash was swift, and many author organizations sprang into action, including The Alliance of Independent Authors (ALLi), who were instrumental in mobilizing people against the measure.

Audible relented quickly and offered some concessions, but the issue is still ongoing at the time of this writing.

I'm proud of ALLi for their efforts in this area, and that's exactly why I pay them yearly dues. (If you're not a member, join using my paid link at www.authorlevelup.com/Alli).

PAYMENT SPLITTING: A NEW TREND
TO WATCH

I was delighted to see Draft2Digital offer a payment-splitting option this quarter. I wrote about PublishDrive's Abacus in the previous volume of this series, which offers a similar function.

The nice part about Draft2Digital's service is that it *actually* splits the payments, whereas Abacus simply tells you what is due to your collaborator. Also, there's no cost, which makes this far more compelling than Abacus, which requires an annual fee. There's also no hassle, as your split payments are automatically reflected in both your and your co-author's monthly sales reports.

That's the proper way to do it.

Oooh, healthy competition! How often do you see that in the self-publishing space?

Payment splitting is now officially a trend. It's hard not to imagine every major distributor offering this feature now. It's also a market opportunity for any new retailers in the future—"Publish with us and we'll split your royalties with co-authors at no cost."

Ultimately, payment splitting is an important trend to

watch because it minimizes risk. Instead of worrying about whether your co-author is stealing from you, you can simply look at the accounting that both of you agreed to. It also makes it easier to create box sets and other collaborative works.

DIRECT AUDIOBOOK SALES

Book Funnel expanded its services this year, branching into delivering audiobooks as well as ebooks.

Audiobooks are difficult to deliver. They often contain chapters that are very large MP3 files, and you can't host them on your website without getting in trouble with your hosting provider.

It makes sense that Book Funnel would want to help with the hosting. Now you can sell audiobooks directly on your website through a service like Payhip or Gumroad and let Book Funnel handle the fulfillment.

I implemented direct ebook sales onto my *Author Level Up* site early in the quarter, but I didn't incorporate direct audiobook sales, even though I could have. There are still too many problems, namely the listening experience.

Book Funnel will deliver the book as a series of MP3s to the customer, who then has to load them into their music player and sync the music to their mobile device, which is not terribly difficult. But your average reader may not know how to do that. They also lose the ability to listen to audiobooks with:

- speed tracking
- 15- or 30-second skip-aheads and replays
- the ability to jump around the audiobook easily
- sleep timers

These are common features on audiobook and podcast apps, and readers are accustomed to them. They may not have an appetite for listening to an audiobook on, say, Apple's Music app.

There is another service called Authors Direct that allows you to sell audiobooks directly to your readers, and they can download and listen via a dedicated app that functions similar to most major audiobook apps. In my opinion, this is a more reader-centric option, more preferable for me. I still applaud Book Funnel for offering an alternative, as there will be readers who are fine with just receiving the MP3s and don't want to fuss with *another* app on their phone. It's much like readers who prefer PDFs—they usually don't need any help getting the book onto their device of choice.

The ideal solution would be to give the reader a choice at the point of sale how they want to consume the audio. Some may want a dedicated app, and others may just want the MP3s. Depending on what they choose, the author can flex accordingly —send them a Book Funnel link or send them a code so they can download the book onto the Authors Direct app.

This gets more complicated when you consider AI-narrated audio. That would likely need a dedicated app. Can Authors Direct handle such technology? Probably not yet, but that's asking a lot at this early point in the technology's life.

So, as I think about direct audio sales, I think about:

- The buying experience and how easy it is to make a purchase.

- The ability to add coupon codes.
- The ability to upsell and cross-sell.
- The logistics of getting the audio from point of sale to the reader's preferred method of listening, which is still a difficult challenge right now.
- Future capabilities. If I want to sell AI-narrated audio *and* human-narrated audio directly to readers, will I have to use separate services? Or will this service manifest itself in ways we're not thinking of yet, such as Audible offering the service as a value-add to its existing app, with no real alternatives for doing this direct for a few years until others catch up?

I will probably pursue Authors Direct in the near future, but long-term, I'd like the ability to sell *everything* direct under a unified storefront. If you want to sell direct today, you have to use *at least* three different storefronts on your website:

- An ebook storefront such as Gumroad or Payhip.
- A paperback storefront such as Ae.rio or Bookshop.
- An audio storefront such as Authors Direct.

Very, very clunky right now. It's hard to be a world-class content creator and marketer when you offer such vastly different buying experiences. It's also harder to service your customers.

This is a developing area that I'm tracking closely, because it will get better.

IDEAS YOU CAN STEAL

PART-TIME EMAIL ONLY ASSISTANT

I'm almost at the point where I need to hire an assistant to help with my email. Ironically, I am *not* in a position to need an assistant in other areas of my business because the work load isn't high enough yet.

I priced an assistant who can provide a la carte email service. I can pay them for an hour or two to clean out my inbox when it overflows.

I've been able to achieve inbox zero and stay there for about a month at the time of this writing. I find that if I can get to inbox zero, I can stay there for a long time. But the moment my emails rise past one hundred, I'm buried. All it takes is a vacation, busy season at work, or law school exams—and in less than a week, my inbox is a disaster.

I'm considering hiring a virtual assistant as needed when:

- I'm on vacation for longer than one week with no laptop access. The emails that cause me the most trouble are the ones I can't reply to right away because I need to be at my laptop to answer it.

- During the two weeks leading up law school exams and the week after.
- When I'm overwhelmed and need help.

Sure, it's an expense, but it's worth paying to dig myself out of that hole. The last time my emails rose over one hundred, the following things happened:

- Reader fan-mail went unanswered for almost a week, which is unusual for me.
- I missed sales opportunities.
- I overlooked important emails, making me look unprofessional.

Paying an assistant for a couple hours of work to achieve peace of mind is worth it.

THE INDIE AUTHOR BOUNTY HUNTER

No, I'm not advocating for hunting authors and taking them to jail. "The Indie Author Bounty Hunter" is the catchiest title I could come up with for what is really a "quality assurance professional."

When you have as many books as I do, it's difficult to keep track of everything. Imagine if I could pay a "bounty hunter" to review the following for typos or errors:

- my website(s)
- my social media profiles
- my books' sales pages
- my books' samples
- my books' interiors

I'd pay them a flat fee and then a "bounty" for every error they find. They would return a list of errors along with an invoice. Then, I could fix the problems and rest assured that my platform is as error-free as possible.

Of course, you could also pay an assistant to do this work,

but it would be expensive. A bounty hunter could do it faster since it's the only thing they do.

This could be a great way for someone with superior attention to detail to make some money on the side. It's also an idea that an existing author-centric virtual assistant could incorporate into their service offerings.

WRITING WHILE MOVING

I recently bought a recumbent exercise bike so I could get healthier. The bike includes a desk attachment so I can put a laptop or a book on it while I exercise. I've used the bike while calling into webinars and meetings that don't require me to participate.

One day while pedaling, I had an interesting idea—what if I wrote a book *only* while moving? What if, every time I got on the exercise bike, I wrote a book (or dictated one)? What if exercise time was the only time I could work on the book? How many words would I write each session, and how long would it take me to write the book?

What would my book look like in terms of "miles," "calories," and "pounds lost?" What would one book represent in each of those categories?

Posture issues and health concerns aside, it's such a cool idea if I could do it safely. It would also be great content for my YouTube channel.

Don't be surprised if you see a chapter in a future volume about "writing while moving." The idea won't let me go.

AUTHOR IT COOPERATIVE

Every author has a need to hire an IT professional at some point in their career. Websites crash. WordPress doesn't cooperate. You want a new feature on the site. All of that requires money, and website programmers aren't cheap.

The idea is for authors to pool their resources for IT support. The group would contract with a dedicated programmer who would perform monthly routine services on the authors' website, and they'd troubleshoot any issues that come up. They'd also offer one-off services at a discounted rate per author.

This could be an affordable way to pay for IT services that would ordinarily price smaller authors out of access.

21-DAY CHALLENGE

I encountered a "21-Day Diversity and Equity Challenge" on the Internet. The goal was for a person to become more sensitive to issues around diversity and inclusion in 21 days through a series of online exercises, webinars, and videos.

While I don't know how effective an idea like this is in combating the diversity and inclusion problem, I liked the idea itself.

What's the most important thing you need to learn as an author right now, and can you design a 21-day challenge around it?

If you're a nonfiction author or content creator, what's the most important idea that your audience faces right now, and can you develop a 21-day challenge and invite them to join you as you help them solve the problem? Even better, can you time it around the new year?

That's why I like the idea. It takes 21 days to develop a habit, so a challenge like this can make a real difference in your life.

YEAR OF CHALLENGES

In the last chapter, I discussed 21-day challenges. What if you spent an entire year doing 21-day challenges?

That would be around 17 challenges!

What if each challenge leveled up your writing game just a little? What if you did each challenge publicly? How would you grow?

If I were new to the industry, knowing what I know now, here would be some of my 21-day challenges:

1. Read 3 bestselling books in my subgenre similar to my book
2. Scrivener mastery challenge (or substitute your favorite writing app)
3. Time management challenge
4. Half-novel challenge (1500 words per day)
5. Short story challenge (21 short stories in 21 days)
6. Back-in-time challenge (pick your favorite writing podcast and listen to one backlist episode you've never heard per day)

7. Study the masters challenge part 1 (pick your favorite contemporary author and spend 21 days learning from their interviews and content about writing, like a mentorship)

8. Study the masters challenge part 2 (for that same contemporary author, study one of their books and find one new writing craft technique to use per day)

9. Book formatting challenge (learn one new thing about book formatting each day)

10. Website creation challenge (learn one new thing about websites so you can build yours afterward)

11. Email marketing challenge (learn one new thing about email marketing per day)

HISTORY OF A CERTAIN SUBGENRE

The literary world is full of genres and subgenres, and each one has its own unique history. You can probably find a book that has the "history of romance novels" for example, but what about the history of romantic suspense? Who were the pioneering authors in the genre? How did they market their work? What did readers think about the first books? What did the covers look like? What does the genre look like today?

In my opinion, that's fascinating fodder for a book, podcast, or YouTube channel. You become a "historian" of a genre and piece together a history of a subgenre through thorough research, interviews, and travel to conferences. If done correctly, it would provide incredible context for authors writing in the genre who don't know the history of it. A lot of that history is dying with older authors.

In my case, I'd love to read a history of the urban fantasy genre—one that includes the contributions of paranormal romance authors *and* self-published writers. I'd also love to follow someone who has their finger on *all* aspects of the genre: readers, writers, and publishers, industry sales, emerging trends, and so on.

Like many of my ideas, this one would require someone with the right personality.

AI FOR SLUSH PILES

I was reading an installment of Jane Friedman's *The Hot Sheet*, which is a bi-weekly periodical of the newest developments in the publishing industry.

In one article, she wrote about the emergence of spelling and grammar apps that are specific to the publishing industry, unlike Grammarly, which is for general audiences. One service was called Fixional, which looks and functions similarly to Grammarly. However, it is designed for editors. Here's what Friedman wrote: "Speaking at Digital Book World, the cofounder and CEO, Pierce Gaynor, explained that Fixional can be taught what kind of writing your publication wants to acquire and publish. For example, the company currently works with a publisher that receives about 1,000 manuscripts per month and has 10,000 manuscripts awaiting review—but only five editors to go through it. (Anyone who works at a literary journal will know the feeling.) Fixional was fed all the work the publisher had already accepted and published, then allowed editors to filter and sort the slush pile based on various criteria from the published work, such as quality, completeness, and clarity. Editors can now scale their judgment and expertise over thousands of manuscripts at a time."

Interesting. So editors can teach the app what types of works they want to read, and the AI filters the works accordingly. If you thought submitting to magazines was hard already...

I see upsides, though. First, if editors rely on the AI instead of, say, a submission assistant, that could mean that they could issue rejections faster, which would be a good thing for authors.

The second upside is what I believe will be the rise of database matching services for literary magazine submissions. A developer could, in theory, create an AI service that authors can submit their work to, and the service would examine the author's work, compare it to open magazine submissions (which use AI too), and then submit to magazines it believes is a good fit. All of this would happen without the author being involved. The author would pay a yearly fee. This could effectively end the submission process as we know it, replacing it with semi-automation. This technology may already exist in some form today.

A downside is cost. This type of software will be expensive for magazines to implement. An equivalent tool would also be expensive for authors. My biggest fear with artificial intelligence is the creation of a have and have-not society. Successful people and businesses will have access to AI and less successful people will not.

SHOWING THE ENTIRE PUBLISHING PROCESS LIVE IN ONE GIANT VIDEO

I've always thought it would be interesting to take the art of writing a book and turn it into a mini reality show. Every time you start working, turn the camera on. Sure, it would be weird, but people would find it endlessly fascinating, especially if you shared your screen. Bonus points if you livestream it.

Start from the beginning and let people watch as you conceive, outline, write, edit, format, work with a designer and editor, and publish a novel.

Put everything into one giant video on YouTube, add some production value, and monetize the hell out of it, with an ad every hour.

I have no idea what would happen, but it would be interesting. Fellow author Garrett Robinson did this a few years ago with his *Nightblade* series. He mostly does Twitch livestreams now.

I believe this idea would work because people are oddly intrigued by seeing "over artists' shoulders." It would also help them see new ways of working.

INCLUDING FAILURES ON YOUR ABOUT PAGE

On a podcast interview, someone talked about including failures on their resume. As a society, we place a premium on people's successes, but we never see the string of failures that led them to success.

What if you include failures on your about page?

Here's what my about page would say:

- Published 50 books and counting and is still not a full-time author.
- Invested $30,000 in a writing business that failed to turn a profit for six years. And he still kept pouring money into it, even with minimal sales and all seemed lost.
- Signed at least six terrible copyright licensing agreements that he's still paying the price for.
- Produced three translated books that make zero dollars per month.
- Started three different podcasts and failed before he found success in the medium.
- Neglected marketing for six years.

- Spent over 15,000 hours devoted to the writing life with only slightly average results.

There are many more.

Seeing people's failures makes it easier to understand what they went through to get to where they are, and how much they had to sacrifice.

THE RETURN OF PERMAFREE?

When I started publishing in 2014, setting a book permanently free ("permafree") was a viable marketing option. The Amazon algorithms treated free books favorably and readers were kinder to free books than they are now (though not by much). However, Amazon changed its algorithms to decrease the visibility of free books, so many authors abandoned the strategy.

My book *Android Paradox* was permafree for about a year. It funneled a lot of new readers into my platform.

I've been hearing people say lately that permafree is still a viable strategy, especially if you are not exclusive to Amazon.

I'm considering trying it again with one of my series in conjunction with Amazon and/or Facebook advertising, just to see what happens. It may work, or it may not, but either way, it would be interesting to see what happens.

TAXES FOR AUTHORS

This is my biannual public service call for someone, *anyone* with a CPA in the United States, to help out the author community and produce practical resources to minimize our tax liability.

Yes, I know it's not sexy, and yes, I know, most authors don't care about taxes.

But I do. I finally hired a CPA this year to help me with my bookkeeping and taxes. We meet monthly, I can call him whenever I have a question, and he does my taxes at the end of the year. And it's expensive. Not every author can afford this kind of service.

Nothing beats a competent CPA who has experience in the author community, but there's a lot of basic information that authors need to know. Taxes isn't just about what you can deduct. There's a lot more to it.

In the previous volume, I recommended someone creating a business called "Your Self-Publishing Accountant." I suggested that this person could carve out a space in the community by offering free tax advice, affordable ebooks, and even paid courses.

Back in 2015, a writer with a CPA started this but stopped for unknown reasons. They published a book that they updated each year with tax law changes. This author also led small virtual workshops during tax season where attendees could ask questions. It was immensely helpful to me as a newbie who knew nothing about taxes or business.

I also believe such a platform would be helpful to new authors today.

CONTENT CREATED WHILE WRITING THIS BOOK

Books

The Reader's Bill of Rights

Every reader has 11 inalienable rights. Respect these rights and you'll transform ordinary readers into superfans. Violate these rights and you'll lose readers and a lot of money. This book is a manifesto on how to treat your readers right and how to stand out in today's crowded market where most authors are taking their fans for granted.

Buy at www.authorlevelup.com/billofrights

250+ Writing Tips, Vol. 1

. . .

This book contains a breath-taking amount of writing, marketing, and publishing tips that will level up your author game. Inspired by Michael's podcast "Writing Tip of the Day," the tips are concise and practical so you can implement them right away.

Buy at www.authorlevelup.com/tips1

The Indie Author Atlas

This imaginative travel guide takes all of the important lessons you need to learn as an aspiring author and turns them into can't-miss vacation destinations across five continents. Journey to The Commonwealth of Craft to discover the secrets of the writing masters, hike through the mountainous land of Market-stan and learn how to market like a boss, and even stop by the sacred lands of Distribution to witness how you can maximize your books' earning potential. You won't find another writing book like this one.

Buy at www.authorlevelup.com/atlas

The Indie Author Bestiary

The hardest side of the writing life is the emotional one. This book takes the emotional "beasts" of the writing world, converts them into actual monsters, and teaches you how to slay them.

Michael will be your guide as you embark on an epic quest against writer's block, fear, self-doubt, and more.

Buy at www.authorlevelup.com/bestiary

The Author Income Problem

Do you stare at a mountain of sales reports every month and sweat about how you're going to calculate your sales? This book will outline how you can track your sales without pulling your hair out. While the solution requires some hard work, you'll glean insights into your sales data that will give you an unfair advantage in today's market where most authors don't even bother with it. The only question you should be asking is: how much money are you leaving on the table by NOT conquering your sales reports?

Buy at www.authorlevelup.com/theauthorincomeproblem

Author Level Up YouTube Channel - Highlights

Watch at youtube.com/authorlevelup.

Writing While on the Road: Watch over Michael's shoulder as he writes books while on vacation and still manages to get an astonishing amount of work done.

. . .

Michael's 2021 Strategy Livestream: Michael outlines his plans for 2021 in painstaking detail.

How to beat fear and self-doubt: An honest talk about how to face the demons of the writing life.

Interviews & Appearances

Mental Models for Authors and the Empowered Author with Michael La Ronn (The Creative Penn): In Michael's second appearance on The Creative Penn, Michael and Joanna discuss a range of interesting topics including mental models, artificial intelligence, and how to be a writing machine.

Control Your Writing Destiny with Michael La Ronn (Growing Intentions Blog): An interview about what it means to be a writer.

Guest Interview with Michael La Ronn (Dark Neon Blog): An intimidate discussion about writing craft.

The Power of Storytelling with Michael La Ronn (Hidden Falls Media Podcast): An in-depth discussion about marketing, something Michael has never talked about on a podcast interview before.

. . .

An Introduction to Scrivener with Michael La Ronn (REWRITE London): Join Michael as he gives an hour-long introduction to Scrivener to a virtual workshop.

How to Use Scrivener to Write Your Novel with Michael La Ronn (REWRITE London): Join Michael as he goes deeper into Scrivener and how to use it at every step of the writing process.

READ NEXT: VOL. 4-7

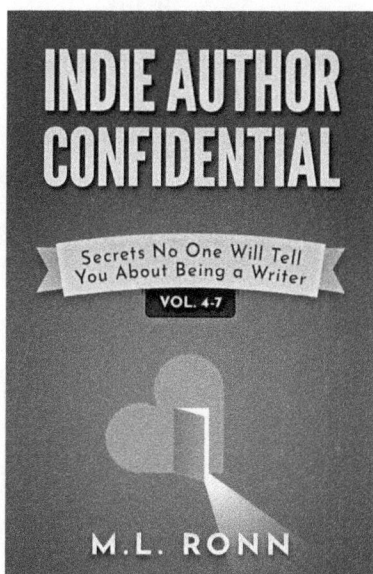

Michael's writer journey continues in Indie Author Confidential, Vol. 4-7!

Grab your copy at www.authorlevelup.com/confidentialcollection2.

MEET M.L. RONN

Science fiction and fantasy on the wild side!

M.L. Ronn (Michael La Ronn) is the author of many science fiction and fantasy novels including *The Good Necromancer*, *Android X*, and *The Last Dragon Lord* series.

In 2012, a life-threatening illness made him realize that storytelling was his #1 passion. He's devoted his life to writing ever since, making up whatever story makes him fall out of his chair laughing the hardest. Every day.

Learn more about Michael
www.authorlevelup.com (for writers)
www.michaellaronn.com (fiction)

MORE BOOKS BY M.L. RONN

Books for Writers

Indie Author Confidential (Series)
    How to Write Your First Novel
    Be a Writing Machine
    Mental Models for Writers
    The Indie Writer's Encyclopedia
    The Indie Author Atlas
    The Indie Author Bestiary
    The Reader's Bill of Rights
    The Self-Publishing Compendium
    150 Self-Publishing Questions Answered
    Authors, Steal This Book
    The Indie Author Strategy Guide
    How to Dictate a Book
    Advanced Author Editing
    Keep Your Books Selling
    The Author Estate Handbook
    The Author Heir Handbook

Interactive Fiction: How to Engage Readers and Push the Boundaries of Story Telling
Indie Poet Rock Star
Indie Poet Formatting
2016 Indie Author State of the Union

More Books for Writers:

www.authorlevelup.com/books

Fiction:
www.michaellaronn.com/books

www.ingramcontent.com/pod-product-compliance
Lightning Source LLC
Chambersburg PA
CBHW022041020426
42335CB00012B/495